Krzysztof Kieślowski: Interviews

Conversations with Filmmakers Series
Gerald Peary, General Editor

Krzysztof Kieślowski
INTERVIEWS

Edited by Renata Bernard and Steven Woodward

University Press of Mississippi / Jackson

www.upress.state.ms.us

The University Press of Mississippi is a member of the Association
of American University Presses.

Copyright © 2016 by University Press of Mississippi
All rights reserved
Manufactured in the United States of America

First printing 2016
∞

Library of Congress Cataloging-in-Publication Data

Kieslowski, Krzysztof, 1941–1996.
  Krzysztof Kieslowski : interviews / edited by Renata Bernard, Steven Woodward.
      pages cm. — (Conversations with filmmakers series)
   Includes bibliographical references and index.
   Includes filmography.
   ISBN 978-1-62846-213-5 (hardback) — ISBN 978-1-62674-574-2 (ebook)
   ISBN 978-1-4968-5793-4 (paperback)
1. Kieslowski, Krzysztof, 1941–1996—Interviews. 2. Motion picture producers and directors—
Poland— Interviews. I. Bernard, Renata, editor. II. Woodward, Steven, 1964– editor. III. Title.
   PN1998.3.K54A3 2015
   791.4302'33092—dc23
                               2015031995

British Library Cataloging-in-Publication Data available

Contents

Introduction

The story of Krzysztof Kieślowski, at least as it is known outside of Poland, is of a filmmaker rooted in the social documentary and politically engaged cinema of his homeland whose original tendencies, by force of personal, political, and economic changes, became grafted onto the wider cinematic tradition of Europe and the stylistics of the art cinema in the 1980s and 1990s. This book strives to give much greater nuance to that story, to represent Kieślowski's hybrid career and oeuvre by mapping his own thoughts and feelings about his work, from 1968, when he was still in film school, to 1996, when the *Three Colors* trilogy had won him global critical acclaim and yet he had announced his retirement from filmmaking, at the relatively young age of fifty-two.

In tracing this psycho-biographical narrative, our selection of interviews ranges across three different languages. Interviews with Kieślowski begin with Polish, expand to French in the late 1970s and 1980s, but only really appear in any number in English in the late 1980s and 1990s, after the international distribution of the *Decalogue* and the two related theatrical films. This development reflects Kieślowski's expanding reputation beyond the borders of what was, until 1989, Eastern Bloc Poland. Kieślowski visited North America for the first time in October 1986, for the screening of *No End* at the New York Film Festival. (*Camera Buff* had been shown at the Chicago Film Festival in 1980 and *Blind Chance* in 1987.) However, only after 1991, when *The Double Life of Véronique* opened the New York Film Festival (and Miramax became involved in the distribution of his films), did U.S. publications take any prolonged interest in him. And even then, he was seldom properly interviewed. Instead, his comments at public screenings and film festivals filled out profiles of the man and reviews of his films. Even Kristine McKenna's interview for the *LA Times*, reproduced here, is focused much more on the man and his beliefs than on the films themselves. This, in short, is one explanation for the rather unusual table of contents of this volume, oriented so heavily towards translations from Polish and French publications.

But there is another reason, too. In seeking interviews for this book, we have carefully considered the merits of interviews in three different languages and their current accessibility. From that perspective, we believe that there is a considerable advantage to publishing translations of interviews that many readers will never have encountered before, even with the apparent accessibility and completeness of information enabled by the Internet. This applies especially to the early interviews in Polish, conducted in the different socio-political reality of Communist Poland, which afford a rare opportunity to trace Kieślowski's filmic trajectory back to its beginnings. These interviews also highlight the difficulty of compartmentalization of his work, with interviewers' attempts to do so even early in his career refused by the filmmaker himself.

As a result of drawing on interviews in three different languages, we believe we have also traced three different tracks of reception to Kieślowski's work, many different registers of engagement, partly owing to significant differences in socio-cultural context. In comparison to English-language interviews, Polish interviews tend to focus on how the films engage with existing Polish discourses on politics, religion, and morality. The Polish interviews reveal the different function of the cinema within Communist Poland where it answered to the dialectical imperative of social betterment central to the social mission of all media. Correspondingly, Polish critics functioned differently in comparison to their Western counterparts, not bound by codes of deference to filmmakers nor fearful of production companies and distributors, but ready to challenge and argue with filmmakers over the morality of their ideas, their engagement with politics, and, occasionally, the aesthetics of their work. Just a quick glance at Bożena Janicka's 1988 interview with Kieślowski, after two of the films of *Decalogue* had been released, films which to Janicka seem to be disengaged from the urgency of contemporary events and emotionally distant, even while dealing with murder and love, will confirm this. (Interestingly, Janicka focuses on the philosophical and social implications of Kieślowski's films, rather than on their particular details.) Kieślowski was quite clearly ready to respond in kind to his Polish critics, not only countering with his own appropriately laden defence, but elaborating on themes and techniques that get very little mention in those interviews conducted for English-language publications (see, for example, his elaboration of a notion of a collective consciousness—or perhaps, subconsciousness—that he describes to Tadeusz Szczepański, 1991). In short, Kieślowski seems to have been intensely aware of both the predilections of his interviewers and the readers of his interviews, and he tailored his responses accordingly.

Perhaps one consistency across all the interviews is Kieślowski's reticence to connect explicitly his films to political and personal developments. Nevertheless, because Kieślowski lived through a period of social, political, and cultural turbulence in Poland that directly affected his life and work, we have included in our chronology far more detail than is typical for books in this series, especially for the benefit of those readers unfamiliar with that part of Polish history. However, readers may wish to consider just how little of the events mentioned in that chronology are made explicit in the interviews and how the subtextual strategies he developed as a filmmaker in a communist context, which he had in common with other filmmakers of the Eastern Bloc at the time, are carried over to the interviews.

Fortunately, before his premature death in 1996, Kieślowski participated in Faber and Faber's book series in which directors, through the intermediary of an editor (and, in this case, translator, Danusia Stok, the wife of Witold Stok, Kieślowski's sometime cinematographer in the 1970s), contemplate their own life and professional accomplishments. Readers of *Kieślowski on Kieślowski* will find some continuity of voice in the interviews collected here, especially in that apparent cynicism (what Tony Rayns interprets as persistent irony) of the man who became determined to go to film school because of his mother's disappointment when he failed the entrance exam for a second time, who continued to make films despite his sense of the foolhardiness of the process because, he claims, he didn't know how to do anything else, and who saw Poland as his home despite his increasing abhorrence of its politics and his amazement at the absurdities of his countrymen. *Kieślowski on Kieślowski* is an invaluable resource for fans and critics, but its mode of address is fundamentally different than will be found in the interviews collected here.

We hope, then, that every reader will find new discoveries in this collection. Ours include Kieślowski's references to "comic-strip cinema" (Sobolewski 1995) and to the difference between anecdotes and stories (Otrębska and Błach 1996). Kieślowski's *Diaries* from 1990, although not strictly interviews, highlight his surprising vulnerability, as when he is defrauded out of all the money in his wallet by a Parisian con artist, and confirm the power of social observation evident in his films, as when he becomes aware of the sifting of races outside the airport in Los Angeles.

Our selection begins with four early engagements with Kieślowski, when he was deciding on his credo as a filmmaker and applying that credo in the filming of ordinary Poles, some of whom were apparently removed from the flow of life (the blind veterans of *I Was a Soldier*) and some who were immersed in, and driving, momentous contemporary events (*Workers '71*). Whatever the subject, though, the young Kieślowski is committed to "The Dramaturgy of the Real" and an authentic engagement with individuals, not types (whether soldier or worker), pushing the production cooperative to allow him to use new methods (particularly 16mm equipment) to do so. In his 1968 dissertation, he refers to Marshall McLuhan's prediction of a post-literate future of children operating cameras in primary school, film libraries, and "accessorized televisions" as an obvious exaggeration, a great irony from our current perspective. His idealistic belief that he can describe the world in his films, bringing "cognizance of what is," is balanced by his experiences with *realpolitik* as film after film of his is "archived" rather than shown. And here, too, we can already detect the yearning that would ultimately drive him to abandon documentary altogether: to supersede the physical, external limitations of the medium with "thoughts and reflections reaching far beyond the photographed picture and recorded sound."

By the time of our fifth selection, a 1976 interview for *Polityka*, Kieślowski was emerging as one of the seminal practitioners of the Cinema of Moral Anxiety (or the Cinema of Moral Concern) and the magazine had chosen him as an influential and provocative figure, the laureate of "Ferment 1976." Nevertheless, he denies that the generation of filmmakers to which he belongs has adopted a new documentary approach. He does admit that "there has come a time when you want to look inside people's skulls," not just to capture their exteriors or their social performances, but he ascribes the possibility of doing so to technical developments. In this same interview, he describes the scope of his ambition for feature films—to make "a fresco, or a mosaic, but not a panorama"—in terms amazingly prescient of the ten-film series and trilogy with which his career would reach its height and end.

Kieślowski's connection with France began long before he made films there since he found a sympathetic French audience in the late 1970s, when he was interviewed by *Jeune Cinema* about *Camera Buff*, and *The Scar* was reviewed in *Positif*. For *Jeune Cinéma*, one of the first magazines outside Poland to pay attention to Kieślowski's work, Kieślowski is able to offer a broader view of the place of *Camera Buff* and his own work within what others would call the Cinema of Moral Anxiety: describing an undescribed reality so that it may be known and possibly changed. Amazingly, here, just two years before the imposition of martial law, Kieślowski can speak of a very liberal attitude among censors and political leaders: "the censor knows, like everyone, that there are many things to change; people in power know it just as well as the population." When Jacques Demeure tried to interview him in the fall of 1979, however, he simply couldn't get Kieślowski into a room, suggesting both Kieślowski's lack of interest in being in the spotlight and the peculiar position he occupied in French critical circles, at that moment, of being both unknown by many and yet much in demand by some. His fame in France was clearly about to break, and Demeure's extensive interview offers an overview of Kieślowski's career to date, an investigation of the relationship between television and cinema, of documentary and fiction, and a more extensive discussion about *Camera Buff*. Here, also, we discover Kieślowski's interest in a persistent theme, since he describes the protagonist of *The Calm* as someone like Julie in *Three Colors: Blue*: as someone who "has only one ambition. . . . He does not want a career, nor money nor friends nor love." And finally, Kieślowski's focus at the end on intergenerational unity among filmmakers and the vitality of Polish cinema suggests his uncharacteristic optimism at this moment, less than a year before the founding of Solidarity.

Even though Kieślowski had begun his career with an insistence on the dramaturgy of the real and, would even tell Demeure that "I think life is smarter than me, that it creates situations more interesting than those I could invent myself," his last four films, the French co-productions, turned away from the kitchen-sink realism and documentary-inflected aesthetics of his earlier work, a shift descried by some critics, especially the Polish. But this turn had been a long time coming and was by no means solely the result of the collapse of government structures of film funding. During the brief period of liberalization after August 1980 and before the imposition of martial law in December 1981, Kieślowski wrote a manifesto, "In Depth Rather than Breadth," announcing that cinema's previous function of description could now be taken over by journalism and that cinema itself must turn to "more universal and sagacious diagnoses" and must develop "a richer vocabulary if accounts of political events, intrigues, captains of industry or delinquent wives are also to be a forceful comment on love, hatred, jealousy, or death." And the forcefulness to which he refers will come from "evoking in audiences feelings similar to my own: the physically painful impotence and sorrow that assail me when I see a man weeping at a bus stop, when I observe people struggling vainly to get close to others, when I see someone eating up the leftovers in a cheap restaurant, when I see the first blotches on a woman's hand and know that she too is bitterly aware of them." In short, here, Kieślowski seems to be envisioning the very images and situations with which his filmmaking career would reach its apogee: the suffering of a range of ordinary Poles would be reflected in *Decalogue* while a more select, beautiful, and effete range of individuals would undergo their own passion in the *Three Colors* trilogy.

After the manifesto, however, we enter a period of ominous silence, the martial law period and its aftermath. Although martial law was only in place for a year-and-a-half, it was a relatively dark period in Polish lives, which further intensified the obvious economic shortcomings and other deficiencies of the system, and which it was aiming to remedy. Martial law also obliterated Kieślowski's remaining interest in serving Polish society. By the time Maria Marszałek interviewed Kieślowski in 1987, she could speak of a turn in his films: characters' fates are now determined by psychological rather than institutional factors. And when Bożena Janicka interviewed him the next year, after the two extended versions of the *Decalogue* films had been released but before the democratizing Round Table talks had begun in Poland, he is speaking bitterly of the world of politics and even of his fellow Poles who "all hate one another," and he is defending his turn to a metaphysical cinema that, although still depicting

Polish individuals, has no interest in commenting on Polish society, "the People's Republic." In a curious echo of British Prime Minister Margaret Thatcher's famous remark in 1987, Kieślowski intones, "What is society? No such thing exists. Only 37 million people exist." In his interviews with French magazines in the same period, as the first of the *Decalogue* films in their theatrical versions were being screened there and his earlier work was being discovered, he insists that he is still a realist director with a technique rooted in documentary, but it becomes clear, as he talks, that the reality to which he is now attuned is one more in keeping with idealist philosophies: "realism is not photographing things as they appear. It's conveying the impression you have when you look at the work, it's re-creating your ways of seeing what's around you" (Tixeront 1988). And from his documentary background he claims that his feature films have taken not a sensitivity for accurate description but their construction around an idea rather than a story. In short, the interviews complicate rather than clarify Kieślowski's turn to a metaphysical cinema. Was it simply the fulfilment of the change of direction he had announced in the 1981 manifesto? Was it a result of the despair he felt at the political turmoil of the 1980s. Or, indeed, was it a response to the government's restructuring of film funding, which began with the 1987 Cinema Act?

Yet another possible answer is revealed in an interview for the French-Canadian *24 Images*. Here, Kieślowski suggests that the *Decalogue* films were really a separate project from the story of *A Short Film about Killing*, which had been conceived much earlier, the other films serving to give relief—in both senses of the word—to the extraordinary brutality of that film. He insists, too, that the brutality is there to comment less on the issue of capital punishment than to make an existential point: "In reality, the death which threatens us every moment is just as horrible for everyone."

Perhaps one of the most remarkable aspects of Kieślowski's career is just how little known he was to English-language audiences before 1989, even though his work had previously shown at Cannes and films like *Camera Buff* and *No End* had been screened and reviewed in Britain on their release. The abruptness of the change in Kieślowski's reputation outside Poland is brilliantly captured by Steve Goldman's reference to how Kieślowski's "twenty-year overnight transformation from an obscure documentarist . . . to Poland's leading director came on November 26 when Kieślowski's *A Short Film about Killing* took the first European Oscar."

Kieślowski's defensiveness and taciturnity ebbed lowest when he was conversing with a genuinely sympathetic interlocutor, and for Kieślowski there was none more sympathetic than Polish film journalist Tadeusz Sobolewski, whose interviews are generously represented here. One notices immediately the balance in their conversations. The first of these Sobolewski interprets as Kieślowski's first serious attempt at re-evaluating "the People's Republic" as a system and his own role within it, calling for clear demarcation of individual responsibilities. While discussing the *Decalogue*, Kieślowski speaks most openly about the connection between his metaphysical turn and his own sense of religious faith, which lies far outside the typical scope of Polish Catholicism (which, they agree, depends upon an economy of suffering and consolation), perhaps also explaining why his late works were received much better outside Poland, where faith is a possibility rather than a necessity. He defines his films as a conversation between filmmaker and viewer, "about finding in someone else what you don't have in you." He also emphasizes how his own expressivity comes through montage, when "the soul of the film reveals itself," while viewers may concentrate more on *mise-en-scène*, thus finding symbols of which he was unaware.

His diary entries after the *Decalogue* reveal a lonely, isolated Kieślowski traveling extensively outside Poland, discovering an uncertain, tawdry world of con artists and young hooligans, of bomb scares and wilful segregation, of disconnection from home and family, and of artistic uncertainty (that he shares with Wajda and Zanussi). He is disgusted with the slander and hatefulness that passes for Polish democracy and dismayed in equal measure by the Polish Catholic Church's attempt to become the moral arbiter for the secular state. As he begins production on *The Double Life of Véronique*, his exhaustion with the process (including the publicity so essential to commercial cinema) is quite evident, though his enthusiasm for the painstaking process of editing continues.

Amazingly, however, once the film was released, Kieślowski seems to have rallied, describing the luminous quality of the film to interviewers as optimistic and speaking with excitement about his next grueling project, the *Three Colors* trilogy. In short interviews, like the one with Stéphane Brisset, Kieślowski appears as uncharacteristically concise and direct. In longer ones, like that with Michel Ciment and Hubert Niogret, he describes how music and warm light add to the sense of mystery in *Double Life*, and he mentions his idea of producing multiple versions of the film for release.

The interview with Tadeusz Szczepański is quite unique, and not only because Piesiewicz is included. But perhaps because of that, the interview probes very large-scale issues, like the import of film, the question of its enduring value, the complementary nature of the two Krzysztofs, the sources of morality and wisdom, the possibility of salvation through love, and the tension between religion and the sacred, between national and universal subjects, a major discussion theme of Polish filmmaking circles at the time.

To Hiroshi Takahashi, in whose Paris flat they used to meet, Kieślowski reveals more directly than anywhere else how the ideals of liberty, equality, and fraternity are a distortion of the truth of human nature and of our real desires, thus explaining the irony of the *Three Colors* films.

Kieślowski's later discussions with Tadeusz Sobolewski are extraordinarily frank and intimate. In a van on the location shooting for *Three Colors: Red*, with a (red) Marlboro cigarette packet as a constant fixture in the conversation, they discuss whether mass culture has ever been or can ever be truly rebellious, ending with the chain-smoking Kieślowski's assertion that an artist can be most provocative not in the social or political sphere but by touching viewers' subconscious with lingering effect. The details of how that might be done in *Red* are the subject of their second conversation. And in a third conversation, this time intended for a Catholic publication, the specifics of how one detail is used—the blue lollipop in *Three Colors: Blue*—allow Kieślowski to explain how symbolism is really at the discretion of the viewer. He also speaks defiantly of the enslavement of religion, the freedom that comes from faith, and the dangers of the Church involving itself directly in politics, a significant trait of post-communist Poland.

If Kieślowski was one of the Polish filmmakers most successful in crossing over into the commercial market outside the Eastern Bloc, his success did not come without suspicion and even hostility, and not just from Polish critics. The "elusive symbolism" of all Kieślowski's work from *Decalogue* on, as Jonathan Romney describes it in his interview for the *Guardian*, could be interpreted simply as a pose, contrived art-house poetics of the kind described by David Bordwell, a cynical calculation designed by Kieślowski to earn himself a place among European auteurs. And Romney's scepticism is just the beginning of what Tony Rayns describes as a critical backlash against Kieślowski, as much fueled by Kieślowski's responses at press conferences, often interpreted as "bitter and arrogant," and his announcement of his retirement, as by the films themselves. Even while probing Kieślowski's integrity with his questions, particularly in terms of the relationship of his stories to his funding sources, Rayns insists that Kieślowski has "pinpointed the mood of Europe in the nineties" better than any other filmmaker.

Katherine Monk's interview with Kieślowski during the 1994 Vancouver International Film Festival focuses particularly on the reasons for his retirement, with Kieślowski ultimately insisting that his films are all of a piece and that none have really enabled him to find the meaning for which he has been searching. Now, he insists, he may as well continue the search in private. On his way home from that festival, he stopped in Montreal and offered John Griffin a slightly different sense of his reasons for retiring, which we could summarize as an exhaustion not just with filmmaking but with the state of the world and the direction it was taking (perhaps signaled in Quentin Tarantino's win with *Pulp Fiction* over Kieślowski's

Three Colors: Red at Cannes in 1994). And finally, to Simon Hattenstone of the *Guardian*, he comes across as a Beckett-like existentialist, having had a happy childhood and achieved success in adulthood, but never being able to escape the awareness of the grave. In that context, filmmaking is neither enjoyable nor honourable, but merely the only thing Kieślowski was trained to do.

As already mentioned, American interviewers took an interest in Kieślowski only late in his career, but that fact produces a happy effect in interviews like Kristine McKenna's, where there is a freshness and directness to her very broad questions and an answering optimism in Kieślowski's responses, even if it is qualified, in this case by his awareness of such pitfalls as the egotism of romantic love or the illusory benefits of personal freedom.

We conclude with a series of interviews with Kieślowski as he moved deeper into his retirement, the first with Sobolewski again, who begins by asking why Kieślowski is still so busy and then compares him to Ken Loach, the filmmaker whom Kieślowski most admired. Loach is going on making films of protest about the "simple man" whom Kieślowski had, according to some critics, abandoned in his elegantly packaged French films. Sobolewski himself wonders, though, whether effective protest is even really possible anymore, given the kind of manipulation of reality that is endemic to the mediated world and perhaps most prevalent in the United States. This, Sobolewski's last one-on-one meeting with Kieślowski, took place in the socio-realist interior of the famed Mozaika café in Puławska Street in Warsaw.

Paul Coates's extended interview offers a survey of Kieślowski's career and themes, and aims to place his work within broader European filmmaking traditions. Here, too, Kieślowski insists that the mystery of our presence in the world is an existential one, for which religions offer one kind of response and his films one possible other. Many of his filmmaking strategies he explains as attempts to touch on that mystery, leaving the viewer enough space of interpretation (as, for example, in not giving interpretive titles to the *Decalogue* or *Three Colors* films) to feel their way into it. The films are also attempts to meditate on foundational concepts, like liberty, equality, and fraternity, to connect those concepts to individual lives in the present and thereby to make those words meaningful again.

At a theatre in Poznań, an ailing, but relaxed and reflective Kieślowski invites questions from the audience, whether about his films or about life itself, and the result is an extraordinarily diverse discussion, of night porters, of old ladies eating donuts, and of the importance of his daughter in his life, among other things. In a TV studio for the taping of the show *I Love Cinema*, Kieślowski once again faces Sobolewski, accompanied this time by Grażyna Torbicka, and the three consider documentaries in general and, in particular, how Kieślowski's early documentaries on the most mundane, unspectacular subjects have endured, especially those that emphasize the fleetingness of life, like *Seven Women of Different Ages*, and those that celebrate achievement in the face of adversity, like *Hospital*.

And finally, in a discussion with two high school students four days before his death, Kieślowski patiently responds to the implications in their questions that he has become a cultural icon, with corresponding responsibilities to the younger generation, that his films have lost any sense of story and specific place, and that the arts are fraudulent because they simply package up the same old material in different form. One particularly strong thread here is that none of us are free—capable of keeping our "neutrality," as the students put it—but absorb the influence of everything and everyone that we contact and, indeed, of everyone that has lived before us. For we carry some awareness of those earlier lives—especially of those who have more or less lived the same life—whether that awareness is a dim apprehension [as in *The Double Life of Véronique*] or a more powerful sense conveyed to us by a force that some identify as God, but that is imperfect and lets us often slip from his hands (just as the judge does not predict the ferry disaster in *Red*, even though his plan for Valentine is nevertheless realized). The recording of this interview ended mid-way so it is now lost in that moment forever, because the excited high school student Jacek Błach had only one tape on him, a fact he came to regret for years to come. And that is where our collection ends, with Kieślowski anticipating his upcoming heart operation during which he, too, somehow slipped from God's hands.

Most interviews are included in their entirety. However, in the cases of interviews that included long introductions to the actual conversation, we have sometimes summarized the preamble in our own brief introduction.

In translating, we have kept some of the rhythms and metaphors more particular to Kieślowski's native Polish, only converting them fully to English patterns and idioms when necessary for the sense. Kieślowski did tend to use eccentric metaphors, which were reflective of his work and worldview. Nevertheless, for the French interviews, Kieślowski's contributions to which were themselves translated from Polish, we have translated more aggressively. Punctuation has been silently altered to correspond to current English practice.

Interviews are presented in the order in which they were conducted, since the publication of some (like Kołodyński's) was delayed by more than twenty years.

Acknowledgments

Krzysztof Kieślowski: Interviews maps out some of the creative processes underlying Krzysztof Kieślowski's filmmaking trajectory, especially those previously obscured from anglophones by language barriers or difficulty of access, and it does so through the lenses of particular socio-cultural moments in which each of the texts included here came into being. The challenge of combining these texts into a coherent entirety was lessened by the generosity of the people who knew the influential Polish film director. Although their recollections are rarely made apparent in the book, their stories of encounters with Kieślowski, relayed in cafés in Warsaw and Kracow by Tadeusz Sobolewski, Stanisław Zawiśliński, and Jacek Błach, permeate the inevitable interpretative choices that had to be made in the translation of Polish interviews. The complexities of untangling the copyright knots tied by the systemic changes in Poland post-1989 and of locating the interviewers and copyright holders were made less cumbersome by Irena Strzałkowska at Tor Film Studio, Adam Wyżyński at Filmoteka Narodowa, Ewa Misiewicz at Fama Films, Maciej Korbut at Polska Federacja DKF, Dorota Dołęgowska at PISM, and the invaluable Paul Coates. In the case of interviews in defunct French film magazines, Jean-Luc Gaignepain pointed out how we might find the interviewers themselves. And to help with translating the French interviews, the meticulous Simon Gilbert devoted many hours of his attention.

The generosity of interviewers and copyright holders in granting their permissions to have the texts included here translated and published without a fee speaks volumes of the Kieślowskian spirit. Maria and Marta Kieślowska, Tadeusz Sobolewski, Andrzej Kołodyński, Professor Marek Hendrykowski, Dr. Mikołaj Jazdon, Bożena Janicka, Maria Marszałek, Tadeusz Szczepański, Maciej Korbut of Polska Federacja DKF, Jacek Ślusarczyk at Tygodnik Powszechny, Marian Turski, Tomasz Raczek at Instytut Wydawniczy Latarnik, Grażyna Torbicka, Jacek Błach, Agata Otrębska, Lucien Logette, Marie-Claude Loiselle, Stéphane Brisset, as well as Hiroshi Takahashi and Paul Coates all made a selfless contribution to this book. Wojciech Druszcz generously agreed for his mesmerizing portrait of Krzysztof Kieślowski, laden with retrospective symbolism, to be printed on the cover (*ad patriae gloriam*, Panie Wojciechu). Bishop's University helped defray some of the costs of preparing the book for publication.

It has been a surprisingly long journey, which could only be navigated safely with an understanding nod from our family members, Steven's wife, Wendy, and son, Jamie, and Renata's husband, John, and daughter, Apolonia Gigi Bernard, as well as her mother, Barbara Murawska-Berkowicz. Especially warm thank you extends to Gosia Murawska for doing the bulk of initial leg work in Poland.

RB
SW

Chronology

"Andrei Tarkovsky was one of the greatest directors of recent years. . . . Unfortunately, he died. Probably because he couldn't live any more. That's usually why people die. One can say it's cancer or a heart attack or that the person falls under a car, but really people die because they can't go on living."
—Krzysztof Kieślowski[1]

The following narrative chronology synthesizes details about Kieślowski's life and progress as a filmmaker from many different sources, including the most extended book on Kieślowski's life in English, *Kieślowski on Kieślowski*, edited by Danusia Stok. Not all films are mentioned, only those that seem to have been critical in developing Kieślowski's unique attitude and approach to filmmaking. For a complete list of films, see the filmography. Events crucial to the general state of Polish cinema and Polish political and social life are also detailed.

1941	June 27: The son of Barbara and Roman Kieślowski, Krzysztof Kieślowski is born in Warsaw.
1944–49	Kieślowski's sister, Ewa Kieślowska, is born in 1944. After the Germans are pushed out of Poland by Soviet forces, the country is promised political freedom through democratic elections, but Stalin manipulates the situation so that the communists take control in 1947 and forge the non-democratic People's Republic of Poland. During and after the war, Kieślowski moves around with his family in search of health for his tubercular engineer father, Roman (whose pessimism Kieślowski felt he had inherited).
1947	Kieślowski begins his elementary school education. Being a sickly child, throughout the first year, he is taught by teachers at home.
1948	March: National Higher School of Film, Television and Theatre is founded at Łódź. The Łódź Film School becomes an important window into the world beyond communist Poland.
1949	The Documentary Film Studio (WFD—Wytwórnia Filmów Dokumentalnych) is established in Warsaw.

c. 1952   Kieślowski sees his first film at the age of around eleven, probably *Fan-fan la Tulipe* (Christian-Jaque, 1952).

1953   March 15: Joseph Stalin dies.

1955   May: Film production is decentralized with the establishment of film units. By 1957, there are eight units with relative independence, each with an artistic head, a literary manager, and a production executive. The units remain centrally funded, so the role of film producer does not exist in Poland until the late 1980s.

1956   June: Large protests in Poznań against poor working and living conditions are violently suppressed. October 19: In an attempt to quell continuing widespread unrest, the Polish United Workers' Party (PZPR) elects the moderate Władysław Gomułka as First Secretary, beginning the "Polish October." In the new climate of relative cultural freedom under Gomułka, the "Polish School" of filmmaking emerges, with filmmakers like Andrzej Wajda, Kazimierz Kutz, and Andrzej Munk contesting the socialist-realist aesthetic imposed during the Stalinist period and re-examining Polish history. It persists until about 1964. October 23: The Hungarian Uprising begins with student protests in Budapest, but very quickly spreads nationwide, eventually resulting in the complete overthrow of the Soviet-directed communist authorities. On November 4, a large Soviet force invades Hungary and a Soviet-approved government is eventually re-established.

1956–57   Having completed his elementary education in Mieroszewo in southwest Poland, Kieślowski decides he wants to work rather than study and attends the Fireman's Training College in Wrocław. He drops out after three months and tries a high school in Wałbrzych, which he also quits.

1957   Kieślowski's father, Roman, dies on February 22, aged forty-nine, and his mother, Barbara, moves to Warsaw with her children. Through the influence of an uncle, Kieślowski is admitted to the State School for Theater Technicians in Warsaw, a school unique in the European context for the intense and practical focus of specialization.

1962–63   Kieślowski graduates from the State School for Theater Technicians. With the goal of becoming a theater director, Kieślowski applies to Łódź Film School. He manages to get through the grueling two-week exam process in an attempt to win one of the fifteen spots available, but without success at first. In September 1962, he starts classes at Warsaw Teachers' College, but soon quits. In the meantime, he tries to make his living by working on the side as a theatrical dresser and a cultural clerk in Warsaw's Żolibórz District National Council, while writing poems and stories and shooting short amateur films with an 8mm camera. In 1963 he makes a second unsuccessful attempt to pass the entrance exams for the Łódź Film School. At the same time, he adopts various ruses, including starving himself, to avoid being drafted into the army (see Stok 23–28).

1964–68   Kieślowski is accepted to Łódź Film School on his third attempt and has the opportunity to see foreign films there that are not accessible by the general public, at the habitual rate of two films a day. He is deeply impressed by Ken Loach's *Kes* and by the films of Federico Fellini, Orson Welles, Robert Bresson, and, to an extent, Ingmar Bergman. Jerzy Bossak, Kazimierz Karabasz, and Jerzy Toeplitz are the teachers who make the strongest impression on him. While studying, he tries different ways of subsidizing his student life, by working as a pollster, photographer, and actor. He makes a number of short films, including *Tramway* (1966), *The Office* (1966) (for which he receives his first festival award at the student film festival in Warsaw), *Concert of Requests* (1967), and *The Photograph* (1968) (his first professional film, for Polish Television).

1967   Kieślowski marries Maria (Marysia) Cautillo on January 21.

1968   January 5: The "Prague Spring" begins when Alexander Dubček is elected First Secretary of the Communist Party of Czechoslovakia and institutes a series of liberalizing reforms. In response, the Soviets and other countries of the Warsaw Pact invade Czechoslovakia on the night of August 20. March: Following the suppression in January of a distinctly patriotic nineteenth-century poetic play by Adam Mickiewicz, used as a canvas for political and anti-censorship statements, student demonstrations in Warsaw are put down with violence, provoking more widespread student demonstrations across the country. In response, the government intensifies its anti-Zionist policies, begun in 1967, with a purge of Polish Jews from positions of authority, including Jerzy Toeplitz and Jerzy Bossak teaching at Łódź Film School, as well as such important cultural figures as Zygmunt Bauman, Leszek Kołakowski, or Bronisław Baczko. Kieślowski participates in the political unrest with other students, for instance trying, if ineffectively, to defend professors expelled from the Film School. Thousands of Polish Jews are forced to emigrate in the next few years. Kieślowski shoots his Łódź Film School graduation film, *From the City of Łódź*, which is partly funded by the WFD, in 1968.

c. 1969   Feeling that there is no easy way into the film industry, Kieślowski bands together with three other young filmmakers to try to found the

Irzykowski Studio, with the goal of supporting young filmmakers in making their first feature for about a sixth of the typical cost. The enterprise fails, apparently because of lack of Party support, but materializes many years later, in 1980, when Kieślowski is no longer involved. At the same time, he is earning a living by making commercials and short films on commission and working as an assistant at the WFD.

1970   February: After defending his MA dissertation *Film and the Dramaturgy of the Real* (a portion of which is reproduced here), Kieślowski receives the Łódź Film School diploma of graduation with top marks and the title of Master of Arts.

1971   Kieślowski starts his first full-time job as a director's assistant at WFD, which significantly improves his financial condition, with a salary well above the national average. At the end of the year, he makes *Before the Rally*. The same year, Kieślowski finishes the documentary *I Was a Soldier* for the Czołówka film studio, which funds projects about the army. December 13: Gomułka raises food prices 30 percent, provoking demonstrations by shipyard workers followed by violent reactions from police, a broadening of demonstrations, and army intervention, the whole resulting in hundreds of deaths. Edward Gierek succeeds Gomułka and begins economic expansion, on credit from the West, temporarily improving the standard of living. *Workers '71: Nothing about Us without Us*, directed by Kieślowski and Tomek Zygadło, documents the hopes of workers who had been involved in demonstrations the previous year and who are still waiting for more radical reform from Gierek, but the film in its original cut is never released. Some of the audio recordings of interviewed subjects are stolen, then mysteriously returned. Despite protests from the filmmakers, a highly edited and slightly longer black-and-white version titled *Housekeepers* is broadcast on Polish television in 1972.

1972   January 8: Kieślowski's one child, Marta, is born. Kieślowski's first prospect for a feature film, based on Kazimierz Orłoś's short story *Camel*, falls through due to the banning of Orłoś's work. (A film based on Kieślowski's treatment would be made by Jerzy Stuhr in 2000, titled *The Big Animal* [Polish: *Duże zwierzę*]).

1973   Kieślowski makes his first professional non-documentary, the thirty-minute TV feature *Pedestrian Subway* about a man from the country searching in Warsaw for the wife he still loves. Shooting conventionally for nine nights, he adopts a documentary and improvisatory approach for the final night to try to create something more authentic. He also makes *Bricklayer*, a documentary about a middle-aged man who had previously been a champion in Stakhanovite competitions, but who has become disenchanted with communist ideology. The film anticipates Andrzej Wajda's *Man of Marble* (1977).

1974   Kieślowski makes the documentary *First Love* over a twelve-month period, about the difficulties faced by a very young couple becoming parents, according to the precepts expressed in his film school thesis (see "The Dramaturgy of the Real," included here). However, he later admits that he manipulated some of the situations he filmed for maximum drama. Hoping to help the struggling parents, he proposes a sequel to the film to state television that will follow the couple for many years of their lives, thereby essentially forcing the authorities to find an apartment for them in order to preserve the illusions of a socialist utopia. (A sequel is later made, *Horoscope* [2000], but by Krzysztof Wierzbicki, and the couple had by then emigrated to Canada.)

c. 1974   The so-called Cinema of Moral Anxiety (or Cinema of Distrust or of Moral Concern) begins to emerge, committed to describing an "unrepresented reality," persisting until 1980. Although Kieślowski is often hailed as one of its key proponents, he offers a highly nuanced view, avoiding the simple equation of communism with evil.

1975   For the documentary *Curriculum Vitae*, Kieślowski puts an actor with a fictitious background in front of a real Party Board of Control and films the Kafkaesque treatment he receives. Some members of the Party are eager for reform and support the film as evidence of the dysfunction of the system. At the same time, some critics accuse Kieślowski of producing the film under Party direction. Ultimately, the film is shelved by the state censors and never seen by the public, though it is screened at Party instructional meetings and at film festivals. *Personnel* is Kieślowski's first full-length feature, for TV, partly scripted and partly improvised, featuring a combination of actors, film directors, and nonactors. Focusing on the behind-the-scenes life of the opera, it reflects Kieślowski's earlier experiences studying and working in the theatre, as well as being a broader commentary on the disparity between ideals (about politics or art) and the disillusionment of actual experience. It wins, among others, the Andrzej Munk Prize for the best debut.

1976   February: On the basis of just a few films, with *Curriculum Vitae* most prominent among them, Kieślowski receives the "Ferment" award from *Polityka* for young Poles who "stir an intellectual ferment." June 24: Gierek raises food prices more than 60 percent, provoking riots and demonstrations once again. September: Jacek Kuroń and Adam Michnik form the Worker's Defence Committee (KOR) to provide legal advice to arrested workers and to monitor their trials.*The Scar*, Kieślowski's first theatrical feature, has a social-realist subject and style but is structured around an idea rather than an action, a persistent structural feature of Kieślowski's fiction films and a carryover from his documentary beginnings. Jerzy Stuhr makes his first appearance for Kieślowski, though in a supporting role. *The Calm (Spokój)* is made for TV, based on reportage by Lech Borski, as a vehicle for Jerzy Stuhr. Although focused on the difficulties of fulfilling the most humble of individual desires rather than addressing a pointedly political subject, it is shelved by the state censors because it includes a scene of a strike, later proclaimed to be "prophetic" in its anticipation of future events. It is not shown until 1980, just after the signing of the August Agreement between Solidarity and the government. The same year, Kieślowski revisits his documentary imperatives in *Hospital*, which expresses both the terrible scarcity of supplies in Poland and the resourcefulness of Poles living in this situation.

1977   The documentary *I Don't Know* is built around the statement of a factory director exposing systematic corruption among officials and Party members. The factory director tries to have the film suppressed following its completion and Kieślowski himself refuses to agree to its release, realizing the harm that it will cause its subject.

1978   Polish Cardinal Wojtyła (John Paul) becomes Pope and tours Poland, inspiring a resurgence of Polish nationalism and desire for civil rights. Kieślowski becomes Vice-President of the Polish Filmmakers Association alongside Andrzej Wajda as its President.

1979   *From a Night Porter's Point of View*, made in 1977, wins a prize at the Kraków Film Festival, despite having been shelved by the state censors. Kieślowski objects when State Television plans to show it in 1980, once again fearful of the effects on his subject. (It is shown on Polish TV only after Kieślowski's death.) *Camera Buff*, a second feature written for Jerzy Stuhr, is about Filip Mosz, an amateur filmmaker who unwittingly becomes an agent of the authorities and whose wife leaves him. Intensifying the autobiographical and self-reflexive nature of the film, Kryzsztof Zanussi appears as himself. The ending depicts Mosz turning the camera on himself, perhaps heralding Kieślowski's own approaching turn to metaphysical films. The film wins the Golden Prize at the Moscow Film Festival, and other prizes in Chicago and Berlin. Kieślowski begins teaching at the Katowice Film School (founded in 1978), continuing until 1982.

1980   "Polish August": Gierek again provokes widespread strikes with an increase in food prices. The government is eventually forced (August 31) to allow free trade unions, civil rights, and freedom of information, and Solidarity is founded (September 17). One million Party members join Solidarity. For the documentary *Station*, Kieślowski films people waiting overnight at a train station. The footage is temporarily confiscated by the police, who are looking for evidence in a murder case, prompting Kieślowski to realize that he is effectively a collaborator with the authorities and that the documentary approach is too invasive of its subjects' lives. He resolves to abandon documentaries altogether.

1981 With *Blind Chance*, filmed in the spring and summer, Kieślowski abandons the attempt to describe the external realities of Polish life and aims to explore the inner world and "the powers that meddle with our fate" (Stok 113). He adopts a method of filming a portion of the whole, beginning to edit it, then returning to shoot the remainder with a better awareness of what is needed to make the film work in the edit. February: In the face of yet another economic crisis and increasing discord within the Party, General Wojciech Jaruzelski, by some seen as a puppet of Moscow, becomes Prime Minister. He declares martial law on December 13. Solidarity is outlawed and the thirty-eight regional delegates are arrested and imprisoned. Serious filmmaking more or less ceases: some filmmakers emigrate or work outside the country; others are forced to follow the government line or are relegated to producing genre films; importing of Western films is severely limited. Both Kieślowski and Wajda resign their positions in the executive of the Polish Filmmakers' Association. In August, Kieślowski's mother dies in a car accident. Kieślowski's friend was driving. Kieślowski makes the TV feature *Short Working Day* at the same time as *Blind Chance*, about a regional Party Secretary who was almost lynched in the 1976 riots. However, he considers the film to be a failure because of its schematic psychology, an inevitable result of the public's and his own hostility to any sympathetic portrayal of the authorities. The film is never shown. Kieślowski and Agnieszka Holland visit the Łódź Film School, but the students there are now more interested in experimental cinema and New Age practices and they reject Kieślowski (Stok 37–38). Under martial law, Kieślowski gives up any hope of making films, considers driving a taxi or participating in violent resistance, and is even offered the chance to head a production house (Stok 120–25). Instead, he later claimed, he sleeps for five months. Despite the dire political and personal situation, he manages to publish the manifesto "In Depth Rather than Breadth" (included here).

1982   In January, Kieślowski puts sound to *Blind Chance* so his colleagues can receive their pay for the film, now considered completed. It is then censored and shelved. In June, under the pretext of contributing to Andrzej Wajda's *Danton*, then being filmed in Paris, Kieślowski visits France for the first time, to see his Polish filmmaking colleagues. After his return home, he focuses on his family and writing a gardener's journal. September or October: Kieślowski proposes two documentary projects to the WFD, one about soldiers who have to paint over anti-government graffiti and the other about the trials of anti-government activists, showing the faces of the accused and the accuser. The second project brings him into contact for the first time with defence lawyer Krzysztof Piesiewicz, who will soon become his co-writer. Kieślowski realizes that the presence of his camera in the courtroom has the effect of intimidating the judges into being very reluctant to impose anything but the most lenient sentences. He "films" with several unloaded cameras for a month-and-a-half, collecting almost no footage, and eventually abandoning any pretence of completing the project. However, he is temporarily out of favor with intellectuals and other filmmakers who once again mistakenly believe he is collaborating with the authorities (see Stok 125–30).

1983   Agnieszka Holland insists that Kieślowski should co-host with her the seminar on auteur cinema organized through the initiative of Berlin's Transformtheater and Künstlerhaus Bethanien for May/June. This is the first of a six-year series of teaching visits. July 22: Martial law ends, a month after the Pope's second visit to Poland.

1984   Kieślowski wants to make a film about how martial law has destroyed any sense of hope among his own generation, envisioning this metaphysical subject in relation to a lawyer who has died, played by Jerzy Radziwiłłowicz, the lead actor from Andrzej Wajda's *Man of Marble* and *Man of Iron* films. Knowing very little of the material details of the profession, he undertakes his first collaboration with lawyer Krzysztof Piesiewicz, and also with composer Zbigniew Preisner, for the film *No End*. (Both Piesiewicz and Preisner work on all subsequent Kieślowski films.). When the film is released after six months, Kieślowski is attacked by the government, opposition, and Church, but the audience responds to it as an accurate portrayal of martial law. At the end of 1984, Krzysztof Piesiewicz accepts an invitation to co-represent in court the family of Father Popiełuszko, following the latter's politically motivated murder by police officers. During the mid-1980s, Kieślowski often functions as de facto head of the Tor Film Unit, especially during the frequent absences of its President, Krzysztof Zanussi.

1986   October: Kieślowski attends the New York Film Festival for a screening of *No End*. On the way there, his taxi hits a cyclist and Kieślowski has to run to the screening through Central Park, pursued by irate and miscomprehending taxi drivers (Stok 207).

1987   The Cinema Act of July 16, 1987, aims at dismantling the state monopoly on film production and grants the film units commercial independence, by which it opens the film market to economic pressures. The act also outlines the new role of film producer, a concept entirely foreign to the system of film production units constituting the Polish film industry until this time. *Blind Chance* is finally released in Poland. At the Festival of Polish Films in Gdańsk, Kieślowski receives the Best Screenplay Award for the film and its star, Bogusław Linda, receives the Best Actor Award.

1987–88   Kieślowski makes the ten episodes of the *Decalogue*, as well as two modified episodes designed for theatrical release, with funding from Polish Television, the TOR production unit, and German television. Filming for the whole cycle takes eleven months, with the filming of *Decalogue 6/A Short Film about Love* making Kieślowski acutely aware of the absurdity of filmmaking (Stok 171). He had undertaken the writing of the cycle at the instigation of Piesiewicz, crafting it so that it would attract TV funding (so, Kieślowski initially thought, allowing ten young directors to make a feature film) and be exportable. While the drab realities of Polish life of the time are inevitably reflected in the series, they provide an ideal framework (without the glamor endemic to Hollywood cinema) for the exploration of universal moral issues.

1988   May: *A Short Film about Killing* wins the Jury Prize and is tied for the FIPRESCI prize at the Cannes Film Festival, beginning an extraordinary run of prize-winning for the two theatrical films of the *Decalogue* and the series as a whole (see the Filmography for more details).

1989   Mirroring reforms occurring all across the Eastern Bloc under Soviet Premier Mikhail Gorbachev, the Round Table talks begin in February and a new system of democratic elections is introduced in April, with Solidarity reinstated and winning the majority of seats. Nevertheless, the economy is decimated and systemic problems persist. The Cinema Act of 1987 is implemented at last. Government film funding is no longer limited to film production units. Polish filmmakers no longer work to answer to social and cultural imperatives, or to serve the nation. Instead, they need to consider economic pressures, which some of them refer to as "economic censorship." July 22: Krzysztof Piesiewicz's mother is murdered, with some details suggesting a link to Father Popiełuszko's earlier murder.

1991   Given the changes in government film funding and increasing costs of film production, Kieślowski produces his first film outside Poland, using French production money, *The Double Life of Véronique*. Originally, Andie MacDowell and Nanni Morretti agree to be the leads, but are replaced with Irène Jacob and Philip Volter. Kieślowski films in Poland and France, but edits the film in Paris with the help of Jacques Witta. The film premieres at the Cannes Film Festival, winning the FIPRESCI prize. It opens the New York Film Festival (September) and is distributed in the U.S. by Miramax (as are all of Kieślowski's subsequent films of the *Three Colors* trilogy). Many Polish critics recognize the extraordinary formal beauty of the film but are simultaneously suspicious of its social disengagement.

1992   Poland joins the Eurimages Foundation, which supports multinational productions of its member countries and contributes to Kieślowski's *Three Colors* films.

1993   September: *Three Colors: Blue* ties with Robert Altman's *Short Cuts* for the Golden Lion at the Venice Film Festival.

1994   February: *Three Colors: White*, which includes satirical commentary on post-communist Poland, wins the Silver Bear (for Best Director) at the Berlin Film Festival. May: Kieślowski attends the Cannes Film Festival at which *Three Colors: Red* is in competition for the Palme d'Or and announces (though not for the first time) that he is retiring from filmmaking. Quentin Tarantino's *Pulp Fiction* wins the Palme d'Or. Kieślowski begins teaching at the Łódź Film School.

1995   Kieślowski attends the Academy Awards as *Three Colors: Red* has been nominated in the Best Director and Best Original Screenplay categories (Piotr Sobociński has also been nominated for Best Cinematography on the film). In summer, while spending time with his family in the Masuria lake district in Poland, he suffers a heart attack. At the request of his daughter, he gives up smoking.

1996   February 24: Despite ill health, Kieślowski attends a retrospective of his films in Poznań, organized by Teatr Ósmego Dnia. This will be his last public appearance. March 9: Two high school students conduct Kieślowski's last interview, for a school publication, *Incipit* (included here in an edited version). March 13: Kieslowski dies while undergoing heart surgery in a Polish hospital. As he is dying, the Manhattan Film Centre in New York is screening his *Decalogue*, and a cinema on Lake Geneva, *Blind Chance*. After Kieślowski's death, it is revealed that he had been working again with Piesiewicz on the writing of a new trilogy, this time based on the Dantean notions of Paradise, Purgatory, and Inferno.

Note

1. Danusia Stok, ed., *Kieślowski on Kieślowski* (London: Faber and Faber, 1993), 33–34.

Filmography

FACE (TWARZ) (1966)
Production: Państwowa Wyższa Szkoła Teatralna i Filmowa (Łódź)
Director: Piotr Studziński
Production Manager: Tadeusz Lubczyński
Cinematography: Zdzisław Kaczmarek
Editing: Janina Grosicka
Mentoring: Wanda Jakubowska, Janusz Weychert, Kazimierz Konrad, Barbara Mazurek
Cast: **Krzysztof Kieślowski**
Black and white feature, 7 minutes

As Director

TRAMWAY (TRAMWAJ) (1966)
Director: **Krzysztof Kieślowski**
Production: Państwowa Wyższa Szkoła Teatralna i Filmowa (Łódź)
Cinematography: Zdzisław Kaczmarek
Mentoring: Wanda Jakubowska, Kazimierz Konrad
Cast: Maria Janiec (Girl), Jerzy Braszka (Boy)
35mm black and white feature, 5 minutes 45 seconds

THE OFFICE (URZĄD) (1966)
Working title: PENSION (RENTA)
Director: **Krzysztof Kieślowski**
Production: Państwowa Wyższa Szkoła Teatralna i Filmowa (Łódź)
Production Manager: Tadeusz Lubczyński
Cinematography: Lechosław Trzęsowski
Editing: Janina Grosicka
Sound: Marta Stankiewicz
Mentoring: Jerzy Bossak, Kazimierz Karabasz, Kurt Weber

Cast: Krzysztof Kowalewski (Priest)
35mm black and white documentary, 6 minutes

CONCERT OF REQUESTS (KONCERT ŻYCZEŃ) (1967)
Director: **Krzysztof Kieślowski**
Production: Państwowa Wyższa Szkoła Teatralna i Filmowa (Łódź)
Production Manager: Tadeusz Lubczyński
Screenplay: **Krzysztof Kieślowski**
Cinematography: Lechosław Trzęsowski
Editing: Janina Grosicka
Sound: Marta Stankiewicz
Mentoring: Wanda Jakubowska, Kazimierz Konrad
Cast: Ewa Konarska (Ewa), Jerzy Fedorowicz (Andrzej), Ryszard Dembiński
(Bus Driver), Waldemar Korzeniowski, Roman Talarczyk, Andrzej Titkow,
Jerzy Rogalski (uncredited), **Krzysztof Kieślowski** (a bike rider leading a cow,
uncredited)
35mm black and white feature, 17 minutes

THE PHOTOGRAPH (ZDJĘCIE) (1968)
Director: **Krzysztof Kieślowski**
Production: Telewizja Polska, Zakład Produkcji Filmów Telewizyjnych
Production Manager: Zofia Małkowska
Screenplay: **Krzysztof Kieślowski**
Cinematography: Marek Jóźwiak, Wojciech Jastrzębowski
Photography: Józef Rybicki
Editing: Jolanta Wilczak
Music: Andrzej Trybuła
Sound: Włodzimierz Wojtyś, Marek Jóźwik
16mm black and white documentary, 32 minutes

FROM THE CITY OF ŁÓDŹ (Z MIASTA ŁODZI) (1968)
Working title: ŁÓDŹ-SIDERS (ŁODZIANIE)
Director: **Krzysztof Kieślowski**
Production: Wytwórnia Filmów Dokumentalnych (Warsaw)
Production Managers: Stanisław Abrantowicz, Andrzej Cylwik
Cinematography: Janusz Kreczmański, Piotr Kwiatkowski, Stanisław Niedbalski
Editing: Elżbieta Kurkowska, Lidia Zonn
Sound: Krystyna Pohorecka, Ryszard Sulewski
Mentoring: Kazimierz Karabasz

Cast: Cezary Juszyński
35mm black and white documentary, 17 minutes 21 seconds

I WAS A SOLDIER (BYŁEM ŻOŁNIERZEM) (1970)
Director: **Krzysztof Kieślowski**
Additional Direction: Andrzej Titkow
Production: Wytwórnia Filmowa Czołówka
Production Manager: Jan Harasimowicz
Screenplay: **Krzysztof Kieślowski**, Ryszard Zgórecki
Cinematography: Stanisław Niedbalski
Editing: Walentyna Wojciechowska
Sound: Jan Strojecki, Jacek Szymański
Other production credits: Elżbieta Werner
35mm black and white documentary, 16 minutes 31 seconds

FACTORY (FABRYKA) (1970)
Director: **Krzysztof Kieślowski**
Additional Direction: Marcel Łoziński
Production: Wytwórnia Filmów Dokumentalnych (Warsaw)
Production Manager: Halina Kawecka
Cinematography: Stanisław Niedbalski, Jacek Tworek
Editing: Maria Leszczyńska
Sound: Małgorzata Jaworska
Consultation: Edward Margański
35mm black and white documentary, 17 minutes 14 seconds

BEFORE THE RALLY (PRZED RAJDEM) (1971)
Director: **Krzysztof Kieślowski**
Production: Wytwórnia Filmów Dokumentalnych (Warsaw)
Production Manager: Waldemar Kowalski
Cinematography: Jacek Petrycki, Piotr Kwiatkowski
Editing: Lidia Zonn
Sound: Robert Wiśniewski, Małgorzata Jaworska
Other Production Credit: Grzegorz Skurski
Cast: Krzysztof Komornicki
35mm black and white/color documentary, 15 minutes 9 seconds

REFRAIN (REFREN) (1972)
Director: **Krzysztof Kieślowski**

Production: Wytwórnia Filmów Dokumentalnych (Warsaw)
Production Manager: Waldemar Kowalski
Cinematography: Witold Stok
Editing: Anna Maria Czołnik
Sound: Małgorzata Jaworska, Michał Żarnecki
35mm black and white documentary, 10 minutes 19 seconds

BETWEEN WROCŁAW AND ZIELONA GÓRA (MIĘDZY WROCŁAWIEM A ZIELONĄ GÓRĄ) (1972)
Director: **Krzysztof Kieślowski**
Production: Wytwórnia Filmów Dokumentalnych (Warsaw)
Production Manager: Jerzy Herman
Cinematography: Jacek Petrycki
Editing: Lidia Zonn
Sound: Andrzej Bohdanowicz, Henryk Kuźniak
35mm color documentary, 10 minutes 35 seconds (although listed at 17 and 19 minutes in some sources)

THE PRINCIPLES OF SAFETY AND HYGIENE IN A COPPER MINE (PODSTAWY BHP W KOPALNI MIEDZI) (1972)
Director: **Krzysztof Kieślowski**
Production: Wytwórnia Filmów Dokumentalnych (Warsaw)
Production Manager: Jerzy Herman
Screenplay: **Krzysztof Kieślowski**
Cinematography: Jacek Petrycki
Editing: Lidia Zonn
Sound: Andrzej Bohdanowicz, Henryk Kuźniak
35 mm color instruction documentary, 20 minutes 52 seconds

WORKERS '71: NOTHING ABOUT US WITHOUT US (ROBOTNICY '71: NIC O NAS BEZ NAS) (1971, released 1972)
Director: **Krzysztof Kieślowski**
Additional Direction: Tomasz Zygadło, Wojciech Wiszniewski, Paweł Kędzierski, Tadeusz Walendowski
Production: Wytwórnia Filmów Dokumentalnych (Warsaw)
Production Managers: Mirosław Podolski, Wojciech Szczęsny, Tomasz Gołębiewski
Cinematography: Witold Stok, Stanisław Mroziuk. Jacek Petrycki
Editing: Lidia Zonn, Anna Maria Czołnik, Joanna Dorożyńska, Daniela Cieplińska

Sound: Jacek Szymański, Alina Hojnacka
Consultation: Bohdan Kosiński
Other Production Credits: Andrzej Arwar, Bogdan Stankiewicz
16mm color documentary, 46 minutes 39 seconds (broadcast in 1972 as GOSPO-
DARZE, unapproved by the directors, in 35mm, black and white documentary)

BRICKLAYER (MURARZ) (1973, released 1981)
Director: **Krzysztof Kieślowski**
Production: Wytwórnia Filmów Dokumentalnych (Warsaw)
Production Manager: Tomasz Gołębiewski (also listed as Gołębiowski)
Cinematography: Witold Stok
Editing: Lidia Zonn
Sound: Małgorzata Jaworska
Other Production Credits: Jacek Maziarski
Cast: Józef Malesa
35mm color documentary, 17 minutes 39 seconds

PEDESTRAN SUBWAY (PRZEJŚCIE PODZIEMNE) (1973, released 1974)
Director: **Krzysztof Kieślowski**
Additional Direction: Joanna Krauze, Paweł Mann, Halina Słobodzin
Production: Film Studio Tor
Production Manager: Tadeusz Drewno
Screenplay: Ireneusz Iredyński, **Krzysztof Kieślowski**
Cinematography: Sławomir Idziak
Cinematography Assistant: Krzysztof Pełczyński
Production Design: Teresa Barska
Costumes: Ewa Braun
Editing: Elżbieta Kurkowska
Sound: Małgorzata Jaworska
Other Production Credits: Wiesława Dyksińska, Tadeusz Chojnacki
Cast: Teresa Krzyżanowska (Lena), Andrzej Seweryn (Michał), Anna Jaraczówna
(public toilet minder), Zygmunt Maciejewski (teacher), Jan Orsza-Łukaszewicz
(down-and-out man), Janusz Skalski (decorator), Marcel Łoziński (French man
asking for directions, uncredited), Wojciech Wiszniewski (on-looker, uncredited)
35mm black and white feature, 29 minutes

X-RAY (PRZEŚWIETLENIE) (1974)
Director: **Krzysztof Kieślowski**
Production: Wytwórnia Filmów Dokumentalnych (Warsaw)
Production Manager: Jerzy Tomaszewicz

Cinematography: Jacek Petrycki
Editing: Lidia Zonn
Sound: Michał Żarnecki
35mm color documentary, 12 minutes 63 seconds

FIRST LOVE (PIERWSZA MIŁOŚĆ) (1974)
Director: **Krzysztof Kieślowski**
Production: Wytwórnia Filmów Dokumentalnych (Warsaw), Telewizja Polska
Production Manager: Jerzy Tomaszewski
Cinematography: Jacek Petrycki
Editing: Lidia Zonn
Sound: Michał Żarnecki, Małgorzata Jaworska
16mm color docudrama, 30 minutes

CURRICULUM VITAE (ŻYCIORYS) (1975)
Director: **Krzysztof Kieślowski**
Production: Wytwórnia Filmów Dokumentalnych (Warsaw), Telewizja Polska
Production Manager: Marek Szopiński
Screenplay: Janusz Fastyn, **Krzysztof Kieślowski** (Maciej Malicki original concept)
Cinematography: Jacek Petrycki, Tadeusz Rusinek
Editing: Lidia Zonn
Sound: Spas Christow
Other Credits: Krzysztof Wierzbicki, Józef Zduńczyk, Maciej Pacuła
35mm black and white docudrama, 45 minutes 10 seconds

PERSONNEL (PERSONEL) (1975)
Director: **Krzysztof Kieślowski**
Additional Direction: Taduesz Walendowski
Production: Telewizja Polska, Studio Filmowe Tor
Production Manager: Zbigniew Stanek
Screenplay: **Krzysztof Kieślowski**
Cinematography: Witold Stok
Camera Operator: Ryszard Jaworski
Editing: Lidia Zonn, Alina Siemińska
Production Design: Tadeusz Kosarewicz
Sound: Michał Żamecki
Costumes: Izabella Konarzewska
Cast: Juliusz Machulski (Romek Januchta), Irena Lorentowicz (stage designer), Włodzimierz Boruński (theatre technical manager, old friend of Romek's aunt), Michał Tarkowski (tailor Sowa), Andrzej (singer Andrzej Siedlecki), Tomasz

Lengren (cutter Romek), Tomasz Zygadło (youth organization president), Janusz Skalski (costume workshop manager), Krystyna Wachelko (girl on the train), Ludwik Mika (theatre director), Wilhelm Kłonowski (tailor), Jan Torończak (tailor), Jan Zieliński (tailor), Edward Ciosek (tailor), Henryk Sawicki (ballet master), Waldemar Karst (dancer), Krzysztof Sitarski (singer), Mieczysław Kobek (uncredited), Helena Kowalczykowa (Romek's aunt, uncredited)
16mm, color TV drama, 72 minutes
Awards: Grand Prix (International Film Festival) Mannheim, 1975; International Catholic Film Award (International Film Festival) Mannheim, 1975

HOSPITAL (SZPITAL) (1976)
Director: **Krzysztof Kieślowski**
Production: Wytwórnia Filmów Dokumentalnych (Warsaw), Telewizja Polska
Production Manager: Ryszard Wrzesiński
Cinematography: Jacek Petrycki
Editing: Lidia Zonn
Sound: Michał Żarnecki
Other Credits: Piotr Morawski, Jerzy Snoch, Piotr Latałło, Henryka Dancygier, Aleksander Goldbeck
35mm black and white documentary, 21 minutes 4 seconds

SLATE (KLAPS) (1976)
Out-takes from THE SCAR
Director: **Krzysztof Kieślowski**
Production: Wytwórnia Filmów Dokumentalnych (Warsaw), Telewizja Polska
Cinematography: Sławomir Idziak
Editing: Eugeniusz Dmitroca
Sound: Michał Żarnecki
Other Credits: Marek Piestrak, Krzysztof Wierzbicki, Agata Miklaszewska, Mirosława Sada, Zbigniew Stanek, Janusz Szela, Krzysztof Szopa, Andrzej Płocki, Ewa Kowalska, Marta Woźniakowska, Franciszek Pieczka, Mariusz Dmochowski, Jerzy Stuhr, Michał Tarkowski, Jan Skotnicki, Halina Winiarska, Joanna Orzeszkowska, Andrzej Skupień, Stanisław Igar
35mm color documentary, 5 minutes 20 seconds

THE SCAR (BLIZNA) (1976)
Director: **Krzysztof Kieślowski**
Additional Direction: Marek Piestrak, Krzysztof Wierzbicki, Agata Miklaszewska, Mirosława Sada
Production: Studio Filmowe Tor

Production Manager: Zbigniew Stanek
Screenplay: **Krzysztof Kieślowski**
Dialogues: Romuald Karaś, **Krzysztof Kieślowski**
Cinematography: Sławomir Idziak
Camera Operator: Witold Stok
Editing: Krystyna Górnicka, Eugeniusz Dmitroca
Production Design: Andrzej Płocki, Ewa Kowalska
Music: Stanisław Radwan
Sound: Michał Żarnecki
Costumes: Izabella Konarzewska
Cast: Franciszek Pieczka (Stefan Bednarz, director of the works in Olecko),
Mariusz Dmochowski (Bolesław, committee head in Olecko), Jerzy Stuhr (Bednarz's assistant), Jan Skotnicki (Stanisław Lech, transport manager), Stanisław
Igar (minister), Stanisław Michalski (Ministry employee, Bednarz's friend),
Michał Tarkowski (Michał Gałecki, TV journalist), Andrzej Skupień (employee of
the National Committee in Olecko), Halina Winiarska (Bednarz's wife), Joanna
Orzeszkowska (Bednarz's daughter), Jadwiga Bryniarska and Agnieszka Holland
(Hania, Bednarz's secretary), Małgorzata Leśniewska (Mrs. Małgosia, Olecko
resident at the meeting with Bednarz), Asja Łamtiugina (Olecko resident at
the meeting with Bednarz), Ryszard Bacciarelli (architect at the meeting with
Bolesław), F Barfuss and Bohdan Ejmont (participants of the meeting with
Bolesław), Henryk Hunko (Olecko resident), Jan Jeruzal, Zbigniew Lesień
(sociologist), Konrad Morawski (Ramowicz), Jerzy Prażmowski (engineer), Jan
Stawarz (participant of the meeting with Bolesław), Paweł Kędzierski (sociologist, uncredited), Halina Rasiakówna (uncredited), Tomasz Zygadło (sociologist,
uncredited)
Dubbing: Barbara Horowianka (for Halina Winiarska, Bednarz's wife,
uncredited)
35mm color feature, 104 minutes

THE CALM (SPOKÓJ) (1976, released 1980)
Director: **Krzysztof Kieślowski**
Additional Direction: Krzysztof Wierzbicki, Lech Sołuba, Ewa Ociepa
Production: Centralna Wytwórnia Programów i Filmów Telewiyzjnych Poltel
Production Manager: Jeremi Maruszewski, Zbigniew Romatowski
Screenplay: **Krzysztof Kieślowski** (based on Lech Borski)
Dialogues: **Krzysztof Kieślowski**, Jerzy Stuhr
Cinematography: Jacek Petrycki
Camera Operator: Zbigniew Wichłacz, Włodzimierz Krygier, Stanisław Świątek
Editing: Maria Szymańska, Bogumiła Grzelak

Production Design: Andrzej Rafał Waltenberger
Music: Piotr Figiel
Sound: Wiesław Jurgała
Costumes: Renata Własow, Ewa Parys-Płowik
Cast: Jerzy Stuhr (Antoni Gralak), Izabela Olszewska (Jedynakowa, Gralak's
landlady), Jerzy Trela (Zenek, building site's manager), Michał Szulkiewicz
(Mietek), Danuta Ruksza (Bożena, Gralak's wife), Elżbieta Karkoszka (Kryśka
Stańczak, Gralak's ex-girlfriend), Jerzy Fedorowicz (prisoner leaving prison
together with Gralak), Stefan Mienicki, Ryszard Palik, Marian Cebulski (Cracow
workers' hotel's manager), Edward Dobrzański, Janusz Sykutera (manager's
friend), Ryszard Dreger (Jasiek, Gralak's neighbor), Feliks Szajnert (clerk),
Michał Żarnecki (Bożenka's father), Stanisław Gronkowski, Ferdynand Wójcik
(possibly mistaken for Wiesław Wójcik), Jan Adamski, Stanisław Marczewski,
Jan Niziński, Lech Sołuba, Krzysztof Wierzbicki (clerk, uncredited), Wiesław
Wójcik (Gralak's prison mate met in the cinema, uncredited)
35mm color feature, 81 minutes

FROM A NIGHT PORTER'S POINT OF VIEW (Z PUNKTU WIDZENIA NOC-
NEGO PORTIERA) (1977)
Director: **Krzysztof Kieślowski**
Production: Wytwórnia Filmów Dokumentalnych (Warsaw), Telewizja Polska
Production Manager: Wojciech Kapczyński
Cinematography: Witold Stok
Editing: Lidia Zonn
Music: Wojciech Kilar
Sound: Wiesława Dembińska, Michal Żarnecki
Other Credits: Krzysztof Wierzbicki, Jerzy Snoch, Alina Siemińska
Cast: Marian Osuch
35mm color documentary, 16 minutes 52 seconds
Awards: Jury Prize at International Short Film Festival, Lille, 1979; Silver at
International Film Festival *Visions du Reel*, Nyon, 1979

I DON'T KNOW (NIE WIEM) (1977, released 1981)
Director: **Krzysztof Kieślowski**
Screenplay: **Krzysztof Kieślowski**
Production: Wytwórnia Filmów Dokumentalnych (Warsaw), Telewizja Polska
Production Manager: Wojciech Kapczyński, Ryszard Wrzesiński
Cinematography: Jacek Petrycki
Editing: Lidia Zonn
Sound: Michał Żarnecki

Other Credits: Piotr Morawska, Jacek Latałło, Jerzy Snoch, Alina Siemińska
35mm black and white documentary, 46 minutes 27 seconds

SEVEN WOMEN OF DIFFERENT AGES (SIEDEM KOBIET W RÓŻNYM WIEKU)
(1978)
Director: **Krzysztof Kieślowski**
Production: Wytwórnia Filmów Dokumentalnych (Warsaw), Telewizja Polska
Production Manager: Lech Grabiński
Cinematography: Witold Stok
Editing: Lidia Zonn, Alina Semińska
Sound: Michał Żarnecki
Other Credits: Piotr Morawska, Jacek Latałło, Jerzy Snoch, Alina Siemińska
35mm black and white documentary, 16 minutes

CAMERA BUFF (AMATOR) (1979)
Director: **Krzysztof Kieślowski**
Additional Direction: Krzysztof Wierzbicki, Michał Maryniarczyk, Michał
Żarnecki
Production: Studio Filmowe Tor
Production Manager: Wielisława Piotrowska
Screenplay: **Krzysztof Kieślowski**
Dialogues: Jerzy Stuhr, **Krzysztof Kieślowski**
Cinematography: Jacek Petrycki
Camera Operator: Stanisław Szabłowski, Krzysztof Jachowicz, Włodzimierz
Krupa, Andrzej Archacki, Krzysztof Buchowicz
Editing: Halina Nawrocka, Teresa Miziołek
Production Design: Andrzej Rafał Waltenberger, Barbara Kociuba
Music: Krzysztof Knittel, Frédéric Chopin
Sound: Michał Żamecki, Mirosław Dobek, Marian Redlich, Marek Wojtaszewski,
Zygmunt Nowak
Costumes: Gabriela Star-Tyszkiewicz, Janina Wierzbicka
Cast: Jerzy Stuhr (Filip Mosz), Małgorzata Ząbkowska (Irka, Filip's wife),
Ewa Pokas (Anna Włodarczyk of Amateur Film Federation), Stefan Czyżewski
(plant's director), Jerzy Nowak (Stanisław Osuch, Filip's manager), Tadeusz
Bradecki (Witek Jachowicz, Filip's friend), Marek Litewka (Piotrek Krawczyk,
Filip's neighbor), Bogusław Sobczuk (Kędzierski, television journalist), Krzysztof
Zanussi (Krzysztof Zanussi), Andrzej Jurga (Andrzej Jurga), Alicja Bienicewicz
(Jaśka), Tadeusz Rzepka (Wawrzyniec), Aleksandra Kisielewska (Hania's secre-
tary), Włodzimierz Maciudziński (Stelmaszczyk), Roman Stankiewicz (Czesław,
a participant of Amateur Film Festival), Antonina Barczewska (Mrs. Katarzyna),

Feliks Szajnert (emergency doctor), Jolanta Brzezińska (Wawrzyniec's wife), Teresa Szmigielówna (Teresa Szmigielówna), Jacek Turalik (Buczek), Andrzej Warchał (television journalist), Danuta Wiercińska (Grażyna), Tadeusz Huk (shift doctor), Zofia Framer (singer filmed by Mosz, uncredited), Marian Osuch (watchman, uncredited), Tadeusz Sobolewski (Tadeusz Sobolewski, uncredited), Krzysztof Wierzbicki (participant of the meeting with Krzysztof Zanussi, uncredited)
35mm color, 117 minutes
Awards: Gold Medal, International Film Festival, Moscow, 1979; FIPRESCI, International Film Festival, Moscow, 1979; INTERFLIM, International Film Festival, Berlin, 1980; Grand Prix, International Film Festival, Chicago, 1980

TALKING HEADS (GADAJĄCE GŁOWY) (1980)
Director: **Krzysztof Kieślowski**
Production: Wytwórnia Filmów Dokumentalnych (Warsaw)
Production Manager: Lech Grabiński
Cinematography: Jacek Petrycki, Piotr Kwiatkowski
Editing: Alina Siemińska
Sound: Michał Żarnecki
Other Production Credits: Krzysztof Wierzbicki, Grzegorz Eberhardt
35mm black and white documentary, 15 minutes 32 seconds

STATION (DWORZEC) (1980)
Director: **Krzysztof Kieślowski**
Production: Wytwórnia Filmów Dokumentalnych (Warsaw)
Production Manager: Lech Grabiński
Cinematography: Witold Stok, Jacek Latałło
Editing: Lidia Zonn, Alina Siemińska
Sound: Michał Żarnecki
Other Credits: Piotr Morawski, Jerzy Snoch
Other Production Credits: Krzysztof Wierzbicki
35mm (and 16mm) black and white documentary, 13 minutes 23 seconds

BLIND CHANCE (PRZYPADEK) (1981, released 1987)
Director: **Krzysztof Kieślowski**
Additional Direction: Jerzy Braszka, Teresa Violetta Buhl, Michał Żarnecki, Maciej Drygas, Małgorzata Wichlińska
Production: Studio Filmowe Tor
Production Manager: Jacek Szeligowski, Stanisław Rudowicz, Zbigniew Dobrowolski, Lidia Durajczyk, Dariusz Struszczak, Alicja Skorupa

Screenplay: **Krzysztof Kieślowski**
Cinematography: Krzysztof Pakulski, Marek Januszewicz, Józef Letkier, Tadeusz Gąsiorowski
Editing: Elżbieta Kurkowska, Dorota Madej
Production Design: Andrzej Rafał Waltenberger, Barbara Kociuba, Zbigniew Pakuła
Music: Wojciech Kilar
Sound: Michał Żarnecki
Costumes: Agnieszka Domaniecka (and Beata Banasik, Grażyna Hałupka)
Cast: Bogusław Linda (Witek Długosz), Tadeusz Łomnicki (communist Werner in the first version, an appearance in the third version), Zbigniew Zapasiewicz (Adam, Werner's friend, a party activist in the first version), Bogusława Pawelec (Czuszka Olkowska, Witek's girlfriend in the first version), Marzena Trybała (Werka, Daniel's sister, Witek's beloved, in the second version), Jacek Borkowski (Marek, Opposition activist in the second version), Jacek Sas-Uhrynowski (Daniel, Witek's childhood friend, 1968 emigrant, in the second version), Adam Ferency (Father Stefan, Opposition activist, in the second version; an appearance in the third version), Monika Goździk (Olga Mitwyszyn, Witek's wife in the third version), Zygmunt Hübner (Dean in the third version, an appearance in the first version), Irena Burawska (daughter of the dying old woman in the third version, uncredited), Irena Byrska (Witek's daughter in the second version, an appearance in the third version), Janusz Dziubiński (Party activist holding Witek up in Adam's office in the first version, uncreited), Bohdan Ejmont (Party activist in the first version, uncredited), Stefania Iwińska (Opposition's activist to whom Witek brings money, uncredited), Jerzy Jończyk (uncredited), Krzysztof Kalczyński (Werka's husband in the second version, uncredited), Sylwester Maciejewski (youth activist in the first version, an appearance in the third version, uncredited), Borys Marynowski (Jacek, youth activist in the first version, uncredited), Aleksander Mikołajczak (youth activist in the first version, uncredited), Jerzy Moes (militia officer arresting Czuszka in the first version, uncredited), Bogdan Niewinowski (Witek's father, uncredited), Kazimiera Nogajówka (Kasia, a friend of Witek's father, uncredited), Jolanta Nowińska (uncredited), Ludwik Pak (sailor in the second version, uncredited), Edward Rauch (Party activist in the first version, uncredited), Mirosław Siedler (Dean's son in the second version, uncredited), Piotr Skarga (drug addict in the first version, uncredited), Jerzy Stuhr (youth activist in the first version, uncredited), Włodzimierz Twardowski (uncredited), Krzysztof Zaleski (man at the airport in the first version, uncredited)
35mm color feature, 122 minutes
Awards: Soviet Filmmakers Society, International Film Festival, Moscow, 1987

SHORT WORKING DAY (KRÓTKI DZIEŃ PRACY) (1981, released on TV 1996)
Director: **Krzysztof Kieślowski**
Additional Direction: Henryk Schoen, Teresa Violetta Buhl
Production: Studio Filmowe Tor, Telewizja Polska
Production Manager: Jacek Szeligowski, Stanisław Rudowicz, Marek Depczyński
Screenplay: **Krzysztof Kieślowski**, Hanna Krall
Cinematography: Krzysztof Pakulski
Camera Operator: Marek Januszewicz, Józef Letkier, Tadeusz Gąsiorkiewicz
Editing: Elżbieta Kurkowska, Grażyna Hałupka
Production Design: Andrzej Rafał Waltenberger, Marta Woźniakowska
Music: Jan Kanty Pawluśkiewicz
Sound: Michał Żarnecki
Costumes: Renata Własow, Ewa Parys-Płowik
Cast: Wacław Ulewicz (First Secretary of the Workers' Party in Radom), Lech Grzmociński (chief police officer in Radom), Tadeusz Bartosik (executive member of the Party in Radom), Elżbieta Kijowska (Bogusia, secretary of the First Secretary), Marek Kępiński (chief of the Party's Headquarters in Radom), Paweł Nowisz (Henio, the First Secretary's driver), Barbara Dziekan (wife of the slogan's destroyer), Marian Gańcza, Wojciech Pilarski (judge), Jan Konieczny, Tadeusz Płuciennik, Zbigniew Bielski (worker building the barricade, in the retrospective, Solidarity activist reading a statement), Mirosław Siedler (Opposition activist), Leon Charewicz (worker at the Party building, uncredited), Janusz Dziubiński (watchman at the Party Building in Radom, uncredited), Anna Grzeszczuk (secretary in the Party Headquarters in Radom, uncredited), Eugeniusz Korczarowski (Central Committee's Representative with the list of price increases, uncredited), Tadeusz Mazowiecki (trial observer, uncredited), Marek Nowakowski (doctor in the Party building in Radom), Stefan Paska (worker destroying the slogan, in the retrospective of the trial, uncredited), Remigiusz Rogacki (Central Committee's Representative with the list of price increases, uncredited), Michał Szewczyk (militia captain, uncredited), Eugeniusz Wałaszek (Central Committee Secretary recommending the hero for the position of Party Secretary in Radom, uncredited)
35mm color feature, 79 minutes 22 seconds

NO END (BEZ KOŃCA) (1984, released 1985)
Director: **Krzysztof Kieślowski**
Additional Direction: Elżbieta Oyrzanowska, Maciej Dejczer, Anna Stempi
Production: Studio Filmowe Tor
Production Manager: Ryszard Chutkowski, Paweł Mantorski, Wlodzimierz Bendych, Jerzy Janicki, Andrzej Cebula, Anna Kowalska, Bożenna Mrówczyńska

Screenplay: **Krzysztof Kieślowski**, Krzysztof Piesiewicz
Cinematography: Jacek Petrycki
Camera Operator: Roman Miastowski, Janusz Całka, Piotr Obłoza
Editing: Krystyna Rutkowska, Beata Chichocka
Production Design: Allan Starski, Elżbieta Łupińska-Stępniak, Grażyna Tkaczyk, Joanna Lelanow
Music: Zbigniew Preisner
Sound: Michał Żarnecki
Costumes: Wiesława Starska, Małgorzata Bursztyńska, Henryka Ciok, Jolanta Włodarczyk
Cast: Grażyna Szapołowska (Urszula Zyro), Maria Pakulnis (Joanna Stach, Dariusz's wife), Aleksander Bardini (Mieczysław Labrador), Jerzy Radziwiłłowicz (Antoni Zyro), Artur Barciś (Dariusz Stach), Michał Bajor (Miecio, apprentice lawyer), Marek Kondrat (Tomek, the Zyros' friend), Tadeusz Bradecki (hypnotist), Daniel Webb (American), Krzysztof Krzemiński (Jacek, Zyro's son), Marzena Trybała (Marta Duraj), Adam Ferency ("Rumcajs," Opposition activist), Elżbieta Kilarska (Antek's mother), Jerzy Kamas (judge Biedroń), Hanna Dunowska-Hunek (Justyna, Opposition activist), Jan Tesarz (Joanna's father), Andrzej Szalawski (solicitor, Labrador's friend), Jacek Domański (Opposition activist, uncredited), Katarzyna Figura (hypnotist's assistant, uncredited), Jacek Hilchen (uncredited), Katarzyna Jungowska (uncredited), Małgorzata Kaczmarska (uncredited), Andrzej Krasicki (judge, uncredited), Bogdan Niewinnowski (Mr. Kazimierz, cloakroom man, uncredited), Tomasz Taraszkiewicz (uncredited)
35mm color feature, 107 minutes

A SHORT FILM ABOUT KILLING (KRÓTKI FILM O ZABIJANIU) (1987, released 1988)
Director: **Krzysztof Kieślowski**
Additional Direction: Teresa Violetta Buhl
Production: Studio Filmowe Tor, PRF Zespoły Filmowe
Production Manager: Ryszard Chutkowski, Paweł Mantorski, Włodzimierz Bendych
Screenplay: **Krzysztof Kieślowski**, Krzysztof Piesiewicz
Cinematography: Sławomir Idziak
Editing: Ewa Smal, Urszula Rekłajtis
Production Design: Halina Dobrowolska, Grażyna Tkaczyk, Robert Czesak
Music: Zbigniew Preisner
Sound: Małgorzata Jaworska
Costumes: Małgorzata Obłoza, Hanna Ćwikło
Cast: Mirosław Baka (Jacek Łazar), Krzysztof Globisz (advocate Piotr Balicki),

Jan Tesarz (Waldemar Rekowski, taxi driver), Zbigniew Zapasiewicz (President of the Bar), Barbara Dziekan (cinema cashier), Aleksander Bednarz (executioner), Jerzy Zass (prison warden), Zdzisław Tobiasz (judge), Artur Barciś (worker with a measure), Krystyna Janda (Dorota Geller), Olgierd Łukaszewicz (Andrzej Geller, Dorota's husband), Leonard Andrzejewski (drunken guy's friend at the taxi stand, uncredited), Wiesław Bednarz, Zbigniew Borek, Władysław Byrdy, Ryszard W. Borsucki, Andrzej Gawroński, Henryk Guzek, Iwona Gębicka, Elżbieta Helman (Beatka, grocery shop assistant), Bogusław Hubicki, Helena Kowalczykowa (old woman feeding pigeons), Krzysztof Luft, Henryk Łapiński (member of solicitors committee), Bogdan Niewinowski, Borys Marynowski (guard), Marzena Manteska, Maciej Maciejewski (barrister), Andrzej Mastalerz (Jacek's brother), Jolanta Mielech, Marlena Miarczyńska, Lech Pietrasz, Małgorzata Pieczyńska, Zbigniew Plato, Zdzisław Rychter (street artist), Krzysztof Stelmaszyk, Karol Stępkowski, Maciej Szary (taxi driver's neighbor), Cezary Świtkowski, Alicja Wolska, Sylwester Maciejewski (Jacek's brother)
16mm and 35mm color feature, 85 minutes
Awards: Jury Prize, International Film Festival, Cannes, 1988; FIPRESCI, International Film Festival, Cannes, 1988

SEVEN DAYS A WEEK—WARSAW (SIEDEM DNI W TYGODNIU—WARSZAWA) (1988)
Director: **Krzysztof Kieślowski**
Additional Direction: Piotr Mikucki
Production: Rotterdam Films/Rijneke & Van Leeuwaarden
Executive Producer: City Life (Rotterdam)
Production Credits: Jacek Petrycki, Dirk Rijneke, Mildred van Leeuwaarden
Other Production Credits: Marcin Kwiatkowski, Janusz Krzepkowski, Jan Heijs, Paul Steinhauser
Cinematography: Jacek Petrycki, Zdzisław Wajda
Editing: Dorota Wardęszkiewicz
Music: Zbigniew Preisner
Sound: Michał Żarnecki
35mm color documentary, 18 minutes

A SHORT FILM ABOUT LOVE (KRÓTKI FILM O MIŁOŚCI) (1988)
Director: **Krzysztof Kieślowski**
Additional Direction: Teresa Violetta Buhl, Paweł Rzepkowski
Production: Studio Filmowe Tor
Production Manager: Ryszard Chutkowski, Paweł Mantorski, Włodzimierz Bendych
Screenplay: **Krzysztof Kieślowski**, Krzysztof Piesiewicz

Cinematography: Witold Adamek
Camera Operator: Witold Adamek
Editing: Ewa Smal
Production Design: Halina Dobrowolska, Grażyna Tkaczyk, Robert Czesak
Music: Zbigniew Preisner
Sound: Nikodem Wołk-Łaniewski
Costumes: Małgorzata Obłoza, Hanna Ćwikło
Cast: Grażyna Szapołowska (Magda), Olaf Lubaszenko (Tomek), Stefania
Iwińska (Tomek's housekeeper), Piotr Machalica (Roman), Artur Barciś (man
with a suitcase), Hanna Chojnacka (waitress, credited as Mirosława), Stanisław
Gawlik (postman Wacek), Rafał Imbro (Magda's lover), Jan Piechociński (Mag-
da's lover), Krzysztof Koperski (gas company employee in Magda's apartment),
Jarosława Michalewska (cashier at the post office), Małgorzata Rożniatowska
(postoffice master), Emilia Ziółkowska (old woman at the post office)
35mm color feature, 87 minutes
Awards: Special Jury Prize, International Film Festival, San Sebastian, 1988;
FIPRESCI, International Film Festival, San Sebastian, 1988; OCIC, International
Film Festival, San Sebastian, 1988; Prize of the City of Schiltigheim, Film Festival, Strasburg, 1989; Best Director, Festival "Tomorrow's Stars," Geneva, 1989;
Olaf Lubaszenko as Best Actor, Festival "Tomorrow's Stars," Geneva, 1989; Audi-
ence Prize, International Film Festival, São Paulo, 1989; Film Critics' Prize, In-
ternational Film Festival, São Paulo, 1989; Silver Hugo for Grażyna Szapołowska,
International Film Festival, Chicago, 1989

DECALOGUE (DEKALOG) (1988, released 1989)
Series of ten one-hour dramas for TV. Credits for individual episodes follow.
Director: **Krzysztof Kieślowski**
Additional Direction: Teresa Violetta Buhl
Production: Studio Filmowe Tor, Telewizja Polska, Sender Freies (West Berlin)
Production Manager: Ryszard Chutkowski
Screenplay: **Krzysztof Kieślowski**, Krzysztof Piesiewicz
Editing: Ewa Smal
Production Design: Halina Dobrowolska, Grażyna Tkaczyk, Robert Czesak
Music: Zbigniew Preisner
Costumes: Małgorzata Obłoza, Hanna Ćwikło
Awards: Silver Film, Italian Film Critics Association, 1990; FIPRESCI, Interna-
tional Film Festival, Venice, 1989; Young Cinema, International Film Festival,
Venice, 1989; Critics' Choice, International Films Meeting, Dunkirk, 1989; OCIC,
International Film Festival, San Sebastian, 1989; Critics' Choice, International
Film Festival, São Paulo, 1989; National Society of Film Critics, USA, 2000

DECALOGUE I (DEKALOG I)
Director: **Krzysztof Kieślowski**
Director 2: Dariusz Jabłoński
Cinematography: Wiesław Zdort
Camera Operator: Jerzy Rudziński
Sound: Małgorzata Jaworska
Cast: Henryk Baranowski (Krzysztof, uncredited in part 3), Wojciech Klata
(Paweł, Krzysztof's son), Maja Komorowska (Irena, Krzysztof's sister), Artur
Barciś (man on the ice), Agnieszka Brustman (chess player), Maciej Borniński
(Jacek's father, credited as "Bormiński"), Maria Gładkowska (Ania, Krzysztof's
friend, Paweł's English tutor), Ewa Kania (Ewa Jezierska, Marek's mother) Alek-
sandra Kisielewska (Jacek's mother), Aleksandra Majsiuk (Olga), Magda Sroga-
Mikołajczyk (journalist interviewing the headmaster), Anna Smal-Romańska,
Maciej Sławiński (headmaster), Piotr Wyrzykowski, Bożena Wróbel
35mm color feature, 53 minutes

DECALOGUE 2 (DEKALOG II)
Director: **Krzysztof Kieślowski**
Director 2: Dariusz Jabłoński
Cinematography: Edward Kłosiński
Camera Operator: Edward Kłosiński
Sound: Małgorzata Jaworska
Cast: Krystyna Janda (Dorota Geller), Aleksander Bardini (doctor), Olgierd
Łukaszewicz (Andrzej Geller, Dorota's husband), Artur Barciś (laboratory
worker), Stanisław Gawlik (postman Wacek), Krzysztof Kumor (gynaecologist),
Maciej Szary (caretaker), Krystyna Bigelmajer (nurse), Karol Dillenius (patient
next to Andrzej), Ewa Ekwińska (Mrs. Basia), Jerzy Fedorowicz (Janek Wierz-
bicki, Andrzej's friend), Piotr Siejka (doctor), Aleksander Trąbaczyński (friend of
Dorota's lover), Piotr Fronczewski (Dorota's lover, only the voice, uncredited)
35mm color feature, 58 minutes

DECALOGUE 3 (DEKALOG III)
Director: **Krzysztof Kieślowski**
Director 2: Dariusz Jabłoński
Cinematography: Piotr Sobociński
Camera Operator: Dariusz Panas
Sound: Nikodem Wołk-Łaniewski
Cast: Daniel Olbrychski (Janusz), Maria Pakulnis (Ewa, Janusz's ex-lover),
Joanna Szczepkowska (Janusz's wife), Artur Barciś (tram driver), Krystyna
Drochocka (aunt), Krzysztof Kumor (doctor), Dorota Stalińska (railway

employee on a skateboard), Zygmunt Fok, Jacek Kałucki (policeman), Barbara Kołodziejska, Maria Krawczyk, Jerzy Zygmunt Nowak (doctor), Piotr Rzymysz-kiewicz, Włodzimierz Rzeczycki, Włodzimierz Musiał (nurse in chamber detention), Henryk Baranowski (Krzysztof, uncredited in part 3), Edward Kłosiński (Edward Garus, Ewa's ex-lover, Kłosiński's face appears on the photograph shown to Janusz by Ewa, uncredited)
35mm color feature, 55 minutes

DECALOGUE FOUR (DEKALOG IV)
Director: **Krzysztof Kieślowski**
Director 2: Dariusz Jabłoński, Paweł Rzepkowski, Winfried Bolenz
Cinematography: Krzysztof Pakulski
Camera Operator: Krzysztof Pakulski
Sound: Małgorzata Jaworska
Cast: Adrianna Biedrzyńska (Anka), Janusz Gajos (Michał, Anka's father), Artur Barciś (kayaker), Aleksander Bardini (doctor), Adam Hanuszkiewicz (Anka's lecturer at acting college), Jan Tesarz (taxi driver Waldemar Rekowski), Igor Śmiałkowski (man at the airport), Andrzej Blumenfeld (Adam, Michał's friend), Tomasz Kozłowicz (Jarek, Anka's boyfriend), Elżbieta Kilarska (Jarek's mother), Helena Norowicz (eye specialist), Andrzej Chyra (acting student, uncredited)
35mm color feature, 55 minutes

DECALOGUE 5 (DEKALOG V)
Television version of *A Short Film about Killing*
Director: **Krzysztof Kieślowski**
Director 2: Dariusz Jabłoński, Paweł Rzepkowski, Winfried Bolenz
Cinematography: Sławomir Idziak
Camera Operator: Sławomir Idziak
Sound: Małgorzata Jaworska
Cast: Mirosław Baka (Jacek Łazar), Krzysztof Globisz (solicitor Piotr Balicki), Jan Tesarz (taxi driver Waldemar Rekowski), Artur Barciś (worker with a measure), Krystyna Janda (Dorota Geller), Olgierd Łukaszewicz (Andrzej Geller, Dorota's husband), Maciej Szary (caretaker), Zbigniew Zapasiewicz (president of the barristers committee), Zbigniew Borek, Władysław Byrdy, Aleksander Bednarz (executioner), Barbara Dziekan-Vajda (cinema cashier), Iwona Głębicka, Elżbieta Helman (Beatka, grocery shop assistant), Helena Kowalczykowa (old woman feeding pigeons), Borys Marynowski (guard), Maciej Maciejewski (barrister), Sylwester Maciejewski (Jacek's brother), Andrzej Mastalerz (Jacek's brother), Zdzisław Rychter (street artist), Karol Stępkowski (man at the taxi stand), Zdzisław Tobiasz (judge), Jerzy Zass (prison warden), Leonard

Andrzejewski (drunken guy's friend at the taxi stand, uncredited), Henryk
Łapiński (member of solicitors committee, uncredited)
35mm color feature, 57 minutes

DECALOGUE 6 (DEKALOG VI)
Television version of *A Short Film about Love*
Director: **Krzysztof Kieślowski**
Director 2: Paweł Rzepkowski
Cinematography: Witold Adamek
Camera Operator: Witold Adamek
Sound: Nikodem Wołk-Łaniewski
Cast: Grażyna Szapołowska (Magda), Olaf Lubaszenko (Tomek), Stefania
Iwińska (Tomek's housekeeper), Artur Barciś (man with a suitcase), Stanisław
Gawlik (postman Wacek), Piotr Machalica (Roman), Rafał Imbro (Magda's
lover), Jan Piechociński (Magda's lover), Małgorzata Rożniatowska (postoffice
master)
35mm color feature, 58 minutes

DECALOGUE 7 (DEKALOG VII)
Director: **Krzysztof Kieślowski**
Director 2: Dariusz Jabłoński, Paweł Rzepkowski, Winfried Bolenz
Cinematography: Dariusz Kuc
Camera Operator: Dariusz Kuc
Sound: Nikodem Wołk-Łaniewski
Cast: Anna Polony (Ewa, Majka's mother), Maja Barełkowska (Majka),
Władysław Kowalski (Stefan, Majka's father), Bogusław Linda (Wojtek, Ania's fa-
ther), Artur Barciś (man at the train station), Bożena Dykiel (cashier at the train
station in Józefowo), Katarzyna Piwowarczyk (Ania, Majka's daughter), Stefania
Błońska, Dariusz Jabłoński (Wojtek's friend), Jan Mayzel (Grzegorz, Stefan's
friend), Mirosława Maludzińska, Ewa Radzikowska (usher), Wanda Wróblewska
35mm color feature, 55 minutes

DECALOGUE 8 (DEKALOG VIII)
Director: **Krzysztof Kieślowski**
Director 2: Dariusz Jabłoński, Paweł Rzepkowski
Cinematography: Andrzej J. Jaroszewicz
Camera Operator: Andrzej J. Jaroszewicz
Sound: Wiesława Dembińska
Cast: Maria Kościałkowska (Zofia, ethics professor), Teresa Marczewska
(Elżbieta Loranc), Artur Barciś (student at Zofia's lecture), Tadeusz Łomnicki

(tailor), Marian Opania (Dean), Bronisław Pawlik (stamp collector, Zofia's neighbor), Wojciech Asiński (student speaking out at Zofia's lecture), Marek Kępiński (tenant at Nowakowska Street), Janusz Mond, Krzysztof Rojek (rubber man in the park), Wojciech Sanejko (student, credited as Wiktor), Ewa Skibińska (student telling Dorota Geller's story), Wojciech Starostecki (student), Jerzy Schejbal (priest), Jacek Strzemżalski (caretaker at Nowakowska Street), Hanna Szczerkowska, Anna Zagórska (student speaking out at Zofia's lecture), Marek Kasprzyk (student, uncredited)
35mm color feature, 55 minutes

DECALOGUE 9 (DEKALOG IX)
Director: **Krzysztof Kieślowski**
Director 2: Paweł Rzepkowski
Cinematography: Piotr Sobociński
Camera Operator: Piotr Sobociński
Sound: Nikodem Wołk-Łaniewski
Cast: Ewa Błaszczyk (Hanna Nycz), Piotr Machalica (Roman Nycz, Hanna's husband), Artur Barciś (cyclist), Jan Jankowski (Mariusz Zawidzki, Hanna's lover), Jolanta Piwowarczyk (Ania, Majka's mother), Jerzy Trela (Dr. Mikołaj, Roman's friend), Małgorzata Boratyńska (nurse), Renata Berger, Janusz Cywiński (doctor), Jolanta Cichoń, Sławomir Kwiatkowski (ski hire worker), Dariusz Przychoda (Janusz)
35mm color feature, 58 minutes

DECALOGUE 10 (DEKALOG X)
Director: **Krzysztof Kieślowski**
Director 2: Dariusz Jabłoński
Cinematography: Jacek Bławut
Camera Operator: Jerzy Rudziński
Sound: Nikodem Wołk-Łaniewski
Cast: Jerzy Stuhr (Jerzy Janicki), Zbigniew Zamachowski (Artur Janicki, Jerzy's brother), Henryk Bista (stamp collector's shopkeeper), Olaf Lubaszenko (Tomek), Maciej Stuhr (Piotrek, Jerzy's son), Jerzy Turek (stamp collector at the market), Anna Gornostaj (nurse), Henryk Majcherek (stamp collectors' society president), Elżbieta Panas (Jerzy's wife), Daniel Kozakiewicz (dealer at the stamp shop), Grzegorz Warchoł (Bromski), Cezary Harasimowicz (police officer)
35mm color feature, 57 minutes

THE DOUBLE LIFE OF VÉRONIQUE (LA DOUBLE VIE DE VÉRONIQUE, PODWÓJNE ŻYCIE WERONIKI) (1991)
Director: **Krzysztof Kieślowski**

Additional Direction: Gerard Monier, Christine Gaymay, Brigitte Chaussade, Thibault Leflaive, Laurent Salotti, Pierre-Yves Ferandis, Włodzimierz Dziatkiewicz, Teresa Violetta Buhl, Grzegorz Okrasa, Maria Czartoryska
Production: Sidéral Productions, Le Studio Canal+, Studio Filmowe Tor, Norsk Film (Norway)
Producer: Leonardo de la Fuente
Executive Producer: Ryszard Chutkowski, Bernard-P. Guiremand
Production Manager: Daniel Szuster
Screenplay: **Krzysztof Kieślowski**, Krzysztof Piesiewicz
Cinematography: Sławomir Idziak
Art Direction: Krzysztof Zanussi
Editing: Jacques Witta, Urszula Lesiak
Production Design: Patrice Mercier, Halina Dobrowolska
Music: Zbigniew Preisner
Sound: Edith Vassard, Michèle Catonné
Costumes: Laurence Brignon, Claudy Fellous, Elżbieta Radke
Cast: Irène Jacob (Véronique/Weronika), Philippe Volter (Alexandre Fabbri), Halina Gryglaszewska (Weronika's aunt), Sandrine Dumas (Catherine), Jerzy Gudejko (Antek, Weronika's boyfriend), Kalina Jędrusik ("Pstrokata," Cracow choir leader), Aleksander Bardini (conductor), Władysław Kowalski (Weronika's father), Janusz Sterniński (solicitor), Louis Ducreux (professor), Claude Duneton (Veronique's father), Lorraine Evanoff (Claude), Guillaume de Tonquedec (Serge), Gilles Gaston-Dreyfus (Jean-Pierre), Alain Frérot (postman), Youssef Hamid, Thierry de Carbonnières (professor), Chantal Neuwirth (receptionist), Nausicaa Rampony (Nicole), Bogusława Schubert, Jacques Potin, Nicole Pinaud, Philippe Campos, Beata Malczewska, Dominika Szady, Barbara Szałapak, Jacek Wójcicki, Lucyna Zabawa, Wanda Kruszewska, Bernadetta Kuś, Pauline Monier, Katarzyna Gajdarska (uncredited), Anna Kadulska (uncredited)
35mm color feature, 98 minutes
Awards: Irène Jacob, Best Actress, International Film Festival, Cannes, 1991; Prize of the Ecumenical Jury, International Film Festival, Cannes, 1991; FIPRESCI, International Film Festival, Cannes, 1991; Prize of the National Society of Film Critics, USA, 1991

THREE COLORS: BLUE (TROIS COLEURS. BLEU, TRZY KOLORY. NIEBIESKI) (1993)
Director: **Krzysztof Kieślowski**
Additional Direction: Emmanuel Finkiel
Production: MK2 Productions SA, CED Productions, France 3, CAB Productions Lozanna, Studio Filmowe Tor, Canal+
Producer: Marin Karmitz

Production Manager: Yvon Crenn
Screenplay: **Krzysztof Kieślowski**, Krzysztof Piesiewicz
Screenplay Co-operation: Agnieszka Holland, Edward Żebrowski, Sławomir Idziak
Cinematography: Sławomir Idziak
Editing: Jacques Witta
Editing Co-operation: Urszula Lesiak, Michele d'Attoma, Ailo Auguste, Catherine Cormon
Production Design: Claude Lenoir
Music: Zbigniew Preisner
Sound: Jean-Claude Laureux
Costumes: Virginie Viard, Naima Lagrange
Cast: Juliette Binoche (Julie Vignon-de Courcy), Benoit Régent (Olivier), Florence Pernel (Sandrine), Charlotte Véry (Lucille), Hélène Vincent (journalist), Philippe Volter (real estate agent), Claude Duneton (doctor), Hugues Quester (Patrice, Julie's husband), Emmanuelle Riva (mother), Florence Vignon (copyist), Daniel Martin, Jacek Ostaszewski (flute player), Catherine Therouenne, Yann Trégouët (Antoine), Alain Ollivier (solicitor), Isabelle Sadoyan (maid), Pierre Forget (gardener), Philippe Manesse, Idit Cebula, Jacques Disses, Zves Penay, Arno Chevrier, Stanislas Nordey, Michel Lisowski, Philippe Morier-Genoud, Julie Delpy (Dominique), Zbigniew Zamachowski (Karol Karol), Alain Decaux
35mm color feature, 98 minutes
Awards: Golden Lion, International Film Festival, Venice, 1993; Best Cinematography, International Film Festival, Venice, 1993; OCIC, International Film Festival, Venice, 1993; Best Music, National Society of Film Critics, USA, 1993; César, Best Editing, Académie des Arts et Techniques du Cinema, France, 1994; César, Best Sound, Académie des Arts et Techniques du Cinema, France, 1994; César, Best Actress, Académie des Arts et Techniques du Cinema, France, 1994

THREE COLORS: WHITE (TROIS COLEURS. BLANC, TRZY KOLORY. BIAŁY)
(1993, released 1994)
Director: **Krzysztof Kieślowski**
Additional Direction: Emmanuel Finkiel
Production: MK2 Productions SA, France 3, CAB Production Lozanna, Studio Filmowe Tor, Canal+
Producer: Marin Karmitz
Production Manager: Yvon Crenn
Screenplay: **Krzysztof Kieślowski**, Krzysztof Piesiewicz

Screenplay Co-operation: Agnieszka Holland, Edward Żebrowski, Edward Kłosiński
Cinematography: Edward Kłosiński
Camera Operators: Henryk Jedynak, Muriel Coulin
Editing: Urszula Lesiak
Editing Co-operation: Ewa Lenkiewicz, Christian Phan-Trong Tuan, Alicja Torbus-Wosińska
Production Design: Halina Dobrowolska, Claude Lenoir
Music: Zbigniew Preisner
Sound: Jean-Claude Laureux
Costumes: Elżbieta Radke, Teresa Wardzała, Jolanta Łuczak, Virginie Viard
Cast: Zbigniew Zamachowski (Karol Karol), Julie Delpy (Dominique, Karol's wife), Janusz Gajos (Mikołaj), Jerzy Stuhr (Jurek, Karol's brother), Grzegorz Warchoł ("Elegant," exchange bureau's co-owner), Jerzy Nowak (peasant), Aleksander Bardini (solicitor), Cezary Harasimowicz (inspector), Jerzy Trela (Mr. Bronek, Karol's driver), Cezary Pazura (exchange bureau's owner), Michel Lisowski (interpreter), Piotr Machalica (man at the exchange bureau), Barbara Dziekan (Mrs. Ewa, cashier at the exchange bureau), Marzena Trybała (Mariott's employee), Philippe Morier Genoud (judge), Francis Coffinet (bank clerk), Yannick Evely (metro official), Jacques Disses (Dominique's solicitor), Teresa Budzisz-Krzyżanowska (Mrs. Jadwiga, Karol's customer), Krystyna Bigelmajer, Jerzy Dominik, Jakub Grzegorek, Małgorzata Kaczmarska (airport worker), Aleksander Kalinowski, Stan Latek, Joanna Ładyńska, Marianna Grodzka-Marziano, Jan Mayzel, J. Modet, Liliana Okowity, Adam Papliński, Wojciech Paszkowski, Małgorzata Prażmowska, Maria Robaszkiewicz, Zdzisław Rychter (luggage thief), Bożena Szymańska, Bartłomiej Topa (Jacek, Karol's employee), Wanda Wróblewska, M. Verner, Piotr Zelt (Karol's employee), Juliette Binoche (Julie), Florence Pernel (uncredited), Andrzej Precigs (engineer constructing Karol's house, uncredited)
35mm color feature, 91 minutes
Awards: Silver Bear for Directing, International Film Festival, Berlin, 1994

THREE COLORS: RED (TROIS COLEURS. ROUGE, TRZY KOLORY. CZERWONY) (1994)
Director: **Krzysztof Kieślowski**
Additional Direction: Stan Latek, Emmanuel Finkiel, Thierry Mouquin, Roman Gren, Xavier Nicol, Pascal Verdosci, Jean-Jacques Rossman
Production: MK2 Productions SA, France 3, CAB Production Lozanna, Studio Filmowe Tor, Television Suisse Romande

Producer: Marin Karmitz
Executive Producer: Yvon Crenn
Production Manager: Gérard Ruey
Screenplay: **Krzysztof Kieślowski**, Krzysztof Piesiewicz
Screenplay Co-operation: Agnieszka Holland, Edward Żebrowski, Piotr Sobociński
Cinematography: Piotr Sobociński, Piotr Jaxa
Camera Operators: Henryk Jedynka, Muriel Coulin
Editing: Jacques Witta
Editing Co-operation: Urszula Lesiak, Michele d'Attoma, Ailo Auguste, Catherine Cormon, Salvatore Di Meo, Sandrine Normand, Bettina Hofmann
Production Design: Claude Lenoir
Music: Zbigniew Preisner, Bertrand Lenclos
Sound: Jean-Claude Laureux
Costumes: Corinne Jorry
Cast: Irène Jacob (Valentine), Jean-Louis Tritignant (judge), Frédérique Feder (Karin), Jean-Pierre Lorit (Auguste), Samuel Le Bihan (photographer), Marion Stalens (vet), Teco Celio (barman), Bernard Escalon (record dealer), Jean Schlegel (neighbor), Elżbieta Jasińska (woman), Paul Vermeulen (Karin's friend), Jean-Marie Daunas (theatre manager), Roland Carez (drug dealer), Brigitte Raul, Leo Ramseyer, Nader Farman, Cécil Tanner, Anne Theurillat, Neige Dolsky, Jessica Korinek, Marc Autheman (voice), Juliette Binoche (Julie Vignon de Courcy), Julie Delpy (Dominique), Benoît Régent (Olivier), Zbigniew Zamachowski (Karol Karol)
35mm color feature, 99 minutes
Awards: Grand Prix, International Film Festival, Vancouver, 1994; Best Foreign Film, Film Critics Society, Los Angeles, 1994; Best Foreign Film, Film Critics Society, New York, 1994; César, Best Music, Académie des Arts et Techniques du Cinema, France, 1994; Grand Prix, International Film Festival, Valparaiso, 1994

Krzysztof Kieślowski: Interviews

The Dramaturgy of the Real

Krzysztof Kieślowski / 1968

From *Film na Świecie* 3–4 (1992): 7–9. Reprinted by permission.

The Dramaturgy of the Real *is an extract from Krzysztof Kieślowski's master's disser-*
tation supervised by Professor Jerzy Bossak at the Directing Department of the Łódź
Film School and submitted in 1968. It was also published in French in Positif *in 1995.*

André Bazin wrote that when cinema finds no excitation in technical innovations,
when it is not the width of the screen nor the photographic color that determines
the development of the means of expression, when movement and sound cease
to fascinate, then we resort to literature. He did not mean topics or characters; he
meant a language, structural and dramaturgical patterns.

Documentary film, tired and worn-out by its language, should reach out for
reality, within which it should search for dramaturgy, action, style. [It should]
create a new language resulting from an unprecedentedly precise transcription of
reality. It is about taking a step that would be a consequence of all the manifes-
tos written by documentary filmmakers; a consequence of Flaherty's statement
[that] *the camera is a creative tool* [emphasis in the original].

The elements of action, surprise, punch line, so important in classical dramaturgy; the elements of suspense, lack of resolution, disorderly motifs, so important in contemporary dramaturgy: all of this is not invented—it is after all mim-
icking (different perceptions of) reality. [Now] it is about ceasing the mimicry and
pretence, about taking it [reality] the way it is. Precisely with its lack of punch
lines, with its simultaneous order and disorder; it is the most contemporary and
the truest of structures. Apart from documentary film, there is no method of recording this structure. Documentary film should fully utilize its possibilities and
distinctiveness. This is a window of opportunity.

While considering the dramaturgy of the real, I asked several people—a history student in her final year, a welder, and a clerk—to write down precisely everything they do throughout the day. They were not recording conversations,
thoughts, moods, recollections, dreams. Only the events that could be seen and

heard. All the texts were fascinating film scripts. We always say that life is a ready-made script, but only filled pieces of paper present a clear proof. I do not mean (and at this moment this is also impossible for technical reasons) to realize such scripts. Because this project is similar to a practice, popular in the second year of the [Łódź] Film School, of standing a camera at a street corner and filming the traffic for an hour while the author, according to the program's conceptual ideal, should be drinking beer. Not far from that method remain the rebellious film-makers who, at festivals, present eight-hour films about a sleeping man, or ten-hour [ones] about a sleeping child [because a child should sleep longer]. Despite the artistic absurdity of such ideas (films of this type could be useful in medicine, for instance) and their non-existent relations to reality, they are somewhat edu-cational. It appears that people who persevered at the screening for a while would get excited if the man muttered, and the tension reached its peak when he turned onto his other side. This long digression is only to recall the fact that the dramatic and dramaturgical weight of an event can only be judged according to its context. We have to be well aware of this fact when considering filming reality, in which we can invent nothing—neither a significant nor a small event; when the arrange-ment, chronology and the relationship between events will be real and it will not be possible to change them at will.

The examples are of course absurd, because in the films I have described here authorship is limited to the placement of a camera. A camera shoots the film, then a machine develops it, then a copier, etc. A machine is the author. It is pos-sibly an extreme interpretation of the theory of the dramaturgy of the real, and it should not be about extreme interpretations, but about sensible [ones].

The invasion of mass media slowly and inevitably transforms the viewer's awareness. The nature of perception changes. The creator of a theory on the com-ing of the era of post-literary culture, Marshall McLuhan, says that the develop-ment of mass media will lead to a complete extinction of printed communication. McLuhan's vision—more often that of a technician rather than of a humanist—the vision of small cameras that children learn to operate in primary schools, of film libraries and accessorized televisions, is basically a vision of the world in which the printed word will no longer be needed. McLuhan is certainly exaggerat-ing—he is not considering the integration of human culture and its continuity: the invention of television, similarly to print before, will revolutionize percep-tion, but it will not change the continuity and nature of culture.

Contemporary art increasingly more often uses audiovisual means—they lead to changes in the way of thinking. We are starting to think in images, sounds, ed-its. Filmmakers' bias today will be humanity's bias tomorrow. Then it will become a norm.

Despite that, I do not believe that comic strips will replace books. After all, print, whose invention underpinned literature, did not eradicate pre-existing elements of culture, today referred to as audio-visual, such as ballet, theatre, music, dance. Only the hierarchy will change. However even this seemingly obvious statement demands from us specific decisions.

The time I describe above presents a window of opportunity for documentary film, of deriving conclusions out of dramaturgical elements contained in reality. And even though a professional will not be differently equipped than an amateur—the same way today everyone can buy the same brand of pen as that used by Huxley—films will continue to be made by artists.

The auteur in this proposed [idea of] film will continue to be most important. He discovers the world for himself and for us. "When we start a film, we do not know what the essence of its topic is. The film itself helps us to penetrate the topic, to understand the meaning of the matter; to see the threads that connect it" (Richard Leacock). "To be in the right place at the right time, to understand what should happen, what should be photographed at the time of the event taking place, to be receptive and flexible to photograph the necessary. . . . A director's individuality manifests itself much more strongly in the choice of an event and the method of expressing it, rather than in influencing [that] event. It is subjectivity not in directing a scene, but in its reproduction" (Robert Drew). "Conveying the sense of being there is most important" (Richard Leacock). I quote Leacock and Drew's stance so often because it corresponds closely with the views I want to express. Their words came out of practice. A few (different) sources' accounts of their films confirm my convictions.

We have to overcome the stage of looking for pretexts that have always served us when making films. We have to reach for what has been the essence of art since the start of the world—the life of a person. Life itself has to be transformed simultaneously into the pretext and the essence. The way it looks, goes on, continues. With all its inventory.

It is about film without artistic conventions—instead of telling about reality, telling with reality. Instead of a commentary from the author, an equal partnership between the viewer and the filmmaker.

Practically, the topic determines everything—the timing of the shooting, the place, and the length of the film. There is no script and preparation of written materials. The crew strictly records. The author is the material's master of ceremonies—the person who knows the order of events. The function of editing is not to hunt film morsels—editing, similarly to shooting, on the one hand, is conveying accurately the mood and the course of events; on the other, [it is about] the necessary compression of time and space. It is dependent completely on the rhythm and order of events. It never attempts to construct; at most, to organize.

A theory of the dramaturgy of the real leads to obvious conclusions: one can easily imagine a film resulting from its consistent implementation. It will be a psychological film about a person, [constructing] strictly fiction-feature action, using a strictly documentary method. It will compete with a Western, a melodrama, crime film, psychological and social drama. It will not replace Welles or Fellini in film art, but it will replace many contemporary realists. Because reality, and we find that often, is in fact melodramatic and dramatic, tragic and comical. It is rich in surprises and regularities, in psychological tensions and a course of thoughts and reflections reaching far beyond the photographed picture and recorded sound.

Many disappointments await us in our incessant search for the essence of things, the substance and truth, but we have to keep striving for it all the time anew, not only to reach the destination, but also for the road to it itself (Evald Schorm).

16 or 35?

ski / 1970

From *Film* 48 (1970): 2. Reprinted by permission.

This early interview with a young Krzysztof Kieślowski was published under Topics of the Day, *in the front section of* Film, *a popular Polish weekly. The style of young Kieślowski's interview in Polish reflects the stilted patois of the press in communist Poland.*

We have already written about the new and increasingly popular method of producing documentary films. Film is shot in 16mm, which then is copied onto 35mm film. In Poland that method has gained supporters especially among the young. One of them is Krzysztof Kieślowski, who has to his name three documentary films: *A Photograph* (1968, TV production), *From the City of Łódź* (1968, WFD [Documentary Film Studio]) and *I Was a Soldier* (1970, Czołówka, together with Andrzej Titkow). The last one was realized with the new method.

ski: Why do you prefer to shoot in 16mm?
Krzysztof Kieślowski: It has a lot of benefits. There are subjects that are accessible basically only for the 16. We must, therefore, learn to work on a narrow film.

ski: Could *I Was a Soldier* not be shot with the 35mm camera?
KK: I would put it differently: had I been using a 35mm camera during the shoot, a different film would have arisen. Seemingly, it is a traditional piece, realized in the method of "cinematic survey": here are veterans, blind, heavily seasoned by war; they talk to a static camera. It would seem that a light portable camera with narrow film is here utterly unnecessary. But that is so only seemingly. In that film it was not war memories of the veterans that interested us, but above all their feelings, mental states, modes of thinking. So, everything depended on their candor. The blind are sensitive and highly strung people. Narrow film, a portable camera, were essential. It allowed us to film straight after entering the subject's apartment, before he managed to become nervous, before he felt stage-fright. It

also allowed us to change the viewing angle without the necessity to stop filming, which would be lethal to the value of monologues. And, most importantly, it did not happen that we were not able to film something because of technical difficulties.

ski: Will you want to use a narrow-film camera in the future?
KK: I am currently preparing two films. The first, *Million*, will show the trajectory of a man who wins a million in a lottery. The second, *Project*, is devoted to an engineering team at a chemical plant in Tarnów, who work on intensifying production. We would like to follow the story of their improvements from the inception until the moment the project gets delivered to the highest authorities. We will make both films with the method of the "accompanying camera." Sixteen is essential here.

ski: When will you start shooting?
KK: I don't know yet. When I proposed shooting on narrow film to Documentary Film Production [Wytwórnia Filmów Dokumentalnych], the idea met with the management's interest and with objections from the experts on technical issues. As you know, a film shot on 16 must be copied onto 35mm film. It's a technical process rarely practiced here, therefore perhaps risky. Technicians contended that the image achieved that way would be bad, too grainy. Until now, there have been two films made this way in Poland: Królikiewicz's *Fidelity* (1969) and *I Was a Soldier*, both at "Czołówka." Copies on 35mm film seemed utterly accurate. Despite that, objections remained.

ski: Do you think they will disappear in the future?
KK: Probably yes. Experience in other countries indicates that all the imperfections of this process can be eliminated.

A Film about the Working Class

pel / 1971

From *Film* 47 (1971): 2. Reprinted by permission.

Almost a year after the interview on the dilemma of using 16mm or 35mm film, a year of turbulent socio-political events, this interview was also published in the front Topics of the Day *section of* Film. *It is not clear which of the statements belong to Krzysztof Kieślowski and which to his colleague, Tomasz Zygadło. Nevertheless the interview constitutes an interesting document revealing the early idealism of Kieślowski's filmmaking trajectory.*

Krzysztof Kieślowski and Tomasz Zygadło, this year's winners at the Cracow festivals,[1] are finishing work on a feature film, *Workers*.[2] According to Kieślowski's original idea, it was to be a nine-minute film. Then, there was a decision to develop and expand on the subject. There is not much time to realize it: only three months, because the filmmakers as well as the WFD [Documentary Film Studio] are keen to have the film ready before the 6th Party Congress. In the first days of December, we are likely to watch it on TV, and then it might be screened in the cinema.[3]

KK&TZ: *Workers* is intended to be a film synthesizing the portrayal of the contemporary working class. In this approach, the title has to do with a symbol of tremendous social force. We are concerned with portraying a state of mind, the consciousness of the working class most recently, in the fall of this year. We are used to seeing workers on screen at work, in formulaic situations, when they appear anonymously. However, we would like to show to the viewer how they think and feel, what they desire, what their needs and demands are, and—finally—how they see a possibility of fulfilling these needs.

It is a film that is optimistic and bitter at the same time. Optimistic, because it is attempting to show that in the years past, these very people gave most to the country, despite many difficulties and sacrifices, despite the subjectivity with which their efforts have now been judged. The film wants to show that it is this social group that has limitless strength and energy, that really wants something, believes in something, at least that one can live a better and wiser life.

It is bitter because these people understand how much needs to be done to achieve that. The proportion of optimism and bitterness is dictated here by reality. Hopes developed in December,[4] although initially in the mood of skepticism, expect fulfillment. It is now about turning hopes into ardor and sacrifice.

pel: Where did you shoot your film?

KK&TZ: In all of Poland, everywhere. In the mines of Silesia, in the biggest industrial plants of Warsaw, in the Szczecin shipyards, with the metalworkers of Poznań and Elbląg. Those were small and big factories with all sorts of production profiles. The methods we used were also very varied: from "prompted" scenes, when we would supply a topic for discussion, to discussions in front of the camera. Or, we filmed from a hidden camera. We communicated with the heroes of our films—workers—with an extraordinary ease, fairly and squarely. However, it was not uncommon that the political and social organizations operating in the plants we visited approached us with great reserve.

pel: How did you manage to organize such ample material?

KK&TZ: We assumed, supposedly of course, that everything happened in twenty-four hours. From the dawn of one day to the morning of the next. In that time we noted down the events significantly removed from one another, but after all we were concerned with a kind of synthesis. Similarly, as the screen action develops, we move from detailed matters, associated with particular working plants, to more general issues concerning the whole of Poland.

pel: You were shooting on 16mm film. Has this method, provoking many objections even recently, been taken up?

KK&TZ: There are still difficulties with it. The production house admittedly accepted it, but we still lack equipment to copy 16mm onto 35mm film. So, if we wanted to take our film to cinemas, we would have to copy it abroad. We also had issues with material. Suddenly, it seemed that in the whole country there was no sensitive 16mm film in large spools, the type with which you can record 100 percent sound. We had to be satisfied with the less sensitive film. As a result, since we were not in a position at all to light many of the filmed places, we were not able to realize many scenes.

Notes

1. That is, the 11th National Film Festival and 8th International Short Film Festival.

2. The original English title, translated directly from Polish, was *Workers '71: Nothing about Us without Us* (Polish: *Robotnicy '71: Nic o nas bez nas*). The title is a reference to the Nihil Novi constitution from 1505, which limited the powers of the Monarch and granted more rights to the "people" (i.e., nobility) and was seen as the beginning of Polish constitutional democracy.

3. The film was never shown on television or in cinemas in the directors' version. A re-edited version, not approved by the directors, titled *Housekeepers* (*Gospodarze*) was shown on television in 1972.

4. In December 1970, workers protested in the north of Poland against the increase in prices of basic commodities. The protests officially claimed forty-two lives.

Interview Not for Print

Andrzej Kołodyński / 1973

From *Kino* 5.347 (May 1996): 4–7. Reprinted by permission.

This interview was conducted on December 14, 1973, by Andrzej Kołodyński, a film journalist and writer. Krzysztof Kieślowski deemed it inappropriate for publishing at that time. Here he expresses his frustration with the censorship at the time. The interview was only published in 1996, after Kieślowski's death, in Kino, *where Andrzej Kołodyński was then editor in chief.*

Andrzej Kołodyński: In your opinion, what is a documentary, actually?
Krzysztof Kieślowski: It is a type of a film, you see, that should look broadly. Even if it looks narrowly, it should look at those issues that are happening in reality. It should bring cognizance of what is, not what should be.

AK: A film for television?
KK: I am just making one now. Such a narrow topic. But I don't think it will be broadcast. Absolutely not.

AK: Is it not too early to talk about that? I guess it is a secondary issue.
KK: Not at all secondary. It is a fundamental issue.

AK: If they gave you money . . .
KK: I take it, and I make it. However, we'll see how much longer it is going to continue. Out of the films that I made for WFD [Documentary Film Production] . . . and I can count them . . . I have made six for WFD. Out of those, four were shelved. So, they don't feel like having more films like that. *From the City of Łódź* cannot be taken out of the archives, I don't know why. *Factory* absolutely cannot be taken out, the title marked in red. . . . *Workers*, one wouldn't even want to mention. *The Bricklayer* also cannot be taken out. There you have four films. Two others: a film about public servants and about Fiat's preparations for the Monte Carlo rally, which has never screened in cinemas, because the Director of FSO

[Passenger Car Factory] took care of that. Admittedly, it is not a good film, but this is not the issue. This is about a trend, about matters that you can address and those you can't.

AK: But you are like a roly-poly toy since this hasn't stopped you from making the film *Child*.[1]

KK: Now, it would seem that this topic would not clash with the official propaganda, because it is a film about people wanting to have children, giving birth to babies, striving to bring those children up. . . . In one word, it is an expression of the official propaganda. But if you see that film, and you will see it at some stage, you will see that it may not be so after all. . . . Because I respect my profession and record what appears to me to be true and deserving of recording. In that film, there is, unfortunately, a whole heap of issues that do not suit propaganda. From the way things appear, the way people appear, because of some kind of revelation of their mentality, their views. . . . In summary, all this presents a rather frightening picture.

AK: So how do you explain documentaries made by other people, whom we know and know to be honest, which bring us an optimistic hymn of progress?

KK: Maybe they are made by those who believe in their reality. Simply so. They were and remain idealists, they believe in it. . . . For instance, in their nation. But I don't believe.

AK: Since you are making films, don't you have to reach the viewer, because otherwise what sense would it have?

KK: You certainly know that essentially I'm not especially interested in that . . . reaching the viewer.

AK: So a documentary is there mainly to record something for an archive?

KK: I wouldn't ponder the function of a documentary; it's too complex a matter.

AK: But you are making a film for a purpose.

KK: Yes.

AK: For what?

KK: For myself. Of course, never in a lifetime can I tell anyone that.

AK: Isn't it the case that every director dreams, even subconsciously, of reaching the broadest [audience] with his work?

KK: Yes, of course, for instance I would like my film to be liked by a few friends.

. . . Ten-odd people who are important to me. Recently we were in Sopot with my friend Z. [Tomasz Zygadło], we wrote a script at ZAiKS [Polish Society of Authors and Composers], so you can see how splendidly grown up we have become. We ate breakfast in our room, sat with the authors of the song *Hippopotamus* at the same table. . . . We were in a very pleasant social situation. And then we analyzed our professional lives until that point, my four years and Tomek's [Zygadło] three. I came to the conclusion, once I thought it through, that apart from two minor social transgressions,[2] which essentially came out of a misunderstanding rather than malice, I have never compromised in what I have done with what I think, what surrounds me. That's why my films cannot be taken out of the archives.

AK: Passive resistance; are you not afraid it is a somewhat counterproductive stance?
KK: Absolutely classical stance, not calculated with the future in mind.

AK: Something in it is not right. . . .
KK: So suggest something. I am certainly not lying to you.

AK: Maybe you were disappointed by the way your first film was received? A kind of chip on your shoulder?
KK: I was absolutely not disappointed. The first film is the best I have managed to make so far. It was a film for television—*The Photograph*—which doesn't exist now, not even the negative. Not to spite me, but in all life's simplicity because it was f***ing swiped. First, two copies that were made disappeared. And at this moment—because I have been there to recreate that film, with my own money to make a copy for myself—at this moment there is no negative. And two years ago it was still there; I enquired. You see, the first copy disappears, then the second one, and now the negative. I paid PLN200 to this archivist to find it. All this is unimportant, of course. . . . Now I am thinking only about the film I am making, about the script I am writing now, and that's all. You see how much—apart from the idiotic nineteenth-century, not-only-unfashionable, but also moronic, attachment to self-respect . . . to the conviction that you are quite all right—how much success, career progress, and money I sacrificed. You probably understand that if for four years I had been making films that were expected of me . . . couldn't I be making now, without any problems, big films, well-paid, screened everywhere?

AK: Aren't you too young to be bitter?
KK: That I can't help. Maybe it's a matter of a mental attitude, not only the external conditions.

AK: It's good that you make films despite . . .

KK: Yes I do, but I have been wondering for about a year and a half when this will give. Because how many more fools will give money to see later the deletions of the censors.

AK: So, what's next?

KK: I don't think so far ahead. I simply imagine that if they ban me from making what I want, then until I no longer feel like it, I will be making films about OHS on the railway and a buffalo's naked arse in the mines in Lubin. . . . And if not, it won't matter, I'll simply stop. Despite there being an awful attachment to luxury. Luxury, which I have, you know that—I earn not 2.5 thousand a month like in other professions, but six or seven . . . The luxury that has come out of it is such that I had nothing and now I have a flat, I have a wife and a child. That's the type of luxury, but it still counts.

AK: Would you like me to give you an example of a documentary maker who, in this situation, started to make honest films, but completely barren? You don't have to look far—as a matter of fact, among your masters. . . .

KK: I understand this attitude: to make films that cannot possibly go to the point . . . the point that could provoke conflict. There is a way of approaching filmmaking to eliminate any potential for controversy.

AK: Maybe that is nevertheless a way of discovering other subjects—for instance, psychological?

KK: Have you forgotten what you said about it yourself a moment ago?

AK: The crux of the matter is this: do you or don't you want to be a film director? If so, you have to find a way of making something conscionable, something that doesn't repulse you. Find a place like that. Don't you think that WFD is such a place?

KK: I am of the opinion that it is simply impossible.

AK: Don't you take documentary too narrowly?

KK: Perhaps—however, at the same time, also broadly, because I have tried to make things differently, thematically and in other ways. . . .

AK: You are touching only on the sociological matter. Maybe you should show something else—an idea on the screen? Not only people's lives.

KK: I don't think so. To me, documentary is there precisely to show the lives of people.

AK: So, should we talk about Ken Loach?

KK: Of course, about Loach, but you can turn it [recorder] off. You see, this [conversation] hasn't worked out at all. . . .

Notes

1. Most likely *Child* refers to *First Love*.

2. AK's comment: "Kieślowski probably means the two already mentioned films about public servants and preparations for a race."

Conversation with the Laureate

Zygmunt Kałużyński and Marian Turski / 1976

From *Polityka*, March 6, 1976, 1, 10. Reprinted by permission.

In 1976, Krzysztof Kieślowski was awarded the title of "Ferment 1976" *by* Polityka, *an influential Polish broadsheet, for* "activity that provokes thought." *In the rationale for the decision printed on* Polityka's *front page,* Curriculum Vitae *was named as the most provocative film, socially and culturally, of then-recent times.*

Polityka: If you had not become a filmmaker, would you have chosen the career of a political activist?
Krzysztof Kieślowski: Never. Why this conjecture?

P: You search for social tensions, you are able to perceive things at the intersection of economics and social issues, you are interested in human relations and—one might say—civic stances. The majority of the films you've made suggest that you have the temperament of an activist.
KK: No, I don't. I simply live in this place, in this country, in this time, and at the same time I look for a means of expression in a language that I know.

P: Could you please remind us of the films you have made.
KK: I started with the graduation [film] *From the City of Łódź*, then there was *Factory* and three failed films—*Refrain, Before the Rally, X-Ray*—a series of films [that were] humanistic in a way. I suppose the foundations were faulty. Next, I made a few advertising-instructional films because of the lack of ways to make a living in that period, and then *Workers* with Tomek [trans: diminutive of Tomasz] Zygadło, finally *First Love, Personnel, Pedestrian Subway*. Besides that, for "Czołówka" [Film Production Company]—together with Andrzej Titkow—a somewhat successful film *I Was a Soldier* about blind soldiers and their current mental state.

P: Which film do you value most?
KK: It's difficult to say, but I have a sentimental attachment to the film that

—coincidentally—has gotten lost. I mean *The Photograph*. Well, in 1968 I got an old photograph from Kazimierz Karabasz: two boys, poorly dressed, four years old; they stand in a backyard in Brzeska Street, in soldiers' caps, with rifles. It was a film about how we looked for these boys, now adult men, brothers. I took them by surprise because first we switched the camera on, and then we knocked on their door. We showed them the photograph, which they hadn't seen. We caught in the film their emotion, attachment, and love for that place, [for] the backyard, for that time.

P: Is this your main method, that is this filming by surprise?

KK: No, I did it once and have never repeated it. You have to have an appropriate topic that would justify this working method, [which is] probably overused. We see it often on television, and it is reminiscent—in a sense—of an investigation. The person with a camera presses the suspect—"Why have you acted this or that way"—and the latter squirms in front of the camera out of shame and fear.

P: In the debate on *Curriculum Vitae* relayed in *Polityka*, one of the speakers praised the film for being "a life without camouflage, without directing." Is that your artistic credo? Is it at all possible? Do you like to rely on a happening, on letting things run their course, or are you of the opinion that one needs some preparation, including of people?

KK: You can make a film using either method. Generic or methodological divisions are not important. It depends on what you want to achieve, what subject [you want] to touch on. With *Curriculum Vitae* I made of course a thing that is, in some way, staged. A hero who faces the party control committee received a script, which was an amalgamation of a few authentic cases. It was easier for him to empathize with the role because he had lived through a similar case.

P: And in *Factory*, which is nothing else but a highly dramatic production meeting, don't you think that, after all, people a c t e d [spacing in original] a little bit because there was a camera in the room?

KK: No, those people didn't act at all. They were busy and consumed by their own very important business. It's like a girl from *First Love* who is to give birth. She is not acting, her belly simply hurts, regardless of whether there is or there isn't a camera in the room.

P: They often say that what you are doing is a kind of a signature of the young generation.

KK: What young generation? I am thirty-five. . . .

P: They say that what you or your colleagues, such as Tomasz Zygadło, propose is a new formula of documentary filmmaking.

KK: No, I think it is developing old formulas. Of course, it is natural to attempt to find a different way of looking, a different way of photographing, a different way of editing, but it has nothing to do with a generational change.

P: Wait a minute. . . . Critics and observers are saying something different. That in your work, together with that of some of your colleagues, a different way of seeing social issues through cinema has appeared. The first quality listed, for instance, is that you allow your characters to speak, that you give them a voice. Old documentaries observed them instead, or taped them and fixed them with a written comment.

KK: There has simply come a time when one wants to peer a little bit inside people's heads, not only to see what they look like [on the outside]. Of course, you can edit, you can contrive, you can engineer conflict, you can make up commentary. There have been superb films which function that way. But there has come a time when you want to look inside people's skulls.

P: The influence of television?

KK: I don't believe television has anything to do with it. The films you are talking about were fundamentally about events, issues, less so about people. We have come to . . . no, we haven't. A technology has come along that's a little bit better, simply newer; you can take a camera, go somewhere, switch it on when the subject doesn't know it is switched on. Not to surprise him, but he doesn't have to tense up in front of the camera as in the past; there is no need for preparation; you don't have to bring in a chair with a sign "Director" and scream at people through a megaphone. You can simply come in quietly, sit in an armchair, as we are sitting and talking, and simply chat. . . . So, I don't agree with having that way of seeing opposed to mine, which has come about, as I suppose, from technological development.

P: You stubbornly insist that you are not a rebel but a continuator.

KK: Yes, decidedly. At some stage, I was qualified as an "anti-Karabaszean." It was a mistake and a misunderstanding. I have never been anti-Karabaszean, I have never been against the documentary film tradition with which I engaged after graduation from film school. Assigning me—in that time—to a group of the young who insisted on clearing "the old" off the field was essentially unsound, and also it caused me ordinary human hurt.

P: Supposedly, you are not concerned with critics, but a critic managed to hurt you.

KK: Because I was afraid that an injustice might be directed at the man I like and value, that is Kazimierz Karabasz. I don't like to be squeezed into some place where I don't feel like being.

P: Do you find ideas for your films yourself, or is it a result of the thinking and inspirations of a team of people?

KK: It differs a lot. For instance, *Curriculum Vitae* is a typical film that was proposed by WFD [Documentary Film Studio]. They came up with an idea and an initiative to make such a film. Of course, how to make it was my task.

P: Where do you look for collaborators and concepts? Does a film come about as a result of discussions, meetings, group effort?

KK: The atmosphere is the most important thing. I get on well with the studios with which I work. With WFD, with Studio TOR, with the Television Film Studio. To me friendships seem important, [as are] common essential and artistic views in the teams of people with whom I communicate. The films that come into being are to some extent a result of meetings, conversations, arguments, sometimes about matters seemingly small, technical, but coming together to form a common ground. I am thinking here about friends from WFD—Zygadło, Łoziński, Kosiński—about people from TOR—Różewicz, Zalewski, Żebrowski, Zanussi, Krauze, Idziak. In this very atomized environment of filmmakers, the existence of a group of people on whose help and advice I can always count seems to me essential.

P: When you come up with a film by yourself, what gives you a direction?

KK: Whatever interests me. That is, personal passion. When I do what concerns me, I hope there are a handful of people in Poland who are also concerned with it.

P: Do you sometimes have an impression that you are late? I'm thinking of *Factory*, shot in 1969, but screened only in 1971. It could have been more aggressive, it could have been an important discussion piece, but when it [finally] appeared on screens, it was probably no longer satisfying.

KK: Unfortunately. On that subject, my voice was one among many that appeared. Among press articles, [which were]—then—incomparably sharper and wiser. In 1969, it would have been, just as you say, more aggressive, and at the same time it would have uncovered and brought to a public forum what was not spoken about publicly. It is after all a structure [of public commentary] that really appeals to me and is perhaps often the driving force behind my actions.

P: Is what you have done so far an overture to a feature film?

KK: Making a feature film has not been and is not my objective. If I am toying with it, it is only because in documentary there are too many doors closed. . . .

P: Formal considerations?

KK: No. Because of the content. Besides that, there are also genre limitations; you can't talk about certain things with people, because either you cause them damage, or these things are distasteful. You must not spy on people in private or in intimate situations, because how would you, with what right? For that, you have to hire actors and that's how it must be. Maybe this will change some time, I don't know. I doubt it. And content-wise—that platform on which I can fit with my subjects in documentary is too small for me. But I don't want to abandon documentary.

P: There is a popular demand for contemporary film, because we've had enough of adaptations, historical, costume films, and other ersatz. I wonder if Kieślowski and his colleagues should not transfer their documentary experience, their understanding of life and its conflicts, to contemporary feature film.

KK: It's a possibility, and I am not renouncing it. If I say that a feature fiction film has not been my objective, that is because I make feature films precisely the way I make documentary films. I have just finished a feature film. It is called *The Scar*, about a typical moral conflict in the industrial context. You could call it "a production-film," but hopefully without the negative connotations of that genre. A story of a man who with full confidence, with enthusiasm, comes to a place tainted with, let's call it, an ecological fault, and also a social one. My hero realizes that he has little room to manoeuvre and that his mature years have borne no fruit.

P: So, [it's] a drama of the individual? So, it's a less sociological film than your previous ones?

KK: No, because it has a very broad social canvas. Maybe even too broad, which results in it having less action than is typical for a feature [fiction] film, and which I would like to create but can't.

P: One can then make the following generalization: you give your own social take through the view or temperament of an individual.

KK: That's what I'm trying to do.

P: Aren't you drawn by big crowds, expansive landscapes?

KK: So far, no. Perhaps a fresco, or a mosaic, but not a panorama [painting].

P: Aren't you afraid that you will fall slave to a certain cliché?

KK: I hope not. To tell the truth, I'm not very fond of my profession. One of the things that keeps me in it is curiosity. How is it going to end? A film, a take, a scene. This curiosity allows me to persist in a documentary, and bring documentary elements into fiction [film]. If I give a text to an actor, I know beforehand that, with some minor corrections, he is going to say it the way I have written it. If I only sketch a situation for him, provoke his behavior, if I clash him against people from outside of his profession, who bring to the set their issues, their mannerisms, their problems—I wait for the results with anticipation. Maybe for the viewer the method is not most important, [but] for me it very much is so.

P: What needs to be enriched, what additional ingredients are needed, to make a feature fiction film out of a documentary?

KK: Action and artists instead of people who represent themselves. Nothing else is needed. What documentary elements work in feature fiction? Obvious things: a good ear for dialogue, the appearance of things and people, a feeling for the falsehood of situations and acting. But there are also more important elements. Transferring onto fiction film the structure and dramaturgy of a documentary film. Disordered, not always set in stone, with digressions, where we are moved along not by action, but by an issue, sometimes a mood. The dramaturgy of unfinished sentences, sketched characters; the dramaturgy that after all exists in life. One can say that these are bloopers, but one can make a rule, a virtue out of them. Zanussi's *The Illumination* proves that this approach can work.

P: When one watches *Factory*, comparison with the series *Directors* inevitably comes to mind. *Directors* was, among others, your competition for "Ferment 1975." If you were a judge, whom would you vote for?

KK: No, I can't answer that. As a matter of fact, I value that series a lot. It is a very interesting thing, but it is taking one brick out of a huge wall.

P: You have been given credit for achieving a balance between two divergent modes of documentary cinema: observation and reconstruction. Documentary authenticity is impaired, as it were, by matter-of-factness, dryness; and reconstruction, by theatricality, affectation, stiltedness, and so on. So, in *First Love* and even more so in *Personnel* one can speak of a symbiosis [of the two modes]. A hired actor comes to normal, ordinary people who are doing their job, and you are shooting a film in which it is not easy to separate documentary from reconstruction.

KK: That fusion interests me, and it belongs to the formal sphere that I am investigating, and I have a feeling that one can ferret new things out of it. But I don't see this as something incredibly new.

P: Can your earlier statement that you "expanded your [documentary] platform" relate to *Personnel*?
KK: In *Personnel* I employed a cunning, impudent stunt. I placed the action of a film not in a factory, but in the theater and that setting is easier to digest. I chose a safer setting, where it is easier to present conflict.

P: Still, it appears that you feel comfortable in the setting of the theater.
KK: That's not too far from the truth. I graduated from theatrical [technicians] high school and I was even a wardrobe assistant for a year.

P: In what circumstances? For what reason?
KK: That's how my life worked out, or, more precisely, how it didn't. I had tried for film school twice and was successful only the third time. And in those two years, I had to live on something.

P: So, *Personnel* is also a[n auto]biographical film?
KK: To some degree.

P: You don't have theatrical inclinations?
KK: I am just preparing a television play *Two for the Seesaw*.[1] Whether there will be other attempts with the theater, I don't know. Anyway, I only ever make short-term plans.

P: Occasionally, the press, and also viewers, ascribe to you contrary intentions. Are you in *First Love*, they pondered, advocating for extramarital children? Should this film be seen as healthy and constructive, or harmful? In *Personnel*, are you on the side of the rebellious tailor, who acts in a rather loutish way, or are you dishing out a bureaucratic satire? What is your attitude to those ideological insinuations?
KK: They asked me the most biting questions about *Curriculum Vitae*. Whose side am I on, the defendant's or judges'? I have always answered, on his side.

P: It's strange anyone could doubt that. Even the camera frames characters in *Curriculum Vitae* in a biased way.
KK: Not true. As a matter of fact, I am not biased. I swear that if I imagined that, for instance, a signet ring on a committee member's finger would be read in a particular way, I would have asked him to take it off, because I would see it as

too primitive a trick. And reactions to *Curriculum Vitae* are by no means uniform. Many debaters have said that the "defendant" is a dullard and troublemaker.

P: In *Personnel* there is controlled staging, so there must also be an intention that pushes in a particular direction.
KK: Yes and no, even though I do have a precise view on that matter. In *Personnel*, at the end, I leave the young man with an empty sheet of paper, sad, in wide angle, I leave the question: will he sign or won't he?

P: The decision is marked, because he closes his fountain pen.
KK: He closes the fountain pen, and then there is a shot in which he opens it. I've juxtaposed it on purpose.

P: Let's formulate the matter in this way: you are biased, but you don't prompt the viewer with answers; let them decide within themselves what decision should be made.
KK: That's what I desire. Not to dot the "i's." Not to point people in any particular direction, [to declare] that one should behave this or that way, that I am for marriage or against marriage. I simply want to pose a problem—despite being on a particular side—not solve it.

P: Has any review annoyed you ever?
KK: Never.

P: Is it because you are indifferent to them, or because they are all good.
KK: No, not true. I have plenty of bad ones. Everyone has a right to their own view. I don't see myself as someone who's always right.

P: You are already well acclaimed. Different awards, and now ours. Isn't life spoiling you too much? Won't you get spoilt?
KK: I'm completely at ease [about it]; definitely not. Positive feedback, awards, they make it simpler to make what I want to make. They make life easier.

Note

1. Broadcast in 1976, William Gibson's *Two for the Seesaw* was one of the three attempts by Krzysztof Kieślowski at the popular and ambitious theatrical form of Polish television theater.

Interview with Krzysztof Kieślowski

Ginette Gervais / 1979

From *Jeune Cinema* 123 (December 1979/January 1980): 30–31. Reprinted by permission.

Jeune Cinema *is a monthly film magazine created in 1964 by Jean Delmas primarily for a readership of students belonging to the three hundred school film clubs of la Fédération Jean-Vigo. Remarkably adroit at identifying emerging new talents and movements and fiercely independent of sponsors and advertisers, it was the first French film journal to interview Kieślowski.*

Ginette Gervais: Is your film's [*Camera Buff*] concern with current events an exception within Polish cinema?

Krzysztof Kieślowski: No: many filmmakers have followed the same development.

GG: The new generation?

KK: Precisely; but don't forget that the previous generation of directors, like [Jerzy] Kawalerowicz, also made films about current events.

GG: Before continuing, I would like to ask you about the end of your film, which I'm afraid of not having understood completely. Why has your hero's friend lost his job? Because he acted as an informant?

KK: Not at all. He is the officer of culture, he's supervising the film. The film is being made in the context of a competition organized by TV; towns receive large grants on such occasions to restore their facades, etc. . . . Often they use the grants in a more practical way, such as for organizing kindergartens. A critique made in these circumstances, even if it is founded, can laugh at the negative as much as the positive.

What seems to me important to show is that you only ever discover a part of the truth; you approach it by stages, never all at once; there are several stages. You discover little by little, you question. But we mustn't be fooled; it's rare that a work of art will have a direct impact.

For several years now in Poland, mature, intelligent, young generations have been appearing who haven't known any other regime than the current one. It's in relation to that regime that they live, and not by comparison to the one that existed before the war.

What is striking now, more than criticism itself, is the extraordinary freedom of tone.

This is probably the most important value of films in recent years, and the public is really beginning to come to the cinema.

GG: I was also very interested in your sense of humor.

KK: Since the film deals with reality it is funny, but it is not a comedy; it's funny because life is funny; but sometimes it's the spirit of Kafka, which has nothing to do with comedy. We laugh a lot at first, then the film cools down; it becomes increasingly serious.

GG: A bit like *Bad Luck* [Andrzej Munk, 1960]?

KK: This kind of film has always existed in Poland, but for a long time, it didn't succeed in getting noticed. Whereas now they're around in number and quality. But there has always been this continuity since Munk. I myself once received a Munk prize, which is awarded for first movies.

GG: A bit like our Jean Vigo prize?

KK: Polish cinema experienced a second wave after 1956. Men like Munk, and [Tadeusz] Konwicki also, were critical, but through the lens of history. We must do justice to the generation that showed a whole new reality.

Unfortunately we don't have in Poland either a literature or a drama focusing on describing the world. For a long time we've suffered from this need. We have no description at all, not even the most basic, and yet we would need not only the outward appearance, but also the political, social, psychological aspects. No branch of artistic creation at the moment fulfills this role. It is in this vacuum that film has begun its work. It is necessary to know this in order to understand the imperfection of this cinema that remains for now at the level of description; it is not yet a really precise analysis; there is not, understandably so, any real generalization; only realistic little films that try to fill this gap in the description of reality. And that's why they're having so much success in Poland; many really are experiencing a great success. There is much debate, even in the press, because everyone has realized that film touches on problems about which no one has spoken in public. But I stress the imperfection; it's a start; we have not seen a *La Strada* [Federico Fellini, 1954] yet, but it will come!

GG: And what about censorship? You must touch on hot issues?

KK: There is censorship; it's functioning, but it considers that this type of film is in the interests of all; the censor knows, like everyone, that there are many things to change; people in power know it just as well as the population. Censorship has a rather pragmatic role; it doesn't constitute a real problem.

GG: Authors don't censor themselves too much?

KK: Of course, yes! The problem is knowing to what degree censorship allows you to express yourself. But cinema as it currently exists does not go so far that censorship can eliminate the value of film.

GG: Do you have projects underway?

KK: Right now I'm making documentaries.

GG: By choice or necessity?

KK: I love documentary film: it's what keeps you in touch with life. In fiction, I invent the world; but for fiction to correspond to reality, you have to know the real world well, and this world one learns about through documentary film. It's what's called charging the battery.

First Meetings with Krzysztof Kieślowski

Jacques Demeure / 1980

From *Positif* 227 (February 1980): 23–28. Reprinted by permission.

Positif *had taken an interest in Kieślowski as early as 1978, when* The Scar *was shown at the Berlin and Cannes film festivals. However, Jacques Demeure prefaced this interview with Kieślowski by expressing his frustration at how elusive the increasingly lauded and in-demand filmmaker turned out to be. Demeure had to pursue him over the course of a month to a range of events and screenings in Lille (where* From a Night Porter's Point of View *was shown) and Paris (where* Camera Buff *was screened) before finally being able to meet with him at the Polish Institute in Paris.*

Jacques Demeure: You started as a director even before finishing your studies at the Łódź Film School, and you have since made many films. In addition, have you performed other functions in film production, as an assistant for example?
Krzysztof Kieślowski: No, I have never been anyone's assistant. My ambition has always been to direct, even if only films about cicadas, rather than to be someone's assistant.

JD: Which production unit do you belong to?
KK: To the TOR group, previously headed by Stanisław Różewicz, and now by Krzysztof Zanussi. Filmmakers such as Zanussi, of course, as well as Edward Żebrowski, Antoni Krauze, Filip Bajon, Janusz Majewski, among others, make it, in my opinion, the best production unit, along with the "X" unit headed by Andrzej Wajda.

JD: You have made many documentaries since 1968.
KK: About thirty. Also, some feature films and TV movies. Also, TV drama, which for me represents another form of filmmaking. Also, the theatrical *mise en scène* for a play I wrote, *Biography* (*Życiorys*), based on one of my documentaries.

JD: Among the many documentaries, do you have a preference for some of them?

KK: I have some favorites, of course, but not strong ones. I look at what I have done with a certain detachment; it is difficult for me to have clear favorites. So I quite like *Biography* (*Życiorys*), *The Photograph* (*Zdjęcie*), *From the City of Łódź* (*Z miasta Łodzi*), *Hospital* (*Szpital*), *From a Night Porter's Point of View* (*Z punktu widzenia nocnego portiera*).

JD: Do you have regular collaborators with whom you always work?
KK: Yes. The cinematographer, camera operator, sound operator, editor have almost always been the same. These are people who understand me and whom I understand. Yet now, I feel a need for change.

JD: You also worked on video, for television?
KK: Yes. I directed three shows written by others. There are two that are worth mentioning. *Two for the Seesaw*, by Gibson, an American play that everyone knows, and *The Card Index* [*Kartoteka*] (1979) by Tadeusz Różewicz, the protagonist of which is a man who straightens out his own life. This is not a work in a realistic vein, but a production that abandons theatrical aesthetics to get closer to the real, which seems appropriate for television. It's actually very close to a film, shot in a really ordinary apartment, with very mobile portable video cameras, looking nothing like the recording of a theatrical performance, of which there seem to be a lot in France. If I directed *The Card Index*, it is because the author's thinking was very close to mine, because I could take on the theme of the drama and be a little more than a simple director.

JD: You've also shot TV movies that you've written.
KK: *Pedestrian Subway* is a fairly short movie that happens in a pedestrian underpass; the action takes place between passers-by about whose lives we discover a few fragments; it's a little drama between a man and a woman who separated one day; the man tries to return to the woman, but does not succeed, because he's a little man, a somewhat cynical careerist. But for me it's not a good movie.

Personnel is a feature film set at the opera: a seventeen-year-old guy comes to work in the costume shop and discovers what could be defined as life in a small cell; the theater, backstage, is like a life trapped in a tiny shell; the young man is still a blank page, is full of ideas, aspires to greatness, to art, and his dreams collide with a very cruel reality, because our world is cruel. What's interesting in this film, I believe, is that the theater is real: the theatre director is actually played by the director of the Opera, all the costumers are played by real costumers. There are one or two actors that one could say are professionals, like the one who plays the young man, but whom I prefer to call "my gang"; these are students of the directing program of the Łódź Film School; they carry the dramatic line, the drama of this little drama, but what gives life to this film is real, very real: there are conversations between the costumers about completely banal things, both long and funny at the same time, exactly the tone of ordinary conversation you get between ordinary people in an office or workshop, and which, on the screen, becomes metaphorical or comical. The film traces the downfall of the young man; we leave him at the end, when the director requires him to write a sort of letter of denunciation against one of his friends, without knowing whether he will sign it. This film won the Grand Prize at the Festival of Mannheim, and fifteen prizes in Poland, that is to say nearly all the prizes there are for TV movies. Then I filmed *The Calm*, also a feature film, in which Jerzy Stuhr plays the lead role, a man who gets out of jail and has only one ambition: to get some peace. He does not want a career, nor money nor friends nor love. He wants only a bed and a TV, and to earn two thousand bucks a month so that he has something to eat. And he isn't able to make it happen. . . .

JD: Do you find it very different to shoot for television and for film?
KK: There is no difference, except that television pays less and you have to shoot faster. But since we're shooting in 16mm, we can shoot faster. There's no problem.

JD: *The Scar* is your first feature film.
KK: Yes, if you like, my first feature film for cinema. But in Poland we do not clearly distinguish between films for cinema and television films. Before *The Scar*, there was *Personnel*. For me, then, this is my second feature film.

JD: It's a film that examines power in the context of the most recent history of Poland. Have there been many films that make such references?
KK: Now there are many. The documentaries that my friends and I made refer to contemporary reality. And it's from this documentary current that many directors have emerged, and also many themes for fiction films. These documentaries have opened up access to specific topics that hitherto fiction film did not touch.

JD: You bring television into the plot of *The Scar*, and you do it again in *Camera Buff*. It seems to preoccupy you a lot. . . .
KK: It's one part of our world now, as important as the factory, or agriculture, love, and death. Just kidding, of course.

JD: But could *The Scar* have been made for television?
KK: I'm not sure that this film could have been done for television, but it was broadcast two months ago. Anyway, I did not propose this subject for television.

If there is any difference between films for television and film for the cinema, it's a difference of subject. The whole world over, television is a means of propaganda, while cinema is primarily a cultural element. This fundamental difference between these two means of expression entails the choice of different themes.

JD: The main character of *The Scar* is going through a personal crisis.

KK: He's a man in a position of power, at the head of the largest chemical plant in Europe, a company so big that it is detrimental to the natural environment and the human side of things. Hence the title, *The Scar*. But it's not at all an environmentalist movie; this is a film about the need to protect certain values, perhaps traditional values, but which people feel good to be a part of, because they serve as references, points of support. A man, an honest man comes among them, he wants to bring them happiness. But they imagine their happiness completely differently than him. The drama, the tragedy of the protagonist, arises when he begins to realize that the happiness he has brought is not at all what they were waiting for. Of course, he achieved his goal, since he managed to build the factory, but, morally, he is confronted with failure.

JD: How was the film received upon its release in Poland?

KK: Very well by critics. But it had a very small audience. It was still that period when it seemed to audiences that contemporary films, especially those concerning industrial productivity, could not be interesting. I think that today the reception would be different, because people have gotten used to seeing interesting works on this subject.

JD: Maybe because at the time of the release of *The Scar* they still had in mind other earlier films dealing with production. But, after this work of fiction, you returned to documentaries with *From a Night Porter's Point of View*, which is based on an interview.

KK: It's not an interview, it's a monologue, a monologue recorded before the shooting and organized around a succession of themes. Then I proceeded to shoot and edit the whole thing.

JD: What reactions has this film provoked?

KK: It has not really been shown. It was practically only seen at the Kraków Short Film Festival. In Poland, the distribution of short films is problematic. It is never very large. *From a Night Porter's Point of View* is not an exception to this pattern. Of all my documentaries, only one was really shown, *Seven Women of Different Ages*, because it had the opportunity to be screened with a major feature film.

JD: To continue to make short films in alternation with feature films is an exceptional practice for a French filmmaker. Is it the same in Poland?

KK: No, there are still some Polish filmmakers who do this, and successfully.

JD: Does shifting from feature film to documentary represent for you a change in the form of expression?

KK: Why do I make features? Because there are themes we cannot be dealt with in a documentary, either because they do not fit in a short space, or because the truth doesn't accord with these themes. The documentary, for example, can hardly penetrate into private life: everyone wants to keep that to themselves, and does not want to expose it. And major psychological and political problems are difficult to deal with in a documentary, because it would be necessary to film people as they live, their connection to their profession, their wives. . . . And it is very difficult to ask them to cooperate. That's why I make feature films. But is it another form of expression? Of course, I have to invent for myself, to create the world that I film. Also, when I shoot a feature film, I always know how it will end.[1] When I shoot a documentary, I don't know. And that is exciting: I don't know how the scene that we're in the process of filming will end, and even less the entire film. For me, the documentary is a grander form than the fiction film, because I think life is smarter than me, that it creates situations more interesting than those I could invent myself. This happens very often. For example, I would not have been able to invent a character like the "night porter." And what actor would be able to play the part with his manner of speaking? Such an actor does not exist. It could only be the actual living person.

JD: Your next feature film, *Camera Buff*, refers to the movement of amateur filmmakers in Poland.

KK: It was once a very important movement. And there are still a lot of people who have cinema rather than stamp collecting as a hobby. A number of professional filmmakers have come from this movement: Krzysztof Zanussi, for example. Today, it's less important, partly because it has been institutionalized, partly because there are technical difficulties, lack of cameras, of film. But this is the least important, because if someone has something to say, he will always say it, if he really wants to. It's the problem of institutionalization that's more serious. There are festivals, there are organizations of amateurs. These festivals expect a quite particular type of film, and people, instead of doing what they feel or what they want, make films that are expected by the festivals. And this creates a system running on empty, a completely closed circuit. But, with a few thousand participants, the movement still has some importance, I think. You begin of course by filming your own family, making home movies. And then, sometimes, as is the case with the "camera buff," you become aware of the tool that you have in hand, and you begin to look at the world. If I was able to invent my hero, it was because this phenomenon occurs quite often. Of course, *Camera Buff* is not a film about amateur filmmakers, but they did not see anything false in it, and have often stated that they have had this experience. And there are old amateurs who regret of course not having thrown out their first films, but admit that that's how they started out, before working for television: "You're right, we were wrong."

JD: Why did you use Krzysztof Zanussi and an extract of *Camouflage*, rather than shooting a short sequence of an imaginary feature film and getting an actor to play an imaginary professional director?

KK: Because what interested me was to bring in a real authority, the real authority of Zanussi. Also, I wanted to give the impression that this whole story is real, since there's Zanussi, since there are in the movie some other people famous in Poland. And to make people think that perhaps all of it is true, that the truth of the film comes from reality, that it can be accepted as real. Among the other celebrities, there's Andrzej Jurga, who is really a television producer, who is in charge of amateur cinema, who, in reality, fulfills exactly the same function as in my film. He was my classmate at the Łódź Film School, and is now in the process of directing his first feature film. There is also a television producer among them whom Poles recognize, a bespectacled man, who also played the part of producer in *Man of Marble*. He's not acting under his real name, just because in reality, he's not a producer of TV, but of radio. But for Poles his face is associated with this role, because he sometimes works for television.

JD: Was the debate with Krzysztof Zanussi about *Camouflage* staged or simply documented?

KK: The debate was organized for *Camera Buff*, but was shot like a documentary, because the spectators freely improvized their opinions. This type of debate is held by filmmakers several times a month upon the release of one of their films. Except that, in this particular case, there were technical constraints, the choice of one room rather than another mainly. But the people really came to see Zanussi's film and to discuss it with him. And I filmed them without intervening. The scene was not written in advance.

JD: Your main character is going through a crisis that seems to act as a revelation, as a means of criticism of everyday life, of the social environment.

KK: This crisis is not the main point of the film. It comes at the end, when the character begins to understand that the life of a filmmaker is not so simple, nor so easy, that it's influenced by many things, that it is not enough to aim the camera at reality to film the truth, that truth has many faces, that it all depends on the point of view from which you look, that the personal truth is not always the public truth. This is the problem of the hero, who becomes smarter throughout the film, by way of the cinema, of his own point of view, at his amateur level. He experiences, at the same time, other, personal problems,

JD: Isn't he a kind of devastating character for the people who live around him?
KK: If he is, it's beyond his control. He's certainly an honest man, full of good intentions. If things go against his intentions, it is not because of him, but because of what he suffers. It's not him who is culpable, it's the situation.

JD: If we compare the tone of *The Scar* and of *Camera Buff*, the two seem to be differentiated by the prominence given to humor in the second.
KK: In *The Scar*, I looked at my character with more detachment, from further away. In *Camera Buff*, I'm always with him. This determined the film's aesthetic: the cutting, the montage. The humor here is an expression of sympathy for the human miseries that can be funny. *Camera Buff* is a film about a character, *The Scar* is a film about a problem. Perhaps that's why *The Scar* also had such a small audience. In this film I kept a greater distance, a certain coldness towards my hero, because I cannot identify with him. While I can identify with the "camera buff." The two films are very different: *The Scar* covers twelve years of a man's life, *Camera Buff* concerns only a rather short period, about a year. So the camera can stay with the hero even more, and he can follow it; the dramatic construction, the shooting, the editing are different.

JD: Can you try to situate yourself in Polish cinema?
KK: I think I'm more of a realist than a romantic, but firstly I would like to be an auteur. I do not think at all of the cinema as a profession, but as a means of expression. Film, for me, is not at all the makeup, the lights, the Hollywood star, but only the ideas. There's my problem as a filmmaker today.

JD: What do you think of Polish cinema today? How do you see its evolution in the future?
KK: The future is difficult to talk about, because everything depends on the evolution of each individual. Moreover, it's impossible to speak of that of others, since it's hard enough to speak of one's own. All depends on the way that the world, that life, evolves. I hope to stay active and attentive to life, to know how to speak about it. I try to do what I think is important in the moment. The present situation of cinema in Poland seems to me quite noteworthy, because this cinema has been interested in Polish daily life, thanks to many young filmmakers. The

directors of the older generation and the middle generation were also interested in contemporary Poland, from a political and critical perspective, just like these kids. What is remarkable is that there is no real opposition between generations. They move forward together, we could say on different tracks, but towards a common goal. But what is that goal? It is difficult to define it, as it is impossible to know whether the interest of older filmmakers in contemporary problems is due to the young directors or the reverse. Documentary film and its techniques have helped to radically change cinematographic language, even for Andrzej Wajda, even for Jerzy Kawalerowicz. Of course, Andrzej Wajda, Krzysztof Zanussi influence young directors, but there is reciprocity. That's what I feel is most important, this unity, this community, without there being a manifesto, a group constitution, a chosen label. Criticism, of course, invented for its own needs specific terminology, like currently "the cinema of moral anxiety." But that practice is sometimes dangerous. In the debates currently underway in the press, we see, once the drawer "cinema of moral anxiety" is opened and its contents inventoried, that many remarkable young filmmakers are not included: the poor critics don't know what to do. Do they [the filmmakers] belong? Do they fit or not fit? These are quite empty considerations, because cinema is alive precisely when it knows how to work in very different directions, both thematic and aesthetic. And I have the impression that cinema in Poland today is alive.

Note

1. Though note that, in many later interviews, Kieślowski speaks of his films only taking form in the editing room.

In Depth Rather than Breadth

Krzysztof Kieślowski / 1981

From *Polish Perspectives*, 1981. Reprinted by permission.

This manifesto originally appeared as "Głęboko zamiast szeroko" in Dialog *in 1981, and was reprinted in translated form that same year in* Polish Perspectives, *a publication of the Polski Instytut Spraw Międzynarodowowych. Kieślowski begins by invoking the short-lived liberalizing reforms that allowed the foundation of Solidarity and a much greater freedom of expression.*

It is the fashion at present to write off everything in the arts that antedates August 1980 as dead history and file it away under "Errors." I use the word fashion as I hope that it will eventually pass and sounder judgments prevail, and that in the necessary process of weeding out the bad things we make sure of preserving, and building on, the good. It must be remembered that, though it is politicians who make and supervise arts policy, they are not its executors. No matter how conservative or even retrograde it may be, its final shape springs from the personal beliefs, language and perception of the world of the people directly involved. If this were not so, we would be forced to conclude that published writers like Różewicz, Andrzejewski, Mrożek, or Nowakowski, were collaborators, that Wajda and Zanussi ate the establishment's salt, that the journalism of Krall, Kapuściński, or Bratkowski represented a sell-out.

That there were also a great many casualties and victims is quite another matter. The wrongs and the blank spaces must be set right without delay—even if it is, I fear, going to mean the dreadful business of revising bits of the Encyclopedia. But this, as I say, is another matter. My point here is that, against all the odds, the record in culture was not an unmitigated disaster and that in its own interests we must not on any account let the credit side go to waste.

Declaring an interest, I think there is a case for placing the cinema in this category. It must in fairness be recognized that the filmmakers' position is exceptionally difficult because of the sheer amount of money and industrial effort that go into their work. If they decide to opt out, they opt right out and cut themselves off from the possibility of participation in cultural life, official or unofficial. For them this is where the crunch comes; it is not the risk of losing their livelihood as some kind of existence can always be scraped together. If I quit because I have had a scene cut, a script vetoed, or a film banned I must, if I am not to be left out in the cold, switch to some other fields. As I may not be that versatile, all I can do is keep trying, a second time, a tenth, a twentieth. In the cinema such hammering on the wall was frequent and various chinks in the other side's armor were found, whether as a result of attrition, an off-guard moment or plain incompetence (which is one thing of which the cultural bureaucracy is never short).

So we managed to get a fair number of films made (even if they have had to wait till today for exhibition), partly because by hook or crook we squeezed through the process of script approval or production clearance, but chiefly because many of us considered that mattered more than seeing them actually released and deliberately took the gamble that they probably would not be. I once remarked in an interview that "what's made is mine" (and it appeared in the weekly *Polityka* under this headline) and there were plenty of other directors who made film after film (some of them running into double figures) under no illusion whatsoever that they would belong or be known to anyone but themselves. Of course even that would have been impossible but for the occasional presence of sympathetic decision-makers (most of whom, for that matter, were not around for much longer). I am thinking not only of producers, but also ministers.

We also made a fair number of films which *were* released—in mutilated form, admittedly, but not to the point of complete distortion. They showed our country and its problems in what still seemed to be a truthful light and nailed the things we thought needed nailing. We regarded such tampering as an acceptable trade-off for the ultimate health and survival of culture. So, it appears, did many writers, journalists, and academics.

As I saw it, the artist's fundamental obligation in the seventies was to *describe*. Life operated on a number of planes: the same people or events took on different appearances depending on whether they were viewed from an official or private angle; inequities that were common knowledge but not to be ventilated in public abounded; a variety of languages gained currency. These were the things we had to pinpoint. Only if they were on record could they be subjected to appraisal; but there is no way of doing this outside the sphere of culture in the broad sense. If a particular aspect of reality is to be opposed and an alternative put forward, it must first be delineated. To fight evil—ineffectually, perhaps, but not for want of trying—you must get its measure. You cannot dissent unless you have a clear idea of what you are dissenting from. It is no use saying "we know all about that" unless you do so out loud and are satisfied that everybody *does* know. Skulduggery, raw deals, moral illiteracy, depravity can all occasion protest and revolt—but only after they have been called by the right name. Why else do parish priests in small towns explicitly refer to sins of which their congregations scarcely need reminding? If they did not get down to cases, they would not be able to deplore and condemn.

Obviously, one could not expect masterpieces to follow automatically. This was another of our calculated risks. As a genre realism has never stood as high in Polish culture as in American or Russian; but, in the circumstances, we had to try and raise its stock.

At that moment the artist's inner self, his heart-searchings and angst, were of less importance. I personally considered them valid only if they seemed to resonate with what I could observe around me. So very broad a premise doubtless explains why many filmmakers did not hesitate to adopt an equally broad approach to the necessity in question.

The results developed into a current of cinema that made a mark both here and abroad. Here, it happened to merge with a longing for truth that was universally evident; for that matter, recent events have made it abundantly clear that people will not cheerfully settle after work for ostrich-feathered show girls, that, despite fatigue, hardship, and frustration, or possibly for these very reasons, they want to be drawn into a serious conversation about the surrounding world. Abroad, our picture of life seemed to touch a chord since purchases reached an all-time high and festival awards came on a scale reminiscent of the Polish cinema's bumper years two decades earlier. The fact was that, whatever else might be said about these films, they showed a living country and living human beings. The directors who made them represented different generations and even artistic outlooks— and that also told in their favor.

Though absolutely certain of the sense (if less so of the effectiveness) of what we were doing, we eventually ran into a barrier that brought home to us its limitations. On the one hand, there were many areas that, for fundamental political reasons, were totally out of bounds, while those that were not were in danger of being worked to the ground. On the other, answering the question "what are things like?" begged its corollaries: "why are they like that?" and "what can be done about it?" Description was no substitute for diagnosis and prognosis of the whole system of nexuses in which we are caught up both as a nation and individuals. In the end many filmmakers began to chafe at this predominance of description as they were afraid it might cramp their self-development, stifle their imagination, prevent the articulation of ideas of a more philosophical nature, and militate against experimentation with form.

Looking for ways out of this dilemma, some delved into the nearer or remoter past for the roots of the present situation, though without abandoning the realist vein. Others took a couple of years off altogether to take stock of their options.

I believe both reactions to have been necessary and right since a way round this barrier can and must be found by our own unaided efforts and without prior commitment to either course.

A further complication has—thank God—been the march of events. Freedom of thought, let alone speech, is in our case a mixed blessing. Many subjects, once to all intents and purposes broached only by the cinema, are now being tackled by the press and even television. If we remain locked in the mind-set of a few years ago, we will inevitably end up vying with reporters in, say, tracking down the murkier aspects of life or scanning the social and political upsurge of recent months. The cinema cannot hope to win this race, even if it is prepared, which it is not, to enter in the first place.

Today telling the truth about the world, although still essential, is no longer enough. We must look for more dramatic situations, for morals reaching beyond the everyday, for more universal and sagacious diagnoses. Needless to say, we will have to chart the area previously barred to us, but our frame of reference will have to be broader and our point of view communicated more incisively. In a context of freedom stances polarize more sharply, which is only natural and as it should be. We must advance therefore via dialogue between them, through a clash of differing ideas about people, our country, the world. Freedom offers new opportunities, but it also increases the requirements.

The greatest number of problems will arise, I think, in the sphere of depth. I once gave the following example: from time to time we hear of a student having murdered an old woman, but everything depends on whether the story is told by Agatha Christie or Dostoyevsky. It is all a matter of depth, of language as well as perception because the two are strictly related.

Because of the standardization of the outward appearances of places and people, and the similarity of the issues confronting us, it is necessary to develop a richer vocabulary if accounts of political events, intrigues, captains of industry, or delinquent wives are also to be a forceful comment on love, hatred, jealousy, or death. We must make sure that films about problems are first and foremost films about people, that what is bound to be their surface layer is packaging, not content. We are therefore going to be forced to change the language, protagonists, situations, and words of our films. I am not suggesting a departure from the realist convention, but its development in a direction that can be summed up in the formula: in depth rather than breadth, inwards rather than outwards.

It will be very hard to replenish our language (which in our case consists of images) since much of it has become threadbare. Each one of us will, I repeat, have to map out his own route for himself; at any rate that seems to be the prevailing mood.

I share it. Regardless of the subject of my films (which need not detain us here), I am looking for a way of evoking in audiences feelings similar to my own: the physically painful impotence and sorrow that assail me when I see a man weeping at a bus stop, when I observe people struggling vainly to get close to others, when I see someone eating up the left-overs in a cheap restaurant, when I see the first blotches on a woman's hand and know that she too is bitterly aware of them, when I see the kind of appalling and irreparable injustice that so visibly scars the human face.

I want this pain to come across to my audience, to see this physical agony, which I think I am beginning to fathom seep into my work.

So I sit here laboriously searching for a way. Apart from a few, not necessarily happier individuals, we are all at the moment in the same spot.

About Me, about You, about Everyone

Maria Marszałek / 1987

From *Kino* 8 (1987): 8–10. Reprinted by permission.

This interview was conducted for the organizers of the Pesaro Festival of New Cinema at the retrospective of Polish contemporary cinema in June 1987.

Maria Marszałek: After the premiere of *No End* you said that you were not interested in the opinion of people except for those whose names are in your notebook. Have you revised this position?

Krzysztof Kieślowski: No. I even have the same notebook. But, you might have confused the wording. It was rather "I don't worry about their opinion," and not "they don't interest me." It is, after all, different.

MM: There is a lot of ugliness in your films. The landscape is ugly, people are bleak, even the weather is not favorable. . . .

KK: That's because the world is not too colorful.

MM: Does it mean that even erotic scenes have to be ugly?

KK: Yes, they are not beautiful. They are seen by a person who has opened the door suddenly. And this is what a scene like this looks like in reality. It varies in films. In some movies, erotica looks beautiful, in others close-ups and the wealth of detail intensifies ugliness. In my films erotic scenes will always look the way they do.

MM: Pretty much as if seen by a third person.

KK: Of course. After all, giving them a different meaning depends on that scene's participants, on the people who make love, and not on the voyeur.

MM: But in your films love doesn't belong to the sphere of higher values. It's nondescript like in *Camera Buff*, delayed and muddled up like in *No End*, accidental in *Blind Chance*. . . .

KK: Only very young people commit suicide out of love. Although my protagonist in *No End* dies this way, it is because of a total defeat, because of the inability to accommodate to the world. Maybe even love does motivate her emotions, but what is she to do if her husband was the only tie with the world, and he is dead from the start of the film? Grand love dramas play out outside of my experience. It appears that romanticism was a quality of a different era.

MM: Maybe it's too intimate. It's easier to show a naked person than to express his feelings. The latter always comes with a risk of ridicule.
KK: Agreed. Some things are too intimate even to convey them on the screen.

MM: You've said you cannot see grand emotions around you. However, they do exist: great passions, ambitions, lust for power, desire to be liked, need for acceptance, at last, despite everything, love. They exist and they constitute the engine of life.
KK: Who knows? I am now making a film about grand feelings, about passion, about jealousy. It's called *Decalogue*.

MM: Let's be more precise. The difference between *Camera Buff* or *The Scar* on the one hand, and on the other *No End* or *Blind Chance*, is clear. Different factors decide human fate. In your earlier films, it is about institutional mechanisms; in the recent ones the psychological sketch becomes more defined. The world depicted in *No End* is the world of evil and helplessness. But the grand evil lurks in human weakness, in the lack of faith, even in the obsolescent life instinct, or as with a young interned worker, who pays for his release from prison, in the loss of identity. In one interview you said that those who found themselves in the situation of the oppositionist depicted in the film have survived, but they have [suffered] defeat, so they have to carry their hump. Are there people who have not disowned themselves, and who have still survived and who live without that stigma?
KK: *No End* is not about them. This film is not about heroes, but about ordinary people met in the street. It is a film about a majority, about me, about you, about those like us. Most people carry inside the burden of big and small defeats. It's a film about people with their heads down.

MM: I don't agree with the idea behind this film. I also don't accept the film's heroine, who seems a false character, invented, unconvincing.
KK: Your reaction is very feminine. I'm not coming across it for the first time.

MM: Maybe because it's difficult to identify with this woman's tragedy. She is false as a mother, as a wife, as a human being.

KK: False or ill-favored? I also don't like her. But this is how she is. This film is not a story of the "noble naïve [woman]," cheated by life.

MM: What, in your opinion, determines a defeat? In *Blind Chance*, you showed a young man whose fate could go differently depending on what he comes across along his way. Are you not overestimating the role of the title's blind chance? At the end, that man was formed by a family tradition, by a peer group's atmosphere, by a social environment. All this should enable formation of his basic values. . . .
KK: That's why my protagonist is an honest man in all the variants, even if he follows opposite sides. Of course, the situations I cited in *Blind Chance* are clearer and more condensed than what they would be in life. But shorthand is a film's nature. [Bogusław] Linda playing in *Blind Chance* three embodiments of Witek remains the same trusting and righteous man. The thing is that he cannot find his place in life. Everything turns against him.

MM: There is no absolute honesty. Can faithfulness to oneself, moral purity, exist in an abstract situation, any situation? . . . How can we reconcile the greatness of soul with the weakness of actions? In none of these three template situations does your protagonist make choices; they are beyond him, beyond the reach of his means, and even of consciousness. He is molded by others.
KK: Taking this tack, we won't understand one another. In the factual sphere, the protagonist makes a choice in each situation, he follows a person or a situation, which for him, a young boy, becomes an object of fascination. I agree that, especially in the first variant of fate, many people find it difficult to believe in that fascination, but firstly it is not a film about them, but about Witek Długosz, and secondly let's have the courage to look at ourselves regardless of what costumes we are wearing.

I heard about a substantial gathering of people who, to put it mildly, were disinclined for political reality, to whom someone said: whoever is over fifty and has never been [a member of] the Party or ZMP [Union of Polish Youth], raise your hand. No one did, although three quarters of the gathering were over fifty. I am saying nothing against or for these people. I only want to say that there are many ways.

In the notional sphere. You ask me about integrity and we both know what it's about. The film is concerned with the end of the seventies, and I will tell you that I used to know then honest people who belonged to the Party (or to organizations whose good intentions we doubt). I will tell you more to preempt the next question. I know also today honest people, writing for the official newspapers, working in Ministries, in television. And there are many [people] more honest than they need to be. I even know those whom I can say have a good will. To me the division between fantastic us and always-bad-others is too simple, inhumane, un-Christian. Also untrue and harmful. A person of great kindness who used to take parcels to the camps for the interned and to prisons during martial law told me about prison wardens and guards: listen, they are just like us. Good and bad.

MM: In *Personnel, The Calm, Camera Buff, No End*, acting on noble motives collides with the world's brutality. And the protagonist, almost always, suffers defeat. There is something unsettling in the regularity with which the actions of these people turn against them. Maybe not all is well with them.
KK: Probably not. Maybe it is the world that's not well. It lacks harmony and order. There is no certainty of moral and social norms.

MM: And that is why are you always making the same film, which is an extension of the current called the Cinema of Moral Concern?[1]
KK: I simply make films in touch with my emotions, [films] like me.

MM: So, do you identify yourself with your protagonists? Witek from *Blind Chance* would be an alter ego of the creator?
KK: In the same measure as the protagonists of all the other films. We grew up in the same world, in a similar atmosphere: me, you, our friends. Returning to your previous doubts: in *Blind Chance* it was very important to me to show the protagonist's lineage. Every time when someone tries to manipulate his loyalties, he resists. Why? Just because he inherited something important from home, because he has [good] foundations at his disposal.

MM: But what kind of a choice is that actually? If all the three variants of Witek's life were possible or probable, where can one look for the hero himself? Maybe he is simply a wishy-washy person without a backbone?
KK: Why? Recall even your own school grade. Jacek Kaczmarski[2] sings a song [about it]. What's happened with them? Who are these people today? And then you were all alike.

MM: Which of the three variants presented in *Blind Chance* is closest to you? In the film they are treated as equivalent.
KK: The third one, the shortest one. "Let's do something that we can influence, since there's so much [we cannot] . . ." and so on. That's utopian, but if every one of us took care of life around him? If you felt like making a straight table, a pipe that doesn't leak, cure a person, make a film, or write an article? Even if only in the way you can. Unfortunately, one cannot change the world with that and that's why Witek gets on the plane that waited for him in all the three variants. Because

one has to change the world and in the first two variants the plane takes off and falls apart without Witek inside. And he, bitter, despondent, and still politically active, will stay behind, trying to do something with all that over which, it seems, he has no influence.

MM: In *Blind Chance* a railwayman—and maybe you are hiding behind him?—is a demiurge, he possesses almost godly powers.

KK: Yes, the structure of the entire film rests on that. One day, a railwayman stops drinking tea earlier than usual. If he finished it at his normal time, he would not have met Witek. It seems to me that life's determinism can be traced by going back in time and registering the tiniest events.

MM: You speculate with the life of your hero, you condemn him to hesitation and indecisions, you shove against him different life possibilities, and you keep the same plane up your sleeve. Is there nothing left but determinism?

KK: There is. Not every way leads to that plane. Despite everything, one can choose. The very fact that I give the protagonist three different lives might be a proof of that.

MM: It sounds as if a human life could be analyzed the same way as a finished chess game. A movement of a pawn from C4 to C5 at the beginning of the game at the end leads to check-mate at the end?

KK: Apparently a chess game is based on the rules of life. I constantly have a feeling that even while we are talking, a passenger car assembly worker has just had an argument with his wife, come to work having not slept enough, is putting a car together incorrectly. In a few years, when one of us is running across the road at the red light, this car simply won't manage to stop. And we unconsciously will come close to that critical point.

Notes

1. Polish "kino moralnego niepokoju," also translated as Cinema of Moral Anxiety.

2. Jacek Kaczmarski, an oppositionist poet and singer, wrote a song *Our Class* (*Nasza klasa*) in three stages. The first and most famous part was written in June 1983 as a commentary on displacements resulting from martial law.

Without Me

Bożena Janicka / 1988

From *Film* 43 (1988): 3–5. Reprinted by permission.

This interview was conducted for a popular film magazine by Bożena Janicka, one of the most known and prolific female film journalists in Poland.

Bożena Janicka: Although I don't think that any generations are disconnected from what happened before, I will still remind [everyone] that in the 1970s you were one of the leading figures of Polish cinema, and you were the first to make an on-the-spot film about martial law. In production, its title was *Happy End*. It appeared on screens titled *No End*. Next they released your film [made] in the period between the August [of 1980] and December [1981], *Blind Chance*, which had been shelved for a few years. After *No End*, you didn't attempt a new film for a long while. Some supposed that you were silent because both these films made no impression, which pointed to a fundamental shift in the audience's attitudes. They were saying: Kieślowski is not making a new film because he is afraid of the viewer. Was that really the case?

Krzysztof Kieślowski: That's a natural break; I make a film every few years. And, was I afraid of the viewer? Every director is afraid of the viewer. However, you should also ask how to measure courage. For me courage is saying what you think. In *No End* I said everything I wanted [to say]. I don't know what other type of courage I could have shown. Run onto a barricade, get myself shot? Like the majority of people in Poland, I didn't feel like doing that. Someone could say: and so that's why [Poland's poor state of affairs] is the way it is, but I am not judging [anyone], only saying how it was.

BJ: After that, you began *The Decalogue*, a series of films for television (each relates to one commandment or prohibition from the Ten Commandments). A universal, timeless topic; good for waiting [things] out?

KK: The story of the *Decalogue*'s production is trivial. It was not my idea, but of Krzysztof Piesiewicz, the co-scriptwriter of *No End*. I was then filling in for

Krzysztof Zanussi, who manages "Tor" [Film Studio]. In our studio, we had a group of young people [straight] from film school. I thought it could be a chance to secure a television debut for ten young directors. But when we started to write scripts with Piesiewicz, I started to regret [giving up] some, I didn't want to give them up. I also came to a realization that if each film was made by a different person, the series would drift apart, it would not come together as a whole. So I decided to make these films myself, that's all.

BJ: After all, it's difficult to consider the Decalogue[1] as an idea like any other; it's too significant.

KK: It seemed to us that it was a good, clear-cut topic for contemporary times; that's obvious. When everything around is falling apart, it is worthwhile to turn to fundamental questions. Besides it is always a good time to remember the Deca-logue. Those commandments have existed for six thousand years more or less. No one has ever objected to them, and at the same time, everyday, for thousands of years, we have all been breaking these commandments.

BJ: You saw in the Decalogue only generally accepted ethical norms. Have you taken into account also their religious dimension?

KK: No, the religious aspects we left aside. But I do hope that in the films them-selves one will be able to find something of these values. Certainly metaphysics . . .

BJ: Only two films of the whole ten are known so far, however moral extremism strikes in both. Killing a man is an obvious wrong, even if it is performed under the aegis of law (*A Short Film about Killing*); the lack of goodness is also wrong (*A Short Film about Love*).

KK: Correct. In the subsequent [films], matters may get more complicated.

BJ: The theme of both films is close to the idea that if you don't practice good, you stand on the side of evil. Do you accept this extreme moral stand?

KK: I could be an extremist, but I just don't want to be a pedagogue. I don't in-tend to teach; however I want to warn myself and others. Not because I know better; it's simply that I can be heard better, because I have the appropriate tools: a camera, film, actors, and so on. I think we all should look around and inform one another what we are thinking about, what we are doing, what we are feeling. Hence my right to inform others.

BJ: It seems to me it is essentially a religious thought. It reminds me of a beautiful sentence from *The Letter to the Hebrews*, "stir up one another to love and good works. . . ."

KK: If I really had to define the Decalogue's message, it would sound more or less like this: live attentively, look around you, look to see if you are not troubling others with your actions, not doing harm, not causing pain. This thought—I know well it is neither mine nor new—will be appearing and reappearing through all these films.

BJ: A claim much more restrained than the tone of the films themselves, at least of those we know already. . . .

KK: Because these are matters very simple and very complicated at the same time. Everyone knows how the most important commandment ends: ". . . your neighbor as yourself." However, "as yourself," not more. You can overdo it with evil, but also with good. Tadeusz Sobolewski in his book *Old Sins* shares an interesting observation that martial law awakened in some people an excess of good. This can also be a problem.

BJ: On the basis that if someone helps others at his own expense, he will soon have to ask others for help?

KK: For instance.

BJ: And such values as sacrifice, heroism?

KK: They are beautiful, because they are rare.

BJ: It seems that you blame not so much circumstances, but people themselves, for the condition of ethical decay in which we live today?

KK: You see, the problem is not that we behave especially badly nowadays; the thing is that we don't know what to do. Criteria are falling apart, it's not certain what's good and what's bad, how we should live. There are attempts to define these issues all the time anew, but we have less and less faith in formulations by others. Everyone is clever about their own ends. I don't know if we all have the same Decalogue. Besides, we don't choose between good and evil everyday; a person faces that type of choice extremely seldom.

BJ: Then, what do you think is the essence of the choices we make all the time?

KK: The choice of the lesser evil, that's the essence of almost our every decision. Because it is not only criteria being washed away; also life itself loses clarity, focus. We thought it was worth making the *Decalogue* above all to confront those murky, fuzzy situations that make up our existence, with those simple, unequivocal commandments: don't kill, don't fornicate, don't steal.

BJ: You have said that everyone has their own version of the Decalogue. For instance, living where I live and seeing the local forms of evil, I would tend to consider as most important the commandment that instructs: do not bear false witness. Was that also important to you when you were making the *Decalogue*?

KK: It seems you would like me to portray our reality, and in the *Decalogue* we wanted to escape just that. We rejected a priori everything that was politics, although politics would be a fantastic topic for all ten. Can you imagine?

BJ: Precisely, that's what I don't understand.

KK: We decided to exclude politics because we wanted to eliminate something that is popularly called the People's Republic [PRL].

BJ: So as not to impede the universal character of issues shown?

KK: Yes, but not only [that]. We were of the opinion that there were in the world, including here, problems more important than politics; all this that's the very breath of our lives. The breath of our lives, and not what we talk about. And finally the last reason for forgoing politics: because for a while I have not been able to put up with politics. It annoys me as a thought, a way of life, expending energy. Politicians irritate me, especially those who know exactly how to organize everything. They know, they've organized it, and as a result things are the way they are. Outside [Poland], here. Especially here, because the consequences of good organization of the world can be felt primarily here, right?

BJ: From a film whose action takes place in Poland you can eliminate politics, but the People's Republic? The appearance of things, the folklore of the People's Republic, all this queuing up for meat, and so on. Yes, of course, but the deeper consequences of the way we live? After all, a way of living shapes not only customs, but also mentality, ethics, attitudes?

KK: That's how it works: the way in which people think [that is] shown in the *Decalogue* is from here. For instance, the fact that we all hate one another. I don't want to know why it is this way, but it is. I have always examined, say, a tree, and now I am showing fruit. I don't want to be examining the tree any more.

BJ: Good comparison: a tree. Characters from your previous films have always been strongly related to specific social groups, it was clear whom they represented. Is it going to be different in the *Decalogue*?

KK: There, people represent themselves.

BJ: And society?

KK: What is society? No such thing exists. Only 37 million people exist.

BJ: And collective fate?
KK: I care nothing about it.

BJ: Are you serious?
KK: Utterly.

BJ: However some time ago similar issues concerned you. Politics, which you are rejecting now, constituted a compelling ingredient of your films. Agreed?
KK: Indeed, that was the case.

BJ: It served to ends other than idle politicizing. You used it to defend some values.
KK: Then I thought one could solve things by the means of politics. Now I think that one can't. Politics itself doesn't solve anything; it is too complicated, too relativist for it. That's why I reject it. After all, people want more radical solutions.

BJ: Don't you lose something also as an artist by abandoning writing into your films some collective emotions? The two already known, and exquisite, films of the *Decalogue* exude a cold [detached] manner.
KK: Yes, that's probably true. But I am generally quite distanced. All my films were made as if through glass. I have never delivered emotions. There is no reason I should start.

BJ: Why do you think your films have not been evoking emotions? For instance, I reacted to them very passionately, starting with the first documentary, *From the City of Łódź*, showing the awfully hard life of [female] textile workers, up to *Camera Buff*. Later, not, indeed.
KK: That was a long time ago: *From the City of Łódź*, twenty years ago; *Camera Buff*, almost ten.

BJ: A viewer of a certain age may consent to cold cinema, but a young one? Besides (we keep talking about a viewer who is looking for more than entertainment in cinema), do you think a young person may be indifferent to the political determinants of his fate? After all, they determine his future. Although, maybe it's the natural order of things that only some later generation of filmmakers will be able to express the aspirations of young people. . . .
KK: And do you know what young people's aspirations are? I don't know that. What do young people want from the cinema? What do people want in general today?

BJ: We know that well.

KK: And what are they willing to sacrifice for that? I'm under the impression that, unfortunately, [it's] less and less. Besides, I'm also not prepared to give more. Only one thing has succeeded here: turning a society into 37 million individuals. Regardless of whether we like it or not.

BJ: I think that incompatibility of interests doesn't hinder the existence of a common goal. A common goal may be, for instance, removing an obstacle in the way of the realization of disparate interests. These are, of course, issues outside of the cinema, but Polish film, co-created by you, once upon a time highlighted some processes, wanted to participate in something, influence something.

KK: I've never believed that I can influence anything. I [can] say more: I've never wanted to influence anything. Bringing things to people's attention: yes, indeed. If as a result of their reflection, they wanted to change something, I would be very pleased, but they have to change it themselves, without me.

BJ: Does your attitude come from the fear of responsiblity?

KK: Definitely. But to take responsibility upon yourself, you have to believe that you know what course things should take. And I don't have that certainty, and I've never had it.

BJ: Let's return to your films. While watching the last two, *A Short Film about Killing* and *A Short Film about Love*, I was under an impression, especially so in the case of *A Short Film about Killing*, that you were starting to make films for the few scenes in which you would like to communicate something really important, convey a really important realization or thought. Hence the ostentatious banality of motifs or of secondary scenes. I know, of course, that the banality juxtaposed with important matters emphasizes the latter's importance, but I cannot resist the impression that all the secondary issues above all bore you.

KK: They've always bored me. Unfortunately, I cannot reject them completely. To rebel against all the requirements of professionalism would be stupid. I am, however, trying to search for something beyond professionalism.

BJ: Cinema today, it seems, is going in a different direction. Today even critics, the youngest ones, think that cinema is there to show expeditiously a few simple motifs and situations.

KK: That's how it is today. In the future that trend may turn around. Such shifts are natural in cinema. You have to do your own thing. At least until there are people who are not satisfied with the other cinema. I think there always will be viewers who will say: this cinema is hopeless, boring, stupid, I don't want to watch it. And there will always be filmmakers who will add: God forbid me from making it! A waste of time.

BJ: Politics is a waste of time, collective fate [is], popular cinema [is]. So what is not?

KK: Well, one may not want to answer every question, something has to be left out for oneself.

Note

1. "Decalogue," or Polish "Dekalog," in the Polish original is used in reference to the Ten Commandments, and so it is used in this translation to preserve the terms' original interchangeability.

On *A Short Film about Killing*

Hubert Niogret / 1988

From *Positif* 332 (October 1988): 17–22. Reprinted by permission.

Niogret's introduction to this second interview for Positif *explains succinctly the range of circumstances that delayed broader awareness of Kieślowski's work in France and elsewhere.*

Will the year 1988 be the one in which Krzysztof Kieślowski is finally discovered by the French public? While he has been making feature films for over fifteen years, none of them has been released commercially in France. In 1980, "Positif Week" showed one of his films, *The Scar* (*Blizna,* 1978), in a black-and-white, edited version, then nothing else happened before the screening at Cannes 1987 (Un Certain Regard) of *Blind Chance* (*Przypadek*) and then, in 1988, again in Cannes but this time in competition, of *A Short Film about Killing* (*Krótki film o zabijaniu*), awarded a Jury Prize. Meanwhile, there were many unexpected turns in Kieślowski's career, who, after numerous documentaries, directed his next three movies for television, of which the last, *The Calm* (*Spokój*), was broadcast only five years after completion, most likely because it showed strikers, and has since disappeared from official filmographies. Recognized by his peers (the presence of Krzysztof Zanussi and the documentarist Andrzej Jurga in *Camera Buff* [*Amator*] is proof of that) and by a number of Polish and international festivals for his documentary shorts (Kraków, Lille, Warsaw, Mannheim, Gdańsk, Moscow, Chicago), Krzysztof Kieślowski has, however, made only eight films in fifteen years, of which one is half-banned and another was shelved after the shooting and was not completed until four years later.

The Scar (the first movie to show one of the strikes of 1970 and to refer to the unrests in Gdańsk) and *Camera Buff* attracted the attention of Barthélemy Amengual (No. 207) and Paulo Antonio Paranagua (No. 208 and 227). Passionate about his films, Jacques Demeure went out looking for him and finally managed to interview Kieślowski (No. 227 then 234). Last year in Cannes, after watching *Blind Chance* (No. 317–18) and with the beautiful *No End* (*Bez końca*) in mind (No. 293), we succeeded in meeting up with Krzysztof Kieślowski but too briefly, without having time to hold a real interview.

Along with a retrospective of his work at the festival of La Rochelle in July, Cannon France's distribution of four of his films (*Camera Buff*, *No End*, *Blind Chance*, and *A Short Film about Killing*) is going to raise this filmmaker's profile; we too were finally able to get to know him as he told us about the motivation for his latest film and expressed his outright despair about the Polish situation. Krzysztof Kieślowski, who is neither a filmmaker of compromise nor of silence, is moving towards a greater interiorization to get closer to what he considers essential.

Hubert Niogret: *Krótki film o zabijaniu* is translated into English as *A Short Film about Killing* but the French title is *Thou shalt not kill*, which has a biblical connotation.

Krzysztof Kieślowski: The English title corresponds to the Polish title, the translation is correct, but the title was not translatable into French. I was not against the French title as this is one of the ten verses of the Ten Commandments, which will perhaps yield ten films. At one point I even thought about having the same title with the biblical connotation in Polish, but I gave up the idea.

HN: Why A Short Film . . . ?
KK: This is a short film at ninety minutes since people today are making very long films of two hours. It really is a short film, one hour and twenty-four minutes, to be very precise.

HN: In the structure of the screenplay, the trial is omitted, while generally in movies on such a subject, a relatively large proportion is devoted to the trial.
KK: I was not interested in the trial in itself. The outcome is obvious, since we all know what the lawyer and the prosecutor will say and what the sentence will be. What interested me most is everything that exists in the unseen recesses of the human soul, behind the scenes of murder.

HN: How did you arrive at the structure of this scenario that interweaves the paths of the main characters before they meet, and also the secondary characters, such as the young woman in the store? This young woman crossed paths with the characters but does not affect the narrative.
KK: You remember a scene in *Citizen Kane* (1941) in which a character speaks of two boats that pass each other, with one character on one boat and another on the second. The man and woman cross paths never to see each other again. Had they met again, the life of "Citizen Kane" might have been different. What

interested me the most is how the life of a human being is affected by one event, and how, if something else happens, his life takes a different turn. People are linked to each other. There are invisible threads. Now while we are talking together, there is a worker from an aircraft factory who is fighting with his wife. Neither I nor you know him, and we will never meet him. But because he is furious after fighting with his wife, he will not tighten a screw correctly, even though he does it everyday. It may be you, me, or our wives, in five years, who will take the plane, and it will explode. We are tied to this man but we do not know it now. There is in the depths the idea that the seeds of a future event are being sown. The only problem is finding this thread.

HN: *A Short Film about Killing* has a form of very dark humor: the taxi driver who refuses drunks but agrees to take this young man who seems nice, or the condemned man who is offered a cigarette but who prefers a cigarette without filter. The black humor is an integral part of the moral.

KK: The black humor is there because the absurd is a part of our lives. It affects us. It does not make us laugh. That's what comedy is, good comedy. Very funny things happen to the characters, but that are tragic for them.

HN: What are also interesting are the false leads. The young man is in the café. It's the policeman that he wants to kill. If he was not relieved by the change of shift, he would have been the victim.

KK: I played a sort of game with the viewer, since indeed there was not enough action to fill out this story. There was a need for little events, false leads.

HN: You have the knack of playing with the viewer. In your last completed film, *Blind Chance*, you give us three different versions and we never know which is the real one.

KK: I wanted to make a film about an uncertainty, about doubt. Cinema is a very difficult art. You cannot play with cinematic language in the same way as with literary language. I am speaking of manipulation.

HN: In *A Short Film about Killing* you made the very bold choice of having a deliberately dirty, distorted image, except for the closing scene, in realistic color, about the weeping lawyer. The image is almost monochromatic. And in the scenes with the murderer, there is almost always a shadow to the left or right.

KK: This way of filming was an idea of my cinematographer. We agreed on the idea, but the technique comes from him. The idea was to photograph the world as worse than it is, uglier. I feel that the world around me is increasingly ugly. I feel that God had the ambition to finish his work. Everything is beautiful, too beautiful. Some people regret it when it explodes. I differ from that. I wanted to dirty this world.

On the other hand, when the cinematographer shoots interiors, he can play with the light, to highlight the things that matter. For exteriors, it is difficult to shoot because everything is important. Therefore, to diminish the importance of certain things outside, we used green filters that give this strange effect and that allowed us to obscure in the picture all that was not essential. It was an intervention by my cinematographer to eliminate things that cannot be eliminated in the light of day.

HN: Was the monochrome not also a way of solving the problem of how to show violence?
KK: Yes, also that. But anyway the violence is still just as unbearable.

HN: There are two kinds of violence: the murder of the taxi driver, which is after a moment the murder of someone you don't see anymore, and the legal murder that happens in a very violent moment that is not what we expected. We did not expect that he would resist.
KK: I'm not sure about that. Don't the condemned fight? I have my doubts. The method chosen is more or less humanitarian. But the thing against which I protest is the law.

HN: Did you start with a news item, an actual case?
KK: I believe these types of cases exist everywhere, and they are many. Virtually every day, someone kills. I didn't work from a news item. There is no special case to which I had access as a basis for my idea.

HN: How does the legal profession work? What's the process of becoming a lawyer? In a socialist country, the law is the state. How does a trial work?
KK: Polish lawyers are fighting for their freedom, their independence. Some of these lawyers have obtained this independence, as they appear in political trials where they are in conflict with the intentions of the state. This is very important, very noble.

HN: How do they make a living?
KK: From their clients.

HN: So this is a private system?
KK: There is a kind of cooperation. Several lawyers come together to form a group.

HN: How are their law studies organized?

KK: They complete their law studies over four years, and for another four years, they are assistants, interns of a professional lawyer. Then they take an exam to get their license to practice law. We see the young lawyer of my film pass this exam.

HN: What brought him to take up the case of this young murderer?

KK: Probably officially the Court, as a court-appointed lawyer. If the family cannot afford a private lawyer, it's the Court that appoints counsel.

HN: Once the trial is over, we discover that the character has another side to his life.

KK: He's a whole other person, completely different. That's what's interesting. For the Court, it did not matter that a tractor driver had killed his little sister five or six years earlier. The Court is about justice. Everything seemed clear. But it wasn't. We need to look at everything that was the real cause of the hanging of the young murderer.

HN: Justice is only interested in the law, not people.

KK: Yes. It's a machine. It doesn't have time. It doesn't have the capability. It is us who must interest ourselves in people.

HN: In *Blind Chance*, the character's three lives illustrate three different choices of political attitude that partially represent the situation in Poland.

KK: It's a film that is no longer current [in its references]. I could not shoot this kind of movie now (I speak here only of its political references; on the other hand, I still adhere to its philosophy). Much has changed: the institutions, and also the people. We can no longer make a film the same way. Obviously the factions I had shown in my film still exist: the Party faction, the factions of opposition. But even the Party and the opposition are different today. I think these two factions are less distinct than they were before.

HN: *Blind Chance* is a film about the commitment that each of us can have to a situation. Is it because the situation today is worse that no one wants to get involved anymore?

KK: If I wanted to make this film today, I would first have to ask this question of myself. Would I myself want to get involved in something? The answer is no. I don't want to get involved in anything. I've had enough of politics and politicians. I'm looking for something else. I am looking for calm. I could not make a film like this. I could not show with an entirely clear conscience a guy who commits to something. I do not believe that he could get anywhere, whether with the positions defended by the party or by the opposition. I very much agree with those who think we need to tidy up around us. We must repair faucets so they stop leaking. We must pick up the old toilet paper and not replace it with more of the same old scraps of paper.[1]

HN: *Blind Chance*, which we saw in Cannes in 1987, was already an outdated movie by your reckoning. You speak of it now as a movie you would not make again, but this is a film that has already survived a whole era.
KK: I shot it in 1981, seven years ago. And since then, many things have happened in Poland.

HN: *No End* was shown before we could see *Blind Chance*. It was also a very pessimistic film, very tough, evaluating the state of Poland.
KK: Yes, it was a very tough film. In most movies I do, there are very tough things. To make funny movies, with light, with joy, you must have it inside you, but I get up every morning with gloomy thoughts that get gloomier through the day.

HN: There is a vast difference in style between *Blind Chance*, *No End*, and *A Short Film about Killing*. In *Blind Chance* and *A Short Film about Killing*, we're very close to the character, while *No End* is a more grounded film, with more distance.
KK: I think I am getting further away from pure description of reality, of what is on the outside. And I'm getting closer and closer to the description of what lies inside. This is because I do not care for politics, for the social. That's boring. That's repetitive. What really interests me is how, in this boring, repetitive situation, a human being behaves, situates himself.

HN: In *No End*, there was an element of fantasy: the character who died showed up around his wife in the story.
KK: I call that, rather, a metaphysical element. Probably what interests me is what is in my head, in my gut, in me. I'm getting closer to that which is not clear, is mysterious, is doubtful, is a premonition. The outside does not exist. In most of my films and those I will make, if I'm still making something, these metaphysical elements will be even more prevalent. Maybe it's because I'm older, but I think that young people never think about these things. Young people move away from the problems of existence, but metaphysics is the justification of purpose.

HN: Where do we come from? Where are we going? This is a problem that Poland has partly solved through religion.
KK: Absolutely. This is a very important problem in Poland. It is much more

important than propaganda, ours and yours. In this mess that surrounds us, people look for a certain order. They seek certainty. I'm getting closer to these issues in my life. And it is clear that this has to appear in my films if I consider my vocation seriously, as a professional.

HN: This type of thinking leads increasingly towards doubt. . . .

KK: Not necessarily. It leads to questions, not necessarily to answers. The questions, they're more noble than the answers. It's the politicians who give answers, formulas. But who asks questions? Children.

HN: When you were studying at the Łódź Film School, what idea did you have about your profession?

KK: I imagined myself as a documentary filmmaker, who would only record reality.

HN: In one of your recent documentaries, *From a Night Porter's Point of View*, we no longer know exactly what's real, if there's a degree of fiction.

KK: This is reality pure and simple.

HN: This [night porter] could be a fictional character.

KK: Absolutely, but the problem of this character is precisely that he was real. I believe that you, the French, have a character just like him and you were afraid because he got a number of votes in elections. Imagine the porter becoming president. . . .

HN: Fifteen percent of us now are porters. . . .

KK: This is the real problem. We also have porters. . . .

HN: While making feature films, you continued for some time to make short documentaries. Are you committed, in fiction, to maintaining a fair and objective view of reality inherited from the documentary?

KK: I don't do that anymore. It was a very important balance for me, a professional necessity. When I was making documentaries, I was very close to life, to real people. This allowed me to know how people react, how they function in life. The documentary is a very good school of synthetic thinking in the cinema. That's why I was doing it.

HN: One of the qualities of *Blind Chance* and *A Short Film about Killing* is the very real relationship that you establish between the character and the viewer.

KK: I think it weighs on me a little, that I can't free myself from this way of thinking specific to documentary. It's because of this that I cannot tell a story as one usually does in the cinema. It distances the viewer, because viewers want the story, the incidents.

HN: Your actors have a stripped-down style of acting. . . .
KK: I always look for such actors. When they act too much, I yell at them.

HN: Are they actors who are more involved in theater or in film? Actors are not very numerous in Poland . . .
KK: No, you are wrong, there are many actors in Poland, but most are bad. For my ten films, I needed twenty-five professional actors, very good actors. We have about fifty very good actors [in Poland]. But there are many actors working in television, theater, cinema. Some are out in the country, where they work only in the theater, because there's neither television nor film there. Their lives are completely apathetic, boring. They do not really act at the theater, they exist. At some point, you cannot use them anymore, because they're stuck in a particularly theatrical style.

HN: The actors of *Blind Chance* or the driver and the young murderer in *A Short Film about Killing* are very distinctive. They really seem "soaked" in their social state.
KK: Since *A Short Film about Killing* is a short film, and not at all psychological, especially in the first part, I thought it was very important to have actors who are very legible, so that by means of small scenes, small gestures, you see very clearly what they are. Especially since there was practically no dialogue. When there is little dialogue, it is even more difficult to construct the features of a character.

HN: Is it essentially an on-set job, or a prep job between them and you?
KK: I talk a lot with the actors, especially when I do not know them. I try to explain things to them, and to understand them. Once we're on the set, there's no more time. There are many technical things, it's a mess. I yell at people to hurry. I cannot work slowly because money is always short.

HN: Was *A Short Film about Killing* shot quickly, in difficult conditions?
KK: Usually, I shoot my movies pretty quickly. Otherwise, I get bored. Fortunately, there are cinematographers who support me. When there's a lack of money, it's both good and bad. What's bad is that you cannot do everything you want. What's good is that I can shorten the shooting schedule.

HN: Disregarding the economic context, there are still filmmakers who like to shoot quickly. In some cases, this gives a sense of urgency. Do you think that's what you do? To strike quickly, hard, deep?

KK: Yes, so that things will be clear. I don't have the gift for telling stories. So I aim to make it bold so that it will be clear.

HN: You say you don't know how to tell stories, but the script of *A Short Film about Killing* is a model of story construction.

KK: I think it's a very original scenario, but it's not a film built according to the usual methods of storytelling. This originality stems rather from my weakness, because I cannot do otherwise.

HN: Because you're not interested in traditional narrative?

KK: Viewers have become accustomed to a standard cinematic narration. So if I want an audience in the cinema, I have to adopt this method, and I have not done it.

HN: This is also what other filmmakers are doing, and this is changing the way viewers perceive a narrative. When they do a flashback in a movie today, they do it in a way that people would not have understood a decade ago.

KK: Certainly, I feel that audiences are evolving, that they're getting used to certain methods we use. Gradually the audience comes to see them as natural.

Note

1. Toilet paper in Poland used to be in short supply, so in public toilets, if available at all, it was rationed by "toilet keepers." One could receive, for instance, a 20 cm scrap of harsh gray toilet paper per visit. In more extreme cases, pieces of scrunched-up newspaper would substitute for the toilet paper.

The Key Thing Is to Make a Believable Film

Antoine Tixeront / 1988

From *Cinéma* 452 (December 1988): 11–12.

Tixeront's brief interview, for Cinéma, *the magazine of the Fédération française des Ciné-Clubs, offers some of the most succinct and unequivocal answers from Kieślowski on a number of films.*

Antoine Tixeront: Your films demonstrate a great interplay between fiction and documentary. Is this the result of your training as a documentarist?

Krzysztof Kieślowski: Yes, undoubtedly. The documentary is a very different way of thinking about the cinema, at least the classic documentary, which is the one I prefer and which has virtually disappeared today. . . . The feature film is based on a story, while the documentary depends upon the development of an idea, a thought. And so I always feel like it's my failing not to tell a story, but rather to develop a thought . . . and from this point of view, these films are not that attractive, less so than if a story had been the main component of the narration.

AT: You have claimed to be searching for realism. However the use of color filters in *A Short Film about Killing* works rather towards the sense of unreality, right?

KK: Often people tell me that my films are too documentary. Yet if I try to escape these criticisms by using filters, for example, people think I am running away from realism. Not at all: realism is not photographing things as they appear. It's conveying the impression you have when you look at the world, it's recreating your ways of seeing what's around you. To make a film truly realistic, you need very often to resort to technical tricks. It is not enough to put the camera on the street. We must re-create the world which will be filmed; it's not so much an evasion of realism.

AT: And on the subject of realism, you seem to require very stripped-down acting from your actors to get there?

KK: For me, the key thing is to make a believable film, with characters as realistic as possible in terms of their psychological motivations. And that comes from the actors. . . . So I try to find actors who can give me this credibility. Afterwards, at the shoot, I give them a fair amount of freedom. I think the actor has to be able to get from the director a certain freedom, that of changing the dialogue a little, of including his own experience, his own ideas. He has to be something other than a clever monkey moving to the rhythm of my orders. I actually try during the filming to get the actors doing something more than their job, to remain people above all.

AT: In *Blind Chance*, you propose three possible routes for the life of your hero; you yourself do not seem to want to show a preference for one of the three?
KK: That's true, but not completely so. If you study the film, making an analysis on a purely cinematic basis, you will see that each part is filmed differently. Only the third part is filmed in a traditional way, with shots/countershots. By the play of montage in this final section, I show that it is the most possible, the most normal, and so I perhaps also indicate what my preference is.

AT: The characters in your films are generally very "concrete." So why this ghostly character in *No End*?
KK: This was the first idea for *No End*; the film started with that. I felt that there were around us people who have disappeared and who watch us; that we often refer to what they might say if they were still here. I feel that we must look with these eyes and not just through the camera. And if you look this way, you can see these people, our parents, our grandparents, those we have loved and who have disappeared.

AT: This is what Peter said to Philip in *Camera Buff*: film is a way to keep alive those who have died.
KK: Perhaps it's via this little idea in *Camera Buff* that I came to the idea for *No End*.

AT: Seeing your movies, one has the impression that you view the Poland of today without illusions, almost hopelessly?
KK: I think the situation prevailing at present in Poland justifies this. . . . And then, perhaps this is also my own particular problem: I have come to understand that despair is my subject. . . .

AT: Is *A Short Film about Killing* the darkest of your films?
KK: Yes, but it also conveys hope through the character of the lawyer. He has some humanity in him, and some faith in his convictions. I think that the defeat

he suffered will strengthen him, that he will be a stronger man. He has understood that to realize any idea, you have to fight, to have tremendous strength.

AT: If this film shakes up spectators so much, it's not so much by its theme—the death penalty has already been dealt with in the cinema—as much as by the way of showing it. There is in *A Short Film about Killing* an almost morbid precision of detail.

KK: We've heard all the babble about the death penalty. But nobody really knows how it happens up close. In the same way, a person who has never killed does not know how difficult it is to kill someone. . . . In an American movie, you shoot and instantly kill fifteen people. But in life it's not like that. It's very hard and that's what I wanted to show primarily.

AT: And you leave the viewer alone with his own opinion about the death penalty?
KK: That was in some way my wish.

AT: *A Short Film about Killing* is the first film of a decalogue. Does this mean that the others will also be as "hard" as this one?
KK: *A Short Film about Killing* is indeed the first of the Ten Commandments that I wanted to make of this decalogue, originally intended for television, but the following films will be less hopeless and the last of the series will even be a comedy. . . .

AT: A sign of hope after all. . . .
KK: Yes.

Weapon of Despair

Stanisław Latek and Marie-Claude Loiselle / 1989

From *24 Images* 42 (Spring 1989): 62–64. Reprinted by permission.

This interview in the Montreal-based 24 Images *captures the early enthusiasm of Canadian audiences—particularly those in Quebec—for Kieślowski's work. Some of Kieślowski's documentary and feature films were shown at Montreal's Conservatoire d'art Cinematographique in January 1988, and his work, including the entirety of the* Decalogue, *was showcased at the 1989 Toronto International Film Festival. The ten-episode* Decalogue *was also broadcast on French-language Canadian television in 1989, eleven years before the Sundance Channel was able to acquire the rights for U.S. television.*

When *A Short Film about Killing* by Krzysztof Kieślowski was released in Montreal and the Conservatory presented a retrospective of four feature films of this unjustly little-known Polish director, he came to talk to us about the film that finally enabled him, after twenty years of working, to win international recognition. Between *Camera Buff* made in 1979 and *A Short Film about Killing* there is a singular desire to reveal the deepest mechanisms of a dead-end society, a reality also equally evident in *Blind Chance* (1982) and *No End* (1984). Along with this consistency, there's also a shift, from one film to another, to an increasingly pessimistic worldview, more and more linked to the inescapable abyss threatening his country. With an exceptional rigor, *A Short Film about Killing* shows only the cruel underside of a reality that we avoid looking at.

24 images: Your films deal with moral issues but without being judgmental. What are your reasons not to take a stand?

Krzysztof Kieślowski: I am obviously aware that many people are resistant to this kind of approach but my reason for making films is to ask questions, not to give answers. I present a problem then I see how it plays out. How can I indicate a way forward as I am myself unsure? I certainly don't want to answer any fundamental question.

24i: Is it because you believe that people don't know how to look that you feel the need to show things in as unrelenting a way as you do?

KK: People have always refused to look at reality, to see life as it is. Few people dare to say, "That's the way it is," because reality is dark and no one likes to hear that said.

24i: We know that *A Short Film about Killing* is one of a series of ten films each of which refers to one of the Ten Commandments. What more precisely is this series about?

KK: I prefer to use the term "cycle" rather than "series" because each film is independent of the others. For each one, there are new actors, a stand-alone story, and even, in terms of the photography, ten different directors of photography. So I had to make ten films in two years. Two were made for theatrical release: *A Short Film about Killing* and *A Short Film about Love*. The other eight were for television and will be broadcast in the autumn in Poland.

24i: Is it because of financing that you chose to make only two of the films for the cinema?

KK: This idea of a cycle of films on the Ten Commandments was originally conceived entirely for television. As for *A Short Film about Killing*, I had the idea for this project long before, only I hesitated to shoot it in a manner as raw as I imagined. That's why I felt the need to link it to this cycle, to somehow justify this violence. Outside such a context, I feared that people would find it gratuitous to approach murder in this way. As for the eight films for TV, I could not have made them for the cinema, given the time available. At the same time, it was necessary to shoot two of the films for theatrical release in order to get outside financing. That's how, thanks to the money obtained for these two films, we were able to complete the cycle.

24i: None of the characters in *A Short Film about Killing* allows the viewer to identify with them. Does this approach stem from the sole desire to render social reality as objectively as possible?

KK: It was obviously the main reason, because I wanted the film to have the form of a social analysis, but there's also the fact that I really didn't want to be seduced by the easy way. People tend to identify too much with myths, with characters that you can never become. It was too simple to make the victim a nice character monopolizing the audience's compassion. It's really so much easier to direct the viewer's emotions than to show things as they are. Death threatens all without distinction. That's why I insisted on showing the murder of the taxi driver in as cruel and bestial a way as the hanging of the murderer. In reality, the death which threatens us every moment is just as horrible for everyone, but we do not want to admit it because it would not be possible to live with this awareness.

24i: What importance do you give to creativity? What is your vision of the role of the artist?

KK: To answer that question, we must look back in Polish history, back to the nineteenth century, to the time of Polish Romanticism and even earlier. The artist's role has always been exaggerated and glorified, since we expect him to guide the [Polish] nation. People have long invested all their hopes in that particular idea of the artist, conferring on him an almost magical power, an ability to see things they would be powerless to perceive. Equally, people believed that the artist could change the world. As for me, I don't believe that. He can only make visible what is here, now. The artist's role is also to go along with people, to show them they are not alone, that others live and think the same way as them.

24i: Do you believe that artists try to set the pace, to figure out the single best way?

KK: Yes I do.

24i: Why have you abandoned the documentary form for fiction? Is it because you ascribe more power to fiction?

KK: I like to film reality with a readiness to face all its unpredictability. I concentrated my work for a long time on the documentary because I felt reality was more interesting than anything that can be invented. I stopped making documentaries because on the one hand, this genre has almost completely disappeared, killed by television reporting that is most of the time a superficial and standardized product, but also because I was afraid my films would be used by the police. I realized that in filming what interested me, I was supplying them, despite myself, with a very useful tool.

24i: In relation to the content of the film, one feels that the way of filming always reflects a very deliberate choice. How do you work with your director of photography and how do you explain why you almost never work with the same one?

KK: Until a decade ago, I worked only with two directors of photography, depending on the film, on its subject. I then realized that in order for the worldview that I project in my films to be enriched, so that my film image progresses, I had to work with different directors of photography and to allow them to contribute their own worldview. To this end I have to give him maximum freedom so he can show even what sometimes I do not see. We discuss at the outset the desired effect then I let him get on with it. For *A Short Film about Killing*, for example,

I asked Sławomir Idziak, the director of photography, to create the image of a world where it's impossible to live, where murder seems fated, inevitable. It is always difficult when working on location and with small budgets to tamper with what is in front of the lens. So, by making himself a tinted filter giving a greenish color to the image and messing up its outlines, he was able to enter, with his camera, into this hostile world that we wanted to render.

24i: Despite its subject, it seems that *A Short Film about Killing* did not have the problems of distribution of your previous films. Is discussion of the death penalty now permitted in the official media?

KK: The death penalty is no longer a taboo subject in Poland. When I made *A Short Film about Killing*, everything had already been said on the subject. But on the film's release, the discussions were rekindled. A Polish weekly published a letter of protest against my film, from one of the official executioners. It railed against the fact that his role is presented as on a level with that of the murderer, while his work is socially very useful and in addition, he said, badly paid. My film then did not only reinitiate the discussion of the death penalty, but also allowed the executioner to seize the opportunity to demand a raise . . .

Interview with Krzysztof Kieślowski

Steve Goldman / 1989

Although Kieślowski's work had shown at Cannes before 1988, the prizes that A Short Film about Killing *won there that year awakened a broad European critical and public interest in him and his work. Goldman's interview appeared just after* A Short Film about Killing *was theatrically released in Britain. The entire* Decalogue *cycle would be shown on BBC 2 in the summer of 1990.*

Krzysztof Kieślowski has become the European filmmakers' filmmaker. The twenty-year overnight transformation from an obscure documentarist working with Krzysztof Zanussi's Tor unit to Poland's leading director came on November 26 when Kieślowski's *A Short Film about Killing* (Krótki film o zabijaniu) took the first European Oscar.

Contrasting the brutal murder of a taxi driver with the subsequent execution of the accused, *A Short Film about Killing* forms the first part of Kieślowski's *Decalogue* cycle[1]—ten separate parables which draw thematically from the Ten Commandments and are linked by a common setting, an anonymous Warsaw housing estate.

Says Kieślowski: "The stories are set in Warsaw, the pictures made in Poland, but the situations described are universal. The Commandments relate not only to religion, but to the intercourse between people, which is most interesting to me. If something is well written, one should film it."

Seeking to tap Poland's two primary sources of finance, Film Polski, the state's governing film board, and Pol Tel, the national broadcast network, Kieślowski divided his productions into two groups. *Decalogue V* and *VI*, *A Short Film about Killing* and *A Short Film about Love* were made for the cinema. The remaining eight were made for Polish television. The difference, apart from the lengths (the theatrical versions running at approximately ninety minutes, the television versions at sixty), is negligible. As Kieślowski, who cut his molars on more than thirty documentaries in the seventies, told one French critic: "There's no difference between the two except that television pays you less and you have to work faster."

Remarkably, Kieślowski shot and edited the ten films back-to-back over a twenty-one-month period using different cinematographers on each production.

"Making ten films is truly boring," he says. "If I had worked continuously with the same cameraman, I wouldn't have been able to get up in the morning.

"The decision was to give them a lot of freedom, letting them take the pictures they liked so long as their interpretations were true to the general concept. The result was a kind of competition with each trying to outdo the other."

A Short Film about Killing (Decalogue V) marked its premiere at the 1988 Cannes Film Festival where it was awarded the Jury and International Film Critic's prize. September saw the premiere of the second film of the cycle, A Short Film about Love with top honors at San Sebastian.

By February 1989, following his success at the European Film Awards, Kieślowski had established a formidable reputation. Disqualified from the official competition after "losing its virginity at San Sebastián," the German premiere of A Short Film about Love at the Berlin Film Festival played to packed audiences.

By May, Kieślowski was back in Cannes, this time as a member of Wim Wenders's Jury. Again the films, Decalogues I, IX, and X (the first television versions to be screened), played out of competition to capacity attendance at the small André Bazin cinema. The completed cycle was screened in its entirety for the first time at the Venice Festival this autumn.

Much has transpired in Poland since my two conversations with Krzysztof Kieślowski in Berlin and Cannes—a July election giving a popular mandate to Solidarity (of which Kieślowski is a member), President Bush's tour of the Eastern Bloc, the insubstantial pledge of debt reduction, and the growing economic crisis which now threatens the fragile new government. Still, it is interesting that Kieślowki's pessimistic perceptions of the Polish state, and to a lesser extent its film industry, have remained unchanged.

"Of course, one can say a lot now," said Kieślowki last February in Berlin when asked about the impact of Glasnost. But talking changes nothing, and for now it is only talk. The authorities in Poland understand that talking will not harm them and this gives the Polish intelligentsia a feeling of freedom. So they allowed it. But it is only talk, only words.

"In Poland, the problem is that one can't buy toilet paper. You have to collect old papers and find the special places where they swap them in return for new toilet paper. For three rolls of old paper you get one new roll."

Similar chords of pathos are struck in Kieślowski's A Short Film about Love, where an adolescent voyeur becomes infatuated with an older woman living across the square.

Spying on the woman and her lover from afar with his telescope, he disrupts their encounter by reporting a gas leak in the apartment. But when the gas board make their inspection, they check for the leak with a candle. Similarly, when a rendezvous is finally arranged, a date at an ice-cream parlor, the couple arrive only to find the shop has run out of ice-cream.

"It's funny for you," says Kieślowski, "but for us it's not so funny any more. I think people in Poland are losing their sense of humor and this is very dangerous."

Kieślowski's acerbic critiques of life under communism won little respect from the Party. Few of his films were screened abroad and many suppressed within Poland. Their fate now rests with Solidarity's new communications minister, Andrzej Drawicz, who replaced the hardliner Jerzy Urban.

In Poland, the *Decalogue* has met with impressive results. Kieślowski cites attendances of 200,000 for the initial run of *A Short Film about Killing*, and 400,000 within five months for *A Short Film about Love*.

Initially the Polish press labelled the films "boring," "insipid," "ill-made," and "ill-played." "*They* are now trying to draw back from earlier opinions, but this does not change my opinion of them."

Note

1. *A Short Film about Killing* is, in fact, the theatrical version of the fifth part of the *Decalogue*, as Goldman notes further on in his article.

A Normal Moment

Tadeusz Sobolewski / 1990

From *Kino* 6 (1990): 19–22. Reprinted by permission.

Tadeusz Sobolewski is one of the most universally respected film journalists and writers in Poland. He shared Krzysztof Kieślowski's deeply empathetic approach to cinema, especially Polish cinema, and compassion for individuals, which throughout the years led to many revealing meetings and interviews with Kieślowski.

Tadeusz Sobolewski: Domestic discussions of the *Decalogue* have kept crashing against the reef of religiousness. On the one hand, you hear that it's a deeply religious film, then again, others are saying that it's ungodly. How do you react to that? And generally, how do you react to the fact that in Poland the *Decalogue* has not conjured the expected response?

Krzysztof Kieślowski: You've touched on two issues. Let's start with a minor one, with distribution. How does foreign perception of the *Decalogue* differ from the Polish one? Abroad, until now (March 1990), they've watched these films only in cinemas. Besides that, what's more important, always grouped together. Either they were shown one a day, as in Venice. Or two films in one showing, as in Paris. The Germans have the idea to show them all together, from Saturday to Sunday, serving ham and pea soup. Those films, watched together in a cinema, function completely differently than when you watch them on television once a week. You can then see that they constitute a consolidated whole, you can see a whole succession of details, which disappear in other circumstances. Meanings transfer from one film to another.

I think Piesiewicz and I made a mistake. The *Decalogue* scripts are basically engineered for cinema, not for television. Dense, requiring concentration, filled with detail. I suspect that when they start to be broadcast on various televisions around the world, they will function as in Poland, that is, as single films, better or worse, but not connected to one another.

TS: But the reception of the *Decalogue* in Poland has been specific not only because of television. In Western Europe, especially in France, the *Decalogue* scored terrifically well with critics as well as viewers as a "metaphysical" film. In our country, we are wary of any attempts to break into the topics reserved for the sphere of religion. Religion has become undisputed.

KK: I have read two intelligent theses on this topic. One by Bożena Janicka who has written in *Film* that in our country the *Decalogue* could not have been received as well as in the West because faith in Poland is a certainty, and even a necessity. However, there, faith is only a possibility. As a possibility it is much more interesting than as an obligation.

Krzysztof Teodor Toeplitz has put forward another interesting thesis in *Polityka*. He has written that in the current situation, Poles desire a charitable, patient God, who would forgive us all sins. Meanwhile, in the Protestant West, and—what's interesting—in Israel, the alternative of the existence of a cruel, demanding God is assumed as definite. However, Poles—writes Toeplitz—have lately committed too many serious sins to accept that portrayal of God. They want to have a forgiving Mother above them rather than a fierce Father. Moreover, it is historically justified.

TS: The *Decalogue* encourages "theological" discussions.

KK: I'm afraid of such discussions because there is no theologian in me, and I don't feel too confident on that ground.

TS: However, it can be said that faith in the *Decalogue* is not associated with any particular cult. After all, in every conversation lurks the question: "Are you a believer?" The newspaper *La Suisse* asked you that. You answered, "I haven't attended Church for forty years."

KK: I don't remember that question well; there have been so many similar ones. I referred to the colloquial differentiation according to which a believer is a person who attends Church, devotes himself to some cult. Relatively regularly. Fairly formally. For me, believing in God has nothing to do with Church as an institution. I answer these sorts of questions [by saying] that I don't need middlemen. Furthermore, I think that most of us don't need middlemen.

TS: There are so many definitions of faith. Protestant theologian Paul Tillich, in [his] book *Dynamics of Faith*, published recently by the Dominicans, defines faith as an "ultimate concern." He acknowledges the existence of secular, humanistic faith, next to sacramental, mystical faith. One pursues capturing what's godly, the other centers on the human. But the followers of both faiths have in common "ultimate concern." A provocative meaning of the *Decalogue* and its main value is about leveling out the difference between "a believer" and "a non-believer," religious and non-religious (parts 1, 2, 8).

KK: I wouldn't like to use the designation "Protestant." I am not coming from "Protestant" stances. If we treat the author whom you are quoting not as the Church's representative, but as a writer, a humanist, I agree. What he says is close to me.

TS: It can be said about the protagonist of *Decalogue I* that he is an atheist. Although his gesture of rebellion in Church is a gesture of disappointed faith. In that film there are many unanswered questions, since it chooses this and not another ending, it distributes emphasis in this, not another way. There had been several alternative endings of *Decalogue I*. In one of them, the boy was to be saved. From where does the idea of a film develop?

KK: The final idea? In the editing room. Only then the soul of the film reveals itself. It cannot be prefigured in advance. That's why I often shoot alternate endings. The most appropriate one is the one that emerges logically out of the material.

TS: Michał Klinger has found in *Decalogue I* a unifying idea, a deep symbol.

KK: It's about an analogy with Kafka? Fortunately, Klinger allows for the possibility that the director had not been aware of that. When making the *Decalogue*, I was not reaching out for *The Trial*. It would have never occurred to me to connect these two things. But I do carry that book somewhere inside [me]. The potential similarities may have to do with intuition or with arriving at similar conclusions through similar experiences.

The simplest interpretation of the scene in the church is technical in character. I needed candles so wax could drip on the face of the Holy Mother. That's why I put them there. And I didn't consider whether it's like in Kafka. Nor whether this is how candles are usually placed. I've said already that I am rarely in church.

TS: Paraffin tears on the Holy Mother's portrait are a sign, which is created in front of our eyes, or rather—of the film's protagonist's eyes. It's as if it were a miracle without a miracle. We recognize the technical origin of the sign, which has been caused unintentionally by the protagonist, but soon after, for a short time, we sense the existence of another dimension. This way you justify, or even bless the rebellion of this "atheist," because the Holy Mother weeps over him.

KK: I think, at that point of time, more important than "rebellion" is the word "pain." And it's not important whether the protagonist sees those tears or not.

And if it's him who causes them. It's important that we, the viewers, recognize that somebody else leans over his suffering. And that's the reason we thought it out.

TS: The symbol is recognized in that moment despite an authorial distance. In these films, faith itself, as well as its symbols, is observed with fascination, but always from the outside. That doesn't stop the viewer from creating a symbolic aggregate out of this material.

That's the nature of cinema. When I see a spider on the screen, it necessarily becomes a symbol in my eyes. It's difficult to avoid too deep interpretations, which upset or even irritate you.

KK: They don't irritate me. I've said at some stage that they amuse me. But that's not a good word either. It fascinates me that people notice and interpret some things that are unnamed or even unexpressed in the film. This is how they come to life.

That's why I make films. When they ask me why I make them, I always answer: because I want to have a conversation. How would you define searching for deep and non-existent film meanings if not as a kind of a conversation? After all, a conversation is about finding in someone else what you don't have in you. And that in turn causes you to find in yourself something unexpected.

TS: I am not searching for a deep symbol in your films. In *Decalogue 1*, as well as in the other films of the series, if signs appear, they are always accompanied by irony. Those signs are either misleading or blatantly created by people.

For instance, in *Decalogue 2* you set out a whole net of tiny magical signs around the characters. A woman (Krystyna Janda) has a husband in hospital and wants to guess at any price whether he will live or die. That's a very human desire. Janda has something of the witch about her. When she stands in a window and systematically tears off a plant's leaves, it's as if she wants to influence her husband's fate: let it be what it is to be; let him die!

We await a sign. And signs appear: either a hare falls out of a window, or that red light at the crossroads. . . . On the second viewing of the film, on the door of the elevator, which Janda gets into, I noticed a scratched inscription "Got" (with a "t" [not "d"]). And during Janda and Bardini's conversation in the hospital, in the background there is an empty medicine box with the writing "*Confiance.*" In old melodramas, auspicious or ominous signs always stood in the protagonists' way. In the *Decalogue*, it is somewhat like in those melodramas (a wasp, which extricates itself from "kompot"[1] as a sign that the patient is recovering). But most frequently, signs are set out misleadingly, their meaning is indeterminate. There is some kind of irony in it. And there is no symbol.

KK: Of course there isn't. Although searching and finding—as Klinger does— even of the unintentional is very interesting. Krysia [trans: diminutive of Krystyna] Janda tears off the leaves of the plant we got in at great expense—yes, it was intentional. But the word "Got" (with a "t"?) on the elevator's frame? It's the first time I'm hearing such a thing.

TS: I saw [it].
KK: But it is not me who'd written it. It must have accidentally gotten onto the very elevator next to which we were shooting. I also didn't notice it in the material. The most important thing for me was to know at which point to edit a scene. And you looked at it as a picture whose sense is perceived as a whole. You see how reality breaks into the film independently of the director's intention. What was the writing on the medicine box?

TS: *Confiance*. Trust.
KK: The set decorator arranged these boxes to fill in an empty space. That word is probably the name of some business. He placed the box, and again I didn't notice anything. Apart from everything else, I don't know French.

TS: Still, these are meaningful moments.
KK: You ask how meaning is created? Let's start from the beginning. First, Piesiewicz and I write a script. Later, other people join in. Actors. The designer. And the cinematographer—that one is really important. Edward Kłosiński did the cinematography for *Decalogue 2*. He'd read the script and said: there are a few places in this film where one has to clearly lean on the details and on slow-motion filming. Because with the *Decalogue* , I worked with nine different cinematographers, it was necessary for each of them to mark their participation somehow. So, I said: of course, Edziu [trans: diminutive of Edward], mark the places that need to be photographed in detail and in slow motion. Probably through the way of filming thought out by the cinematographer, understanding what the essence of the film is, the signs that you are talking about appeared.

TS: That would concur with the ironic line of the whole. This method has something of sympathetic magic in it: the desire to look behind fate's curtain. We don't know who is pulling the strings. Director-demiurge? Not quite. You admit yourself how many things happen outside of the director's will. The *Decalogue*'s characters participate in a game. But there is in these films also a link beyond playing with fate. What is the visitor from another world doing throughout? The angel?
KK: Barciś?

TS: I've called him an angel.

KK: I don't mind that at all. But I call him Barciś. Or, more precisely, Artur. If some of the things in the film you are talking about here can be talked about without too many words, without putting a foot on the gas, without pretense, then of course I want to talk about such a thing. I'm only resisting identifying some meanings precisely.

Do you want to know how Barciś got into the film? Again, I am not the author of that character. It was Witold Zalewski, who was then the literary director of the [production] unit. He read our scripts and said that they were missing something. I was trying to find out what. Because I trust his taste, his view, a lot. Then, he told me an anecdote about Wilhelm Mach. It took place at some pre-release screening. The film was over, there was nothing much to talk about. Mach spoke out. He said that he liked the funeral scene a lot, and especially the moment when out of the left side of the frame a man in a black suit appears. Everyone was mortified: Mach always inspired a lot of respect, but everyone in the room, including the director, knew that there was no such man in the film. The director said: I didn't shoot anything like that. Mach: I saw him very clearly, he stood in the background, approached the mid-shot, observed the ceremony. . . . Mach died soon after that pre-release.

When Witek [trans: diminutive of Witold] Zalewski was telling me that, I understood what he was missing in the scripts: that man whom not everyone sees. Connected with a mystery that cannot be explained. That's how it is with mysteries.

TS: If there is a moment of faith in the *Decalogue*, it is associated with the unknown, with mystery. That's contrary to the vernacular notion that faith is a kind of certainty.

KK: You are right; here [in Poland] faith is not associated with mystery. The answers are known. We deserve divine care because we are poor. And it cannot be any other way. So when a trading arrangement exists by which we give suffering and in return get care, there is no room for any mystery.

TS: He who suffers has the right to consolation.

KK: Many, many people suffer. Everywhere. However, I suspect that we as a society have gotten used to that state too much. We've grown to like that arrangement: suffering and care. Just as we cling to the absurd protectiveness of the state, we would not allow what is owed to us—divine care, religion, church—to be taken away from us. We wouldn't consent to it, would we?

TS: You are rejecting the traditional, Romantic thinking about sacrifice as something one (or the nation) has to undertake of oneself, to endear oneself to God. When I spoke to Krzysztof Piesiewicz about the *Decalogue*, he suggested an interesting link, René Girard's *The Scapegoat*. Girard sees in the Gospel above all a protest against ritual sacrifice. The Christian God, says Girard, doesn't demand sacrifice. Everything is determined among people. If they can love, they will be God's equals. They will become Christ's brothers. It's going beyond religion in a traditional, ritual sense.

KK: But isn't people's desire for good and love in itself a religious fact? The immemorial attitude towards God as a being responsible for all the good and all the evil exasperates me. I don't know if a direct line leading up from man to God exists.

TS: But you have also said that you reject brokerage.

KK: I'm not able to understand everything and I don't want to. My attitude towards these matters is associated with a certain trait that Krzysztof [Piesiewicz] also possesses. With a need, or even necessity, to be beside, not inside. I sense that only being beside gives a possibility of clear viewing of matters.

Some time ago, I made the film *Curriculum Vitae*. A contemporary documentary about the workings of a Party committee. The Central Committee of the Party [KC PZPR] had to issue permission for it (although it was not commissioning the film). Why am I saying this now? So there, in the Central Committee, they believed that only a Party member could make a film about the Party. And I was convincing them to the contrary: that only someone from the outside of the Party could make a film about it, someone critical towards it. Then, there were still reformers in the Party who saw evil and were trying to create a warning system. Thanks to them, a critical film, *Curriculum Vitae*, could come into existence. I emphasize: only someone who doesn't belong to the Party could have made it.

The same applies to the *Decalogue*. Only someone from the outside of the charmed circle of ritualized contacts between man and God—and of the complete faith in the possibility of such contact—only that sort of a person can narrate it. Otherwise it would become a sermon.

TS: People need sermons.

KK: People have a need for ideology; if they abandon one, or it is taken away from them, immediately they look for another.

TS: You have never abandoned an ideology?

KK: No, because I have never had any. Unless life itself is an ideology.

I think that misunderstandings surrounding the *Decalogue* stem from ideologizing every phenomenon in Poland. Someone says it's a religious film, somebody else the contrary. But no one utters a different, simple question: is it a good film or not? The same concerns *Curriculum Vitae*. They asked if this was a pro- or anti-communist film, instead of asking if it was good.

TS: Everywhere in the world, creators are asked about their convictions. Although in the West, I suspect, it's a question of a rather social nature. If you introduced yourself as a Mason or as a follower of Zoroaster, they would say: aha, that's interesting! There is a catch also in that equality of grand ideas.
KK: Yes, but of a different type. Here ideologization is a catch.

TS: In the interview for the Strasbourg Festival, you declared: communism lives inside us. How do you understand it?
KK: Communism was sloppy and it taught us sloppiness. I think we would free ourselves of communism more effectively if every one of us cleaned their shoes in the morning, rather than everyone altogether putting a crown on the eagle.[2]

We have a deep desire to reject what was and what we never liked. In society, it finds a symbolic expression: you take Dzerzhinsky, tie him with ropes to a crane, and take him off his pedestal. You do the same with Bierut, Lenin, with many monuments. And you think that's enough to get away from communism. You can also throw out the communist officials who are still active, and [think] that's the end. There is a serious error in this type of thinking. This way, we attain a sense of comfort: that we might have managed something. In the meantime, communism is a virus that lives in everyone who has come into contact with it. It is a type of AIDS. Only it transfers through words, and not blood, through social actions, and not sexual. And although not all of us have AIDS, I'm under the impression that everyone—communists, anticommunists, and the indifferent—had relations with Marxism. And that lingers on.

There is some indelibility, or inability, or maybe a deeply hidden aversion to rejecting all we have lived on for forty-five years. Even if it was not adhered to, communist ideology has infiltrated the way of life itself. In the way we bake cookies, which are lying here in front of us on a plate. It infiltrated everything. Just come out to the street, observe how we live.

TS: But taking another perspective, one cannot reject one's own life, which was connected with that reality. That's precisely [what's in] your first documentaries: *The Photograph* (which I've watched recently), *From The City of Łódź*, *Refrain* show lives of ordinary people as a certain continuity, despite all the social kitsch surrounding them, from which you have always kept your distance. We are now rejecting rituals well-worn throughout the years: women's day, May 1, and so on. Before we used to disdain them, but despite that we lived with them in one system. And we had a sense of freedom. I did.

KK: Everything can be superseded: instead of May 1, May 3![3] Instead of civil marriage, church marriage. Like before the war. It's truly a serious problem: to reject everything that was means to reject oneself. And I want to preserve myself for myself.

TS: I will admit to one more thing: when I watched the moment of the dismantling of the Party [PZPR] on television, although I had never been connected with it, I didn't feel triumphant, but sad. And it is not about the Party itself, but about the whole complex: that was the end of some game in which we had participated. A lost game: lost delusions, buried illusions. That's what the People's Republic [PRL] was.

KK: I was embarrassed to admit similar emotions. But when my anti-communist sister said that when they sang "It's Our Last Battle" [trans: "The Internationale"], she had tears in her eyes, only then I admitted to myself that I was affected similarly. We didn't like that world and we didn't want it, but we lived in it.

If we are ashamed of there being some type of single thread that connects our life through all those years, if we break that thread, there will be a void left. And it will turn out that all we have lived through until now is worthless.

But let's not forget that everyone needs a sense of continuity. Also those who have spent recent years in prisons and interned, all those who were meeting in various secret places, where they printed things, talked, sang. They also have a right to continuity. Those a l s o [trans: original emphasis] have lost something. You hear more and more combatant recollections.

TS: Ten years ago in the film *Blind Chance*, you arranged in one arena, as participants of the same game, communists and anti-communists. The figure of the old dispirited communist believer (Tadeusz Łomnicki) was at the time something unusual; it has had no continuity in the cinema after that. One looks differently at those people today, now without resentment.

KK: Oftentimes, they were people of good intentions. They say hell is paved with them. In a historical sense, most certainly.

Good intentions, impossible to realize, but existing—that's a tragedy. That's why judging these people today is so difficult. I'm curious about what will ultimately be put on the scales: the effects of actions, or intentions? But I don't have a need to stand in for the Last Judgment. If I have a need to talk about human dramas, it's only from an individual perspective.

TS: After martial law you turned away from politics. In the *Decalogue* you talk about people from blocks of flats, but there is no trace in it of what was happening around them at that time.
KK: I am less and less interested in the world, and more and more in people.

TS: Don't you have a need to return to specific life stories? To look at the People's Republic [PRL] from a distance, to see what it is that we participated in?
KK: Maybe there will be a need for that. Even if I don't tell these stories, others will come, and they will tell them. I am noticing how people, a generation or even two younger than me, try to scrabble about in those regions that used to interest me, but today don't interest me any longer. To do something in cinema, you have to really crave it and not have a formulaic program.

TS: What you are writing now touches on those, let's call them, metaphysical regions?
KK: To some degree. But it is also an attempt to tell a story.

TS: When we talk about Polish film, we always start with grand ideas, and we finish with them.
KK: Parties and churches are about ideologies. Critics all over the world go about analyzing films, and people go to the cinema for interesting films.

TS: We have managed to deal with huge wholes, with communism, with religion (NB: how well they coexisted, fighting one another!). And somewhere on the way, we've lost a dimension of our own experience, our own limited consciousness.
KK: We've just spoken about AIDS, or HIV. . . . You are now talking about the same thing. And as for the problem of the responsibility for a whole, recently I watched on TV one of the people responsible for our state's economy: he has Wernyhora's[4] appearance and way of speaking. Again, he orders me to believe in something. He has fiery eyes. He wants me to pick up a bug. And I would prefer he had an abacus, or—even better—a computer. Because it's only about percentages. That's what I also had in mind in talking about a virus that lives in us.

In Poland, we are always waiting for something. Next year, next month, next week, there is to be a general resolution of our situation. And so we have been waiting, since 1945. There is no moment that would not be decisive. There is always a historical decision, or a fundamental change, or a basic regulation. There is no normal moment. There is no normal day.

Notes

1. Stewed fruit drink which traditionally is drunk in Poland the way sodas are drunk in the West.

2. The white eagle is the Polish national emblem. In communist times, the eagle was crownless. In 1989, it regained a crown to symbolize the continuity of the post-communist state with the pre-communist past of Poland.

3. Post-communist national celebration of Poland's first constitution announced on May 3, 1791.

4. Wernyhora is either a historical or mythical foreseer of Polish national demise, depicted in Polish art and literature, usually placed in the eighteenth century.

Diary: 1989–1990 (1)

Krzysztof Kieślowski / 1989–90

From *Kino* 12 (1991): 38–39. Reprinted by permission.

This and the following extracts from Krzysztof Kieślowski's diaries were published first in German in the Zurich magazine Du *and printed in the original Polish in* Kino.

Krzysztof Kieślowski: These will be the simplest notes on Life this coming year. Please, don't expect deep reflections. Something has crossed my path, or something has crossed my mind. That's all.

Sunday: I've arranged a meeting with friends in front of a good hotel in Paris. I am waiting, [it is] morning. The biggest, newest black BMW with an Italian license plate arrives. Inside—an elegant, greyish man. He leans over smiling: are you Italian? I answer with a negative nod of the head and see that I've really upset him. I feel sorry, but at the same time, glad: he's taken me for an Italian! French? He continues to ask and gets worried that I'm not even French. He switches to English, and because he speaks that language worse than me, I have a nice, and nasty, sense of advantage. A tourist? I confirm it. He tells me a story: he is a fashion designer and today he has just finished his show in Paris. He shows folders. Nice. During the closing, his wallet was stolen with money, credit cards; fortunately he kept his passport separately; he also shows his Italian passport. He thought I was a compatriot, and now. . . . And again a worried, doggy, congenial face. I ask what it's about. About money; he has to have some money to get back to Rome, to stay overnight somewhere on the way, to eat something. How much? A lot. More or less as much as what I have. He apologizes that he's intruded, and I feel so good! I am in a way proud that he's addressed me for help, that he's chosen me. I take my wallet out. He gives me his business card, he will pay me the money back and we'll drink wine in Rome, whenever I come there! And he takes out a huge, plastic bag. This is a present for you. Inside: a few leather jackets, these are his designs, whatever is left from the show. I don't want the jackets, I don't look at them, but he definitely has to give me a present. If I don't take [it], he will be offended and he already wants to give me the money back. This is worth a lot more, more than a thousand dollars, he says; it's only a present for you being so good! I feel even better. He pushes the bag on me, and leaves. For the whole day I don't have time, but in the evening I open the bag. The jackets are made of hideous, tawdry artificial leather. Still trustingly, I check his business card: the street in which he lives does not even exist in Rome! I hang the jacket up on a hanger, the seam comes apart.

Tuesday: Bad news this morning. A few months ago, my friend's mother was murdered.[1] He found her in [her] apartment tied up with a very crafty knot; she was dead. My friend is a lawyer. He acted in the trial of the priest Popiełuszko's murderers, milicja officers [trans: "milicja" is the name for the police of the People's Republic; in post-communist Poland "milicja" became "policja"].[2] He was these officers' private prosecutor. That's precisely the knot they used to tie the priest before they drowned him. Yesterday, he had his car broken into. A few days ago, his apartment. Dangerous.

Monday: I'm buying a gas gun. A whole day of work. A purchase permit, fees, photographs, certificates. I'm coming back with a gun; it lies on the car seat next to me. At an empty crossroads, I want to let a motorbike through, even though I have the right of way. On the bike, two young boys in jean jackets. They think that I dawdle, that I dillydally. They go past me and the one on the backseat screams straight into my face through the open window: cunt! For a few seconds I have an unrestrained desire: to turn back, catch up with them and shoot the guy on the backseat straight in his face with the gun that lies next to me. How dangerous! I go back home and put the gun in a drawer. After a few hours I change the place: I put it where it would be handy.

Saturday: Today I'm coming back [home], tomorrow I'm leaving [again]. I don't like travelling. I have a feeling that hours in hotels and on planes are time that stands still. Last week, I got on the plane eleven times. Before, I used to think that I was afraid of flying. Only recently I've understood that I'm afraid that I would be afraid. I return and it turns out, naturally, that time has passed by. Daughter has gotten good marks in math and English, and bad in Russian. Wife has had trouble at work. The dog has puked in the hallway. They will be developing the attic above our apartment. The washing machine has broken down. The grandmother of my daughter's boyfriend has died. So many important things have happened.

Thursday: Morning, 6 am at the airport in America in Los Angeles. A taxi-driver already warns me, seeing numerous people in front of the airport building: a bomb. Indeed, there have been phone calls, they've planted a bomb. The police are throwing everyone out: travellers and staff, even chefs from the airport restaurant. Probably two thousand people. Hot. There is nowhere to go, there is only a building surrounded by the police, and the highway on which they've stopped traffic. We crowd up in bedlam; it's getting hotter. Everything that should be happening is: children are crying, somebody is singing, someone is fainting in the squeeze, and so on. But after an hour, I notice that a strange movement persists among people, or more like a displacement, squeezing through with bundles, step by step. At first it's difficult to understand it, and then it becomes clear. After an hour of that movement the crowd has divided itself: Whites separate, Blacks separate, Chinese, Japanese, and other Asians separate, Mexicans separate. Everyone is standing in harmony, crowded together, but now segregated. Nobody could have planned that, but that's how it's happened. I wonder if I have also moved. Yes. I've moved two meters, because next to me a Mexican child's been screaming. I have moved towards people speaking French; they are probably from Europe.

Friday: At the airport in Warsaw, as usual, a half-an-hour wait for the luggage. The carousel keeps turning and with it go round: a cigarette butt, an umbrella, a Marriott Hotel badge, a suitcase strap buckle, and a white, clean handkerchief. Despite the non-smoking signs, I light up a cigarette. Next [to me], four guys who handle baggage continue sitting on the only four chairs: smoking is not allowed here, chief, one of them says. And sitting and doing nothing is? I ask. Doing nothing in Poland is always allowed, says the other. They roar with laughter. One has no top teeth, no central incisor, nor lateral incisor. The other has no canines. The third one has no teeth at all, but he is older; he might be already some fifty-years-old. The fourth one, about thirty, has all his teeth. I wait for the luggage another twenty minutes, altogether almost an hour. Because we now feel acquainted, the baggage guys say nothing more when I light up a second cigarette.

Thursday: Really, why did I think about censorship yesterday? It's the two conversations I've had in the last few days with the most prominent Polish directors, those who also work domestically. Wajda heavily involved himself in politics for at least two years; he's been a Senator for a year. I've never hidden that I consider it absurd wasting such talent as Wajda's on politics. He says that he wants to do something for Poland, for the new Poland. I've told him that the only truly good thing that he can do is a good film, because he knows how. Recently, he's announced that he won't be running in the next election. I met him, he was sad. What will I be doing? he asked. Films, I answered. What about? He looked at me in such a way that I understood he really didn't know. Two days ago, I met

Zanussi. He'd finished shooting. When asked how it went, he shook his head in displeasure. I've shot something similar to what Wajda did a few days ago. Do you know what they want? Who? I asked. He pointed with his head there, outside. They, people.

Thursday: It has occurred to me that since I've mentioned censorship, it would be good to say how it used to work. I've had, just like my colleagues, a heap of adventures with censorship. Some of my films were not screened for years, others never. Frequently, I cut something out thinking that the change was not destroying the film; frequently, I refused. In 1976 I made the feature film *The Calm* for television. I liked that film, it had a few good scenes, and a thought—that a man couldn't achieve peace even if it meant only home, wife, television—was near to me. The protagonist is a guy who comes out of prison. Once free, he works at a small building site. They bring prisoners there to help. Television objected to that scene. The [television] vice-president was a very intelligent and cunning man. He called me into his office. I knew why. When I approached the building, I noticed that prisoners were working on the railway tracks. They were dressed normally, in prison clothes, around them guards with rifles. I entered the vice-president's office. He said he liked *The Calm* a lot and voiced a truly astute review of that film. Really, he understood everything. He truly liked the film. I was nicely tickled and waited for what was to follow; I knew I hadn't been called in to listen to compliments. Of course. The vice-president with regret informed me that he had to demand the deletion of a few scenes from the film. He believed it would not hurt. On the contrary, the film would be more nimble. Among the scenes for deletion he included also the one with the building site with prisoners. I asked why there could be no scene in which prisoners work on a building site. Because in Poland, said the vice-president, prisoners don't work outside prison. The convention forbids it. . . . He mentioned the name of an international convention. I asked him to come to the window. He did. I asked him what he saw. He said, tramway tracks. And on the tracks? Who is working there? He looked more closely. Prisoners, he said calmly, they're here every day. So, prisoners in Poland work outside prison, I noted. Of course, he said, that's why you have to delete that scene.

That's more or less what those conversations looked like. That one was quite pleasant. I deleted the scene with prisoners and a few more, and the film still would not be shown for four years. When it was shown, it had already become a historical film. In Poland a lot changes fast.

Tuesday: Fourteen years have passed since the conversation with the vice-president. Yesterday I passed through a small town. I slowed down, because the road was being repaved. Like in a bad script, those who were repaving were dressed in prison clothes. Guards with rifles stood next to them. Today I can make a film about it. That's it on censorship, which doesn't exist anymore. And also on how much and how fast things change.

Notes

1. Krzysztof Piesiewicz's mother was murdered on July 22, 1989.

2. Priest Jerzy Popiełuszko's murder in October 1984 was one of the most politically and socially laden murder cases of that era.

Diary: 1989–1990 (2)

Krzysztof Kieślowski / 1989–90

From *Kino* 1 (1992): 29–30. Reprinted by permission.

This is the second extract from Krzysztof Kieślowski's diaries printed in the Zurich magazine Du *and reprinted in Polish in* Kino.

Wednesday: For a few weeks now, or more precisely since the beginning of work on the script, we have been thinking about the film's title. In Poland, it was much simpler: publicity around a film didn't have much significance, so I would find the title when the film was already edited. At least I knew what it was about, which made it easier. Here you have to decide the title as early as possible and the producer is justifiably upset with me that I can't make my mind up. The script is called *Choir Girl*. Admittedly, it doesn't sound the best, although it describes quite aptly the profession of the protagonist; namely, she is a choir girl. It turns out that in France it has bad connotations; someone having read the title said, "oh, God, yet another Catholic film from Poland." The implication is that no one is going to see the film. The protagonist's name is Weronika and from the start I've thought her name to be a good title. However, it's not possible. The ending of her name in French, "nique" (Veronique), describes in not a very elegant way actions that take place between a woman and a man. Obviously, we've abandoned it. The producer is a jazz lover, so he comes up with poetic titles from jazz pieces—"Unfinished Girl," "Alone Together"—which seem to me somewhat pretentious, so we give up. I have about fifty titles in my notebook and really I don't like any of them. The producer is pressing. We both agree that the word *An Understudy* [French: "Doublure"] sounds good and we almost decide, when suddenly someone remembers that men wear "*doublure*" under their trousers. Of course, *An Understudy* is out of the question. Everyone is involved in looking for the title. My wife and daughter propose all sorts of words; assistants read Shakespeare's sonnets, believing that he had not too bad a mind. When I go through the city, I catch myself reading posters, advertisements and newspapers, looking incessantly for some intelligent title. I've announced to a group of colleagues a competition with a cash prize. In the end, we've adopted the title *The Double Life of Véronique*, which will probably not be final. It sounds not bad in Polish, in French, and in English, it's quite commercially viable before you see the film, and after you see it, it describes quite precisely its content. It has one fault: neither I nor the producer are really convinced by it, and no doubt we will have to change it after we start shooting.

Sunday: Shooting continues for *The Double Life of Véronique*. Cinema is not the audience, festivals, reviews, and interviews. It's getting up everyday at 6 am. It's [a] cold [morning], rain, mud, and heavy lights. It's nerve-wrecking activities, and at some stage everything has to be subordinated to it. Including family, emotions, private life. Of course, a train engineer, commercial agent, or banker will say the same about his work. He will certainly be right, but I do my work and I write about my [work]. I'm almost fifty. I probably should not be practicing this profession any more. I am running out of something necessary for making films: patience. I have no patience for actors, camera operators, weather, waiting, for nothing coming out the way I really want it. At the same time I can't let it show. Especially me; I cannot. It's hard work to hide my impatience from my crew. I think the more sensitive ones know that I'm not feeling well in my predicament. What would a reader of the Swiss monthly *Du* care? Not at all, with some exceptions. I quite regularly give classes in Switzerland for younger colleagues, screenwriters and directors. I am writing this to confirm once again what I have already told you. Even if you happen to get satisfaction out of making cinema, there is a high price for that. And satisfaction happens rarely.

Thursday: Fears that the French system of shooting will be completely different to the one I know, ours, have turned out to be unnecessary and premature. People from the crew want to work and they know their job. They are genial and surprised that I arrive on the location first with the cinematographer, and then after the shooting I don't leave by car, but I try to help load up the truck. They don't let me; they think there is a strict division of labor. I have a completely different view. I know that we all make the film, and of course everyone is responsible for their bit, but we are all responsible for the whole. There is another issue, somewhat embarrassing. On the location, everyone has something. The cinematographer has a camera and a photometer, the sound guy has a microphone, gaffers have lights and so on. I have nothing. Straightaway, I give the script to the script girl and I walk around the location empty-handed. That gives an impression, perhaps justifiably so, that I have nothing to do there. Of course, I'm directing. I chat with the cinematographer, I say something to actors, I give some commands, sometimes I change something in the dialogue, sometimes I come up with something. But I have nothing in my hands. Recently, I worked with Wiesiek [trans: diminutive of Wiesław] Zdort; I was making *Decalogue I* with him. He kept watching me; we were working together for the first time and we worked well together. He once said: "The director is a guy who helps everyone." I liked that simple definition. I repeated it to the French assistants who protested when I was carrying boxes to their truck. They nodded their heads and let me do the boxes.

Sunday: I listen to the news from Poland on the radio. I turn it off after a minute. I don't know if this is because I am all-consumed by the film, but I don't care about it. Not at all.

Saturday: We're shooting. We'll be doing it on Sunday also, with a small crew, only a few people. They consent without problems, they don't complain. It's nice to meet people who like their job.

Thursday: A few Italian journalists arrive. They want to know what the difference is between making a film in the East [of Europe] and here, in the West. They shake their heads, displeased, when I say that there aren't significant [differences]. So, I find a difference, to France's disadvantage. I don't like an hour-long lunch break, which distracts people in the middle of the day. They note this down, satisfied. Maybe in their Italy, there is no lunch break? Or, maybe after all they want something in the East to be better.

Friday: Editing is the only period of film production that I truly like. I think that a really good film is created in the editing room. Shooting is only gathering material, creating possibilities. I try to conduct it so I ensure the greatest freedom to maneuver for myself. Of course, editing is about gluing together two pieces of film and at that level there is a series of principles and rules, which have to observed and sometimes broken. But there is another level of editing, and that's the most interesting one. The level of constructing the film, playing with the viewer, a way of guiding his attention, rationing out the tension. There are directors who believe that all these elements are written in the script. These others believe [that], but I know that this elusive, difficult-to-describe soul of the film comes alive only here, in the editing room. That's why I stay [here] evenings and Sundays during shooting, and later, after shooting, however long I can. I try to get the first edited version done as fast as possible, disregarding all details.

This version follows the script or the changes I have introduced on location, during shooting. After the screening of the first version, it becomes apparent how many blunders, repetitions, how shallow the script was. As quickly as possible I make the second [version], sharply shortening scenes, deleting and changing their order. Usually, it turns out I have overdone it. The third version, in which I often return to what I've deleted, starts to look like a film. It doesn't yet have a rhythm, nor linking points, but a shadow of order starts to appear. In that phase, I screen every second day, and sometimes everyday, checking all sorts of possibilities, manipulating the material. This way, seven or eight or more versions come into being, all fundamentally different films. From those changes and frequent screenings emerges a somewhat clear picture and the film shapes up. Only then we start to work in detail, looking for linking points, rhythm, moods.

I am one of those directors who very easily part with whole batches of material. I don't mourn good scenes, or the beautiful, or expensive, or difficult to realize, I don't mourn well-played characters. If they are superfluous in the film, I get rid of them ruthlessly, with a certain dose of pleasure. The better they are, the easier it is for me to part with them because I know they are not thrown out because of low quality, but only because they are unnecessary.

In the editing room I feel a kind of freedom. Of course, I have at my disposal only the material that I have shot, but essentially that material offers unlimited possibilities. I don't feel the pressure of time and money, of actors' moods, of logistics and of inefficient—even if it is the best—cinematographic technique. Nobody anymore has several hundred questions a day for me. I don't wait for the sun to set, or for them to set up the lights. Slightly excited I look forward to the result of every procedure on the editing table.

That's how it's been also today, although it is only the second day of editing. I think with pleasure that the shooting finishes in two or three weeks, and I will be left with Jacques at a good [editing] table, which has a clear picture and sound.

Thursday: We are moving to Paris. Still ten more shooting days. Tomorrow, on a railway siding, in a hired carriage, which will be shaken by assistants using rods, so it looks as if the train is really moving, we will be shooting the scene of Véronique's night journey to Paris. Today, with a few crew we are going to Paris in a real train; it's night. Irène Jacob is sitting behind me. I turn around, she has fallen asleep, she's tired. Her head rests beautifully. The scarf on her neck is quivering slightly from her breath. Tomorrow, when she is pretending to be asleep, I will ask her to sit the same way, and to bow her head the same way.

Diary: 1989–1990 (3)

Krzysztof Kieślowski / 1989–90

From *Kino* 2 (1992): 44. Reprinted by permission.

*This is the third extract from Krzysztof Kieślowski's diaries printed in the Zurich maga-
zine* Du *and reprinted in Polish in* Kino.

Saturday: I am finishing the tenth edit of *La Double Vie de Véronique*. A few more
will still emerge. It is a remarkably difficult film. When writing the script, everything was coming together nicely for us. It is a film about sensitivity, premo-
nitions, and difficult-to-define, irrational relations between people. You cannot
show too much—it would diffuse the mystery. You cannot show too little—no
one would understand anything. Searching for the balance between transparency
and mystery is the reason for so many edits. I am curious myself if we will finally
manage to find the right proportions. Probably, as usual, not.

Saturday: A short, quite depressing stay in Poland. On television and in the
press a whole deluge of insults, slanders, and conflicts. Parties discredit their opponents with completely personal assaults. Strikes, including hunger strikes, and
demonstrations are organized most often under the war-cry of destroying or at
least humiliating somebody. Everyone is arguing with everyone and about everything. A pretext itself is insignificant. Is it a consequence of forty-five years of the
communist system suppressing passions and emotions? I am not an optimist, but
all the time I keep hoping that we didn't need freedom only to show to each other
how much we could hate one another.

Monday: Public polls have shown that Solidarity's and the Church's authority
is failing. The case of Solidarity is entirely clear. It has power now, so whether
it wants to or not, it has to make unpopular decisions. The Church issue must
be considered more seriously. Its achievements cannot be overestimated. I think
that we owe our existence as a nation and a state to a large extent to the Church.
There's a close relationship between the fall of communism in Eastern Europe and

the Polish Church's and the Pope's stance. Today, when communism is no more, the Church, that quiet winner, is starting to make demands. It has demanded the introduction of religious instruction in schools and religion has become, despite the initial resistance from state authorities, a school subject. Now, a quarrel has broken out about the subject of termination of pregnancies. In a country where there are hundreds of thousands of unemployed, and millions of people live on the verge of poverty, in a country with haphazard legislation in the fields of economy and law, they discuss fiercely whether abortion should be allowed or not. Currently, the parliamentarians, the press, and state authorities are busying themselves with it. Catholic activists and parliamentarians very close to Catholic circles demand a legal ban on abortion, even in the cases where pregnancy is a result of rape or incest. Even when a conceived child would come into this world abnormal or heavily impaired. They demand imprisonment for women who undergo abortion and doctors who conduct it. Catholic activists are also demanding an immediate cessation of the production and import of any contraceptives, and even a total ban on their usage. Groups of people burst into pharmacies and buy out all the condoms to burn them ostentatiously. Those who encourage reason, or only call for caution, are called contemptuously "communists" or "reds." In contemporary Poland, that's the greatest insult. One parliamentarian, reasonable and cautious, proposed a referendum on the matter. Soon after, the Church announced publicly its objection to the referendum. The reason: a referendum on moral issues is an abuse [of authority]. The stance of people accepting the idea of pregnancy termination is compared with those stances that in the past led to the acceptance of euthanasia and concentration camps. The Church has compared the consent to terminate pregnancy with crimes against humanity. And so again we have in Poland someone who thinks they know better. Someone who wants to decide on behalf of everyone what's evil and what's good. Just now I am reading old newspapers. Unexpectedly, the word "hypocrisy" comes to my mind. Duplicity. The Church demands a ban on terminating pregnancies, citing the holy right of every person to live. However, it is not opposing capital punishment, which is still in force in Poland. The Church wishes that a great number of new Poles come into the world. At the same time, they seem not to notice that among the real estate taken by communists that they are now demanding back with the utmost sternness, there are also orphanages and kindergartens.

A message of a completely new kind. The highest circles of the Polish Church have cast an official doubt on the separation between the state and the Church that is now in place. The episcopacy represents the view that in the new constitution, state power should no longer be separated from Church [power]. Right now, the whole of Poland claims its right to belong to Europe. However, will Europe be prepared to accept into its midst a Church state with suitably anachronistic legislation? On television you can now see bishops blessing new monuments. They bless army banners as well as newly recruited soldiers. As well as the ball of a newly created soccer team.

Express Meeting with Kieślowski

Stéphane Brisset / 1991

From *Cinéma* 489 (June 1991): 13. Reprinted by permission.

Cinéma *was a review of French cinema published by the Fédération française des Ciné-Clubs until 1999.*

Stéphane Brisset: *The Double Life* . . . appears brighter than your other films, even if it speaks equally of a supreme power that guides us?

Krzysztof Kieślowski: It's true, I feel I've bored the audience sufficiently with my bleak films. All of us live the experiences of Véronique or Weronika, which are the expression of something higher, not religious, maybe simply human. You know, I don't know what it means to be Christian. We all are to some extent.

SB: Are you always so pessimistic?

KK: Of course, my pessimism is innate. Like my hand or my blood, I cannot change it. Life is always so demoralizing in Poland and I know I'll need to find funding abroad. Luckily, living in this part of the world, I feel European.

SB: In this regard, what were the differences of shooting between France and Poland?

KK: I could barely stand the lunchtime break. No, of course materials and organization are better than elsewhere. Changes in the Eastern Bloc have transformed Polish cinema. If you meet the journalists of my country, here, in Cannes, they will tell you it's dead. I don't consider their bleak outlook to be accurate.

SB: Why did you choose to film with colored filters?

KK: At the suggestion of the cinematographer. I like it; I find that they give the film brightness and clarity, a personality.

SB: Why are the characters of the *Double Life* . . . professionals working in the arts?

KK: It was especially important that they do something with their hands: the father and the chairs, the puppeteer with his beautiful profession.

SB: Is this a metaphor for the master manipulator?
KK: I interpret nothing; read into it what you want.

SB: And what about the balance between art and love for the two women?
KK: The problem arises in terms of a choice between the two. We can give ourselves to one or the other, but Weronika and Véronique look for and find something else.

SB: How did you work with your co-writer in terms of aspects of French culture?
KK: As usual: we sit down and talk about cars. Sometimes a few sentences come to us. No, but the actors and technicians helped me enormously for the details of sets, costumes. . . .

SB: Tell us about this project *Liberty, Equality, Fraternity,* with Marin Karmitz.
KK: We already have two treatments. The first (Liberty) will be a drama about a woman in France, the second (Equality), a comedy in Poland, and the third the story of a couple in a francophone country. Just as the *Decalogue* was not intended as an illustration [but as a reflection on the Ten Commandments], these three projects will be a reflection on the meaning of these words today, since many think they are achievable.

From Weronica to Véronique

Michel Ciment and Hubert Niogret / 1991

From *Positif* 364 (June 1991): 26–31. Reprinted by permission.

This interview was conducted in Paris in April 1991.

Michel Ciment and Hubert Niogret: After making the *Decalogue*, a monumental work, how did you envisage the following project [*La Double Vie de Véronique*]?
Krzysztof Kieślowski: It was pretty simple, because after something important, something quite tiring, I realized that I had to make something more intimate, that would take me less time than the *Decalogue*. Anyway I work way too much. It was clear that this should be neither large nor expensive, and undertaken pretty quickly. This film came out of an idea I'd had for several years, but couldn't resolve. And that I wouldn't resolve any further.

MC&HN: What was the first idea?
KK: Making a film about a man from elsewhere. Because over there is just as sad as here. It would be a very pessimistic film. I don't know why he went back there.

MC&HN: Has this project been abandoned?
KK: The film that we now have is the result. A film about two lives: life elsewhere and life here, although they are the same. He was a man, not a woman, but that's not important.

MC&HN: The *Decalogue* was ten films. This film is like the various episodes and could be another story in the *Decalogue*.
KK: Exactly. This could have been a part of the *Decalogue* though told slightly differently. The difference is in the mode of narration and perhaps also in the dramaturgy, in the action. In this film there is almost no action, which does not mean that in the next one there'll be more.

MC&HN: Can you explain the differences from the *Decalogue*?

KK: The film is told in a much more optimistic way; it's sunny, bright. The character of the heroine is clear in both parts; she has no problem to solve. We wonder what she wants; she has everything. She walks calmly, she's talented, she's still a little sick but that can be remedied. What else does she want? What does her intuition tell her? For the characters of the *Decalogue*, we cannot talk this way. Each has an important matter to resolve, she has none. Correspondingly, there's a different style of narration. It's slower, modeled more on the sensibility of the heroine. And of course, there are two modes of narration in the same film, which has some dramaturgic consequences. The Polish part is faster, more choppy, time is indefinite. We do not know if her career developed over a month or a year. The second part, the French part, is more gentle, quieter. We can quite easily imagine how long the action takes. These are small things that the viewer doesn't care about, but for me time is very important. What I call the narration, the manner of telling, comes from time. Camera, editing, actors, music, this is the way of storytelling, the narration.

MC&HN: You said it's a more optimistic film, brighter than the previous films. Does this relate to something in your life or around you?

KK: Nothing has changed in my life because I think I'm more somber than ever. But I realized you cannot always tell somber stories and need to find something light.

MC&HN: There is a very beautiful, optimistic image at the end of the film, when Véronique touches the tree and she's filled with music. This is a character who comes alive with music. At this moment, she links with Weronika, who herself was filled with music. And this optimistic image links with that of the father.

KK: There's a degree of optimism, a bit strained because I don't think her love really works right to the end, an optimism that we seek in life when we've lost something. She's a little disappointed. Despite that, she lives, she can go somewhere, she can touch something stable, consistent.

MC&HN: *Choir Girl* was the first title of the film, which shows that music is a central element of the film. What led you to a musical subject?

KK: We changed the title, because someone said: "Ah! Not another Polish Catholic film." And we didn't want that. Also, I don't think that it was good to indicate in the title that music was so important. I think the current title has many faults, but I haven't found a better one.

MC&HN: Yet this is a film where music plays an important role?

KK: It's because of my work with the composer that music became so important;

the script doesn't highlight it. Of course there was a concert, and many connections between two girls. Sometimes the relationship was very direct, sometimes less so, and all the connections indicated in the script I shot. During editing I realized it was necessary to remove some of them and replace them. That's why music has such an important role. The concert was very good, with music composed before shooting for the playback. I thought it was a bit of a shame to use it only once.

MC&HN: The profession of Weronika and Véronique is music. One becomes a singer, the other is a music teacher. This is in the script; it's not the editing.

KK: The fact that they are both connected to music was already in the script. We looked for what was missing, something beautiful, spectacular and that requires effort, such as heart disease. This idea comes from *Decalogue 9*. I loved this episode and I thought it was a potential subject, but in the *Decalogue*, it was a bit of a separate subject, which was not important for the film's action.

MC&HN: You were speaking of time. Music is a temporal art. Someone said that all art aspires to music, because it's pure form. In music, content and form are the same thing. What's your connection with music?

KK: I have no ear. I never listen to music, except sometimes in the car, to stupid songs. I never go to a concert.

MC&HN: Did you have an idea of the music you wanted, or did you give your composer complete freedom?

KK: Of course I had some requirements, but at the same time I allowed him plenty of freedom. With the delicacy of a bull in a china shop, I stuck my nose into it. I changed things, sometimes even the instruments because there are some that I don't like. I wanted a concert that requires effort, that's dramatic in subject and, above all, that's not modern but that refers to the music of the seventeenth and eighteenth centuries. I think he succeeded because the show is old-fashioned, with some very modern elements. I had another requirement of the composer: that the melody could be sung, even by me, who has neither voice nor ear.

MC&HN: Véronique (Irène Jacob) communicates with Alexandre (Philippe Volter) via sound, since she decodes his message. How were these sound messages developed?

KK: When he calls once, at night, he makes her listen to a bit of this music. She doesn't know who it is, but she had seen him from the window putting his stuff back in his van. We can then understand that she will guess who he is. The scene of the cassette-tape was written very late.

The other sound signals come mostly from the editing and from the later use of the music; they were not described in the script. And the music has to do with Weronika of course, the Polish girl. It was very important for me to make it understood that Weronika still exists somewhere in the French part, and that it's Weronika that says: "Don't sing, do something else even if it isn't a success." To this end, we introduced the music. Because we don't know what the lace is. Perhaps there are two guys, we don't know. Maybe this guy doesn't exist, or maybe it's another person altogether. The lace will bring her to Catherine's house, where she'll ask who the puppeteer is. All this leads her somewhere. As these are small steps, it's hard to call this action in the strict sense of the word.

MC&HN: What is interesting for us French is to see how foreigners look at Paris: Joseph Losey, Roman Polański and now you. Is the Paris you discovered different from what you saw in films?

KK: I feel good here. Despite the fact that I don't know the language, I don't feel foreign. Of course there are many details that I don't know, millions of them. I don't know the ways of being, movements, gestures, and expressions. I was hoping that the actors would bring me that and they did.

MC&HN: We were referring to the visual aspect. Paris ends up looking like Krakow.

KK: With the designer we looked in Paris for similar things. We chose Clermont-Ferrand (of which very little remains in the film) because the town is built on a rather gray volcanic rock, like Krakow. It's difficult for me to explain specifically, but it happened very simply. It was clear to me that I wanted to shoot at the Gare Saint-Lazare. . . .

MC&HN: Why the Gare Saint-Lazare? Why not the Gare de Lyon or other old stations like the Gare du Nord?

KK: I visited them all, but it's the Gare Saint-Lazare that has the best layout. We needed a restaurant with windows through which you see a burning car. The restaurant should not be situated so obviously as at the Gare de Lyon. In the Gare Saint-Lazare, you have to look for the restaurant because it's hidden. Shooting there was very complicated. The people at the SNCF did not want us to, because there's a lot of traffic there. So we adapted ourselves to the timetable and they eventually gave permission.

MC&HN: Clermont-Ferrand is a gray town, but the film is amber?

KK: The light is amber because the background is gray. One thing is so because another is different. To have a bright foreground, you need a gray background, otherwise everything is bright, and that's not good. Furthermore, gray and dark backgrounds create a sense of mystery. It's also the mystery of communication that's not in words, in chatter, in letters, in phone calls, but that comes through another channel. So the mystery had to be conveyed in the film's color.

MC&HN: The *mise en scène* is very pure, very objective. There aren't blatant camera movements, but sometimes there are extremely subjective shots, [creating] a sort of contrast between the general style of the film and these intrusions of extraordinarily formalist shots.

KK: I could not imagine shooting a scene where a woman sings, falls, and dies. That seemed in very bad taste, so I had to come up with an idea to fix it. That's where I got the subjective camera. The cinematographer, Sławomir Idziak, noted that we could not use this type of filming only once, that we would have to find another time in the film to use this technique. In all, four times: the first shot of the film that is upside-down, the shot of the exhibitionist, the concert with the falling camera, and when Véronique, the French one, looks at the camera and it falls over.

MC&HN: The scene where Weronika and Véronique look at each other is very important. It's a very complex scene in terms of staging because of the crowd movements. How did you approach such a complex scene with so many elements to put into play?

KK: This is one of those crowd scenes that you have to shoot from time to time, but that I don't like at all. We had to show, in the background, a little of what is happening in Poland, hence the idea of the protest. We did this very quickly, camera in hand. There were between five hundred and a thousand extras, I don't remember anymore, but I had good assistants. The scene was very much longer and I shortened it in the editing.

MC&HN: In the two stories, the actors echo each other: the aunt in the Polish episode [and] the father in the French episode, the music teachers in Poland and France. Did you choose the physical appearance of the actors with this rapport in mind?

KK: There were Polish actors that I knew and others with whom I had never worked. I did not look for resemblances but rather for matches in the way of being. This is not unimportant. I still tried to put them in pairs, in couples, and not to find physical similarities. I thought it was important that the aunt and father in the Polish part, and the father in the French, convey a sense of tranquility for the people around them. These are people that you can go to knowing that they will always have a bed for you and something for dinner. It seemed important to me that they be put alongside a girl like Véronique-Weronika who has a value system.

MC&HN: Within one part we also see correspondences. The two men in the life of Véronique work with their hands: one is a puppeteer, the other makes furniture.
KK: We wanted to say that it's also possible to make things with your hands. Occasionally we have to make something, to take the hard way, to not have everything readymade.

MC&HN: The actress Irène Jacob is quite remarkable. How did you find her?
KK: I had seen her in the film by Louis Malle, *Au Revoir les Enfants*, in which she appeared for a minute or a minute-and-a-half on the screen. At a seminar in Switzerland, I conducted a test: who remembered a girl in *Au Revoir les Enfants*? Six remembered, the seventh hadn't seen the film. I realized that there was something there: she appears for only a minute, and we remember that minute. She has therefore a personality. That was very important because, for much of the film, she is alone and has nothing to do. She reads a book, she sleeps. I did tests with different actresses in France, all very good, but she was the best, even though she was unknown and very young. We needed to see that personality of hers, of which I was sure. She learned very quickly with the technical directions that I gave her, and I knew that when I asked her to do something, she could do it, she could be really good. She is even much better than I thought. Working with her went very well, magnificently, because she's a very shy person. I realized very quickly that she would give me the strength I needed. Everyone adored her. It is very rare in this business to meet shy, reserved people. We were all very surprised, the French and the Polish.

MC&HN: How could she become Polish without knowing the language, and without having lived in this country?
KK: Seeing her on the street, you could believe that she lives in Kraków or Warsaw. She has a normal face that you can see a lot in France and Poland. What is different is her personality. She quickly learned the Polish language, in a month, a month and a half. She is dubbed but many sentences could have been said by her, because she spoke without an accent. She arrived in Poland before the shooting, asked not to live at the hotel but with some friends. She tried to understand this country and to see it. I was very aware of that and I saw she was very open to the world.

MC&HN: You've worked with Polish and French actors. Did you notice a difference on their part in approaching their work, or a difference of technique?

KK: There is no difference, or maybe just one. The French have more time. In Poland actors come on set for an hour or two or three, and then leave for work in radio, television, theater. . . . They don't earn much, so they work a lot. The French probably earn enough money to be available all day.

MC&HN: Why the choice of profession of puppeteer?
KK: Because of the American puppeteer Bruce Schwartz. A few years ago, I saw on Polish television an excerpt from a movie with him and I realized he was doing miracles. He shows his hands, he moves with the puppet, and three seconds later you forget his hands because the puppet is really coming alive. It's unbelievable. Unfortunately we only used a small fragment of what he did. It's a shame because he's the best. And despite this he cannot live off his work; he stopped two years ago. He works at an art dealer's. He told me he could not live by his work because people did not need what he was offering. I made him read the screenplay; he pulled out his puppets and he came to France.

MC&HN: Why introduce a puppeteer in this story?
KK: This has much to do with Bruce Schwartz. I knew that the hero had to have something special. For our heroine, I thought it would be better if it was something very delicate and very mysterious, and I recalled the movie with Bruce Schwartz. I also knew that if I did not get Bruce Schwartz, I would change the character's profession.

MC&HN: Was working with your co-writer Krzysztof Piesiewicz the same as for the *Decalogue*? What did he bring in particular to the subject?
KK: The same. We can never separate who gives what and that's done by talking about other things. We talk about everything, we go back for five minutes to the film's subject, we digress and the script writes itself.

MC&HN: On several occasions you've said you cut into some sequences. Did you shoot more than usual, whereas you used to be rather thrifty?
KK: This film gave me a lot of trouble in editing and I've never done as many versions as this time around: twenty versions because the subject is difficult, very delicate. It wouldn't have been right to exaggerate one or another aspect of the film. Moreover, there are faults in the script that we cannot eliminate. In the editing we can try to minimize them.

MC&HN: In terms of the cutting, did you shoot more shots than those you edited together in the end?
KK: Much more. The first edit was two hours and thirty minutes long. Afterwards,

I shortened and changed the order of sequences. We had what you call the "service scenes" that are still in the can, and we knew we had them there. Sometimes we put them in, then we'd pull them out for a different cut. One interesting idea that I've never yet told anyone about is to make a few versions of this film, as many versions as theatres where the film is shown. Each version would have its number, and you'd find a slightly different version in another cinema. We thought about fifteen, but I didn't have enough time.

MC&HN: Do you feel like you played with the editing more than in your previous films?
KK: No, but I had more difficulties. I usually make eight or nine versions of a film. And for this we made twenty.

MC&HN: What were the story knots that you were not able to undo? What were the obstacles?
KK: One of the obstacles was the idea of Veronica's friend, Catherine, with all the business of the divorce, highly developed in the script. I love Sandrine Dumas, but I had to shorten the scenes with her. I even made a version completely eliminating this character. It was very simple to do, but it was not good because the heroine became unreal, living always ten centimeters above the ground. If she is no longer an ordinary person, she does not interest us anymore. She must be able to lie, etc. I could not take Catherine out for this reason.

Another difficulty was the ending. We shot seven versions and not one is good; this one neither, but I didn't have another one.

MC&HN: Your film is a little bit like the inverse of the last film of Luis Buñuel in which two actresses play the same character.
KK: This has always fascinated me.

MC&HN: Did you shoot the Polish part before the French part?
KK: Of course. I wanted to be careful about working in France. Furthermore, in Poland, we shot some of the French scenes of interiors. The designer, the actress, part of the technical team (sound) came to Poland.

MC&HN: The differences between the two characters are minimal, [they have] almost the same look.
KK: In the French part, her hair is shorter by about five centimeters. For me, it was clear that they should both look the same.

MC&HN: The most rational artists, Stanley Kubrick, Joseph L. Mankiewicz, Fritz

Lang, or yourself, end up at the fantastic. How did your rational side lead you to fantasy, to mystery?

KK: I try to be as close as possible to the protagonist. The nearer I am to them, the more I discover mystery, phantasms, the imaginary, metaphysics. All this is inside us.

MC&HN: It's not only the inside, it's the irrational. On Earth everybody is different, except in this film where we find what does not exist, absolute resemblance. It's a fantastic, irrational notion, and you are very rational. . . .

KK: Worldwide, many people are alike. If they look alike, why couldn't they be identical?

MC&HN: You will be excommunicated! This is very blasphemous.

KK: We need to move forward. I think people are very much alike, with huge differences. These two girls are like that. One died, the other lives. It's a big difference.

Tree That Is

Tadeusz Szczepański / 1991

From *Film na Świecie* 385 (November–December 1991): 10–17. Reprinted by permission.

This interview was conducted in Mannheim on October 5, 1991, with Krzysztof Kieślowski and Krzysztof Piesiewicz for the periodical published by the Polish Federation of Film Discussion Clubs.

Tadeusz Szczepański: Krzysztof Kieślowski has turned fifty this year. What emotions have accompanied crossing that line?

Krzysztof Kieślowski: You know, they say it is a time when one should take stock, sum up, reflect on what has happened and what may potentially happen in the future, but I have to admit I haven't had any such feelings at all. On the day of my birthday I was simply in Italy with my family. There was some lunch, we poured wine and the only thing that I did was to choke on my first sip. I was choking for a long while, I couldn't manage it, they kept hitting me on the back with full force, I stained a whole tablecloth, I spat over a serviette; everything happened that was meant to happen. Maybe it was a sign? No, I haven't taken stock, neither finished anything, nor started anything. It seems to me that I'm always on my way, and whether I'm forty-six, fifty, or fifty-two makes no difference.

TS: I'm asking because I remember that a few years ago Krzysztof Zanussi was saying that he was approaching that time in his life with great fear.

KK: I was also afraid, but I'm afraid of each day. I'm afraid of tomorrow in the same way I was afraid of yesterday.

TS: I'm interested in this potential sensation of [reaching] a frontier in your life, because I'm curious about your current view of all your films before the *Decalogue*. Don't you regret making them a little bit? When the system fell, those films devaluated. Wasn't it the case that the system embroiled you and your generation in some fight that prevented you from getting in touch with yourselves? For instance, can you imagine what films you would have been making here [in

Germany], not in Poland, because it is a matter of chance that you were born in Poland and not somewhere else?

KK: Obviously, it's a matter of chance, but I don't regret it, to tell the truth. I've made the films that I've made. I've made them the way I could make them, in my state of mind. And this has simply passed, gone, there is nothing to regret. I don't think at all about what I would have done if I were born somewhere else, how my life would have gone. . . . Of course, we reflect on the course of our lives very frequently, but it really doesn't concern work. I think that film is a short-lived thing; it rarely happens that it lasts longer than the moment in which it is screened. Of course these films are anachronistic, unwatchable, and essentially it is now difficult to understand why we were making them then. One cannot understand it, because the situation has changed. But they played their role in their time, they happened, they brought something, good, or maybe also bad, but what they were to do, they did do. That passed and now one has to think about tomorrow, even if I'm afraid of that tomorrow all the time.

TS: I am still bothered by this issue, because the system fell and people haven't changed. Maybe films should be made about a social being not so much struggling against the authorities, but examining himself.

KK: I have never made films about a social being, I've made films about a person in a social situation. Historically speaking, one could explain it most succinctly this way. At the beginning of the seventies, we found out that the world around us is a non-described world. By the way, in the mid-seventies, Kornhauser and Zagajewski wrote a book titled *The Unrepresented World* [*Świat nieprzedstawiony*]. We also understood, more or less at the same time, that that world essentially didn't have its own image. And we had this impression, I think accurate, that one could not understand the world unless it were described. And because people didn't really feel like taking it on, or maybe didn't have the means, then that world really remained for many years completely undescribed. They described how they wanted that world to look, how it could look, but no one described how it actually looked. And we took that task on. It was quite instinctual; I don't think we created any program, nor a manifesto on the subject. And despite that, many of us formed a collective that was important, creative and exciting. We formed a great friendship among people of different generations, which was very interesting and terribly rare in the world, especially here, in the West, where inter-generational contacts really don't exist, or are very desultory, and even if deep, occur only by chance. But if you refer to the conversation in *Literatura*, where we met as a circle of friends, I think that already in 1980 it was really clearly formulated that the era of a collective was ending, and that each of us had to find his own way according to our own criteria, according to our own taste, according to our own views, which also differed somewhat, even though on political matters they were the same. However on most general, non-political issues, in attitudes to life, to the world, to people, to mystery, to love, we were quite different. We declared a desire for individual life, a singular way, and already then we understood that the time of a common duty, common responsibility, was ending, and a different era would begin. And this is what has happened.

TS: You, however, started to look for a commonality of a different kind. I refer here to the role of Piesiewicz in the next chapter of your work. The film *No End*, for which you wrote your first script together, constitutes a clear milestone. For the first time in your films, metaphysical sensitivity appeared.

KK: It's not accidental that we met, although we met by accident and we started to communicate on a certain common wavelength, because such issues as metaphysics, a sense of mystery, had existed, after all, in my earlier films. It's not accidental that I started to work with Krzysztof, because we both had a need for expression. . . . For instance, I had once made a television film titled *The Calm* in which there is a motif of horses. And what are these horses? Are these social horses? Political? No, these are horses as a mystery, maybe some type of longing for a broader, freer life than the one this guy can ever achieve, because his life plan is very simple: a wife, an apartment, a television set, children. But those horses keep appearing in his life, we keep hearing them; the film's end also has to do with these horses. Hypothetically, they are somewhere. Maybe one can dream not only of a wife, a television set, children, but also of something deeper, more buoyant, fierce, spectacular? Maybe that guy cannot formulate it, but he has it in him, since these horses keep appearing to him. There are similar motifs in *Camera Buff*: the protagonist, who directs the camera at himself, begins to understand that essentially someone might possibly need everything he has expressed, but this still doesn't express him [completely], it doesn't express what he really has inside, what hurts him, tortures him, annoys him, makes him bitter. There is also a sequence when he films a woman who then dies, and suddenly it turns out that this [the film] has a huge significance for her son.

But maybe it's worth Krzysztof saying something on the subject. I think I was ready for that sort of a search, but it's interesting how you see it.

Krzysztof Piesiewicz: It's obvious that when we met we had not come from completely different worlds. Although there was something in Krzysztof's cinema that sometimes almost repulsed me. . . .

TS: For instance?

KP: For instance a bent towards a very realistic description of the world, an avoidance of the emotional sphere. . . . Sometimes those emotions would be there, but following our acquaintance they could get articulated more strongly. But the film *No End* was a closure of at least one issue: political cinema. In that film personal, individual issues, emotional matters appeared, with a dose of metaphysics. Although there was a specific reference to the world of politics, when writing *No End* I think we both understood that we had to separate ourselves from that macro view of a society, that we had to get closer to other issues. Not many have noticed it in our work. And even though many reviews and essays appeared about the *Decalogue*, nobody paid attention to a very simple matter: that taking on the Decalogue in 1985 was already a provocation, almost a manifesto, because it was already clear from that idea that we wanted to give attention to a particular person in his circumstances, in situations in which he lives, in conflicts that he lives through, and to cut ourselves off completely from that very general description of the world, from the relation "the political world and a man" or "a political man and the world." This approach was consistently carried out from the start to the end in the *Decalogue*, and in *A Double Life of Véronique* it's even more evident.

I suspect that the difference between us consists of Krzysztof having a greater distance from emotions, rationalizing everything more, but also filtering [it] through a type of sensitivity, which is common for us, and a little bit different. I move in that emotional sphere in a way that's perhaps not more gushy, but more expressive, more open.

TS: And somewhere deeper, in the background in *The Double Life of Véronique*, isn't there also an autobiographical undercurrent. Isn't it also a film about you two, who, after all, share the same name? Indeed, every one of us feels somehow crippled, incomplete, and suddenly you meet in life another person who enriches you with a new tone, a new emotion, new experience. I simply wonder whether you might have written into that topic the nature of your creative friendship.

KK: Maybe that's how it is . . . who knows . . . I think that we never know consciously what's really ours, private, and what is dictated by dramaturgic needs, or simply by the need to qualify characters. I think that in each film, if it's treated seriously or personally, there must be something of us, of our lives. We didn't intend that at all, it never occurred to us, but it doesn't mean that it's not in the film. It may exist out of the nature of things, out of the nature of the space that is cinema. We don't want it at all, and despite that it writes itself in.

KP: I tell you that there has never been a situation in which we knew, when we were starting to write a script, what would come out of it in three months. It's kind of an imperative that something has to be said.

TS: And what is the origin of that unusual idea? Essentially I would like to repeat to you the same question that the puppeteer asks Véronique: is a mental response to a call from an unknown person possible? What specific experience or internal awareness is at the source of that quite risky dramaturgic concept?

KP: It seems to me now that it's difficult to rationalize. If this is how it's come out, that means that it was inside us, an awareness that something like that exists, that such a situation is possible, that there are people who pass one another without any emotions, and sometimes you meet someone with whom you have a very close relationship . . . and it's not worth missing a chance.

KK: I don't have any recollection that would make answering this question easier. And I don't think that it's a realistic situation at all, but I do think it's believable, that it could be this way. Of course, it is made more emphatic to meet the needs of film and its dramaturgy. Then the credibility of that situation relies on almost all of us constantly feeling that we live on other people's experiences. Why do we often know what to do, even though there is no reason for it? But we know.

We know because someone has lived through it before us, because we have received an impulse, a signal, which we cannot recognize, but in our everyday actions, after all, we really can tell good from evil. Where in us is that quiet voice that can tell us that? Where does it come from? It comes from many millions of people before us having tried, wanted, pondered, experienced good and evil and having made an effort to choose. It's a different matter what they ended up choosing, but it is that experience which has happened in the past a billion times. And we live, with these experiences already inside us. It's a different question if we can draw conclusions from that, whether we can at all put good above evil. We can certainly tell them apart, but often we cannot choose good, because it cannot be realized. We are constantly entrapped: we can say less and less often, "we choose good"; we say more and more often, "we choose the lesser evil." But how do we know all that, if we know anything at all? Not from our own experience.

Finally, the issue of communication seems significant to me, that communication which is now so horribly vulgarized. What are we really talking about among ourselves at the moment? Really, instead of discussing, we inform one another. We pass on to one another information, and not emotions any more, nor some gentle, delicate quivers, suggestions, which are inside us. We have less and less time to contemplate some important but delicate matters. We are really avoiding those matters; we inform one another. All the increasingly perfect tools serve to exchange information, and where is an exchange of emotions?

So we thought that we must talk about this possibility, about this possibility still being in us, hypothetically. Because it exists and functions in animals. They haven't forgotten about it, and we have lost it somewhere as a result of the particular development of our civilization. And couldn't we, despite the development of this civilization, still return to communication? It is well illustrated by the example of rats. If you find some rat poison and you poison all the rats in Warsaw, then the next generation of these rats of course won't eat that rat poison: it is a matter of passing on experiences. And that's not interesting. However what's interesting is that the rats in New York will not touch that rat poison, although they don't have the telegraph or teletext, nor do they fly in planes. So some kind of communication exists, about which we people—because we walk around in suits and drive increasingly fast cars and more frequently think about how to set ourselves up than how to live—have forgotten in that race. And now we have to consider if it is still in us. I am convinced that it is, and if we neglected it, if it's worth something, then maybe we should dust it off, water it, so it grows a little bit. In one word, that's what our intentions were, somewhere in the background.

KP: It's very difficult for me to analyze this script and this film. But it is certainly a film about nostalgia for something that has passed, that is passing, that we are missing. And it is in us, in every person, and a particular situation may help you to discover that nostalgia in yourself or to suppress it. Above all, it is nostalgia for a certain desire of collective living, collective in a sense that somebody is thinking about my feelings, thinking about me, that somebody remembers that I exist. By contrast, one may say that it is also a film about loneliness, about how not to be lonely. Still, the problem of loneliness appears in our other scripts. So it is a film about longing for being together. Together with somebody or something that gives joy, an experience of beauty.

TS: Aren't you regretting [not taking up] the title *Choir Girl*? That title really emphasized the concept of community, and also the concept of everyman, [giving it] a morality-play quality. Every one of us is just such a choir member who sings a song of his life, no matter if they have a [good] voice or not, if they sing well or off-key. In any case, that title was very buoyant; this one, on the other hand, commits the sin of a certain literalness.

KP: You are right, but it happened a little bit beyond our control. The title *Choir Girl* was not accepted in France.

TS: It announced a religious film?

KP: Precisely. . . .

KK: You know, since we are making a film with French money, we do have to consider French public opinion. We can't tell ourselves that the French are silly and they eat snails.

KP: It is a little bit amusing, because Krzysztof and I avoid any titles, or any signs, that would be connected with an attachment to any religious system, and especially to Catholicism, in some intrusive way.

KK: One can, however, say that we were not avoiding [that] in the *Decalogue*, although we gave numbers instead of quoting commandments.

KP: After all, we had never associated the title *Choir Girl* with the [church] porch, but in France straightaway . . .

KK: In any case, I often hear and read—and here it is not about the title but the whole film—that it is a compromise, because it is French money, so it has to be commercial so that we can endear ourselves to producers or viewers and so on. Generally, I see this as a horrible Polish complex, which is difficult to explain. I can't accept that way of thinking. We are talking about the title, which is a good example of a discussion about compromise. I liked the title *Choir Girl*. We are taking French money and someone in France tells us: "oh, not another Catholic film from Poland." So, we cannot say: "we object, this title stays because we are the artists who have come up with this title." This is immoral, because this way we stop considering the viewer, who is a human being, who could come to the cinema, because in the background of the qualifier a "Catholic film from Poland" lies a conviction that people will not come to the cinema because they have had enough of Catholic films from Poland and I understand them well. It's a different question if there really have been many Catholic films in Poland, but that's not important.

TS: Krzysztof Piesiewicz has said that it is difficult to analyze this film, and—to tell the truth—viewers leave the cinema deeply moved. This film doesn't leave you in peace, but it's difficult to rationalize; there are many possibilities of interpretation.

KP: If this is true, then this is exactly what we intended.

TS: Also the discomposure of the reviewers attests to it. This film evokes an immensely forceful experience that is not easy to manage. It resounds in us with a growing mental echo, which lasts a long time after leaving the cinema. Of course, I could ask you here about the relation of the script to the finished film, about Irène Jacob, or about certain technical matters, but this is not going to give me an answer to the question with which viewers leave the cinema. To be precise: what does Véronique understand and feel in the last scene of the film, when she touches the tree, hearing the sound of her father's milling machine working on the wood? We are seeing Véronique through a car window, through such mysterious, dramatic light-shadow, and at the same time that nostalgic, heart-rending music blasts, with its fragments spread throughout the whole film, and now for the first time we are hearing them unified. How was that last scene born?

KK: It's a completely accidental scene, it's not in the script. It was Sławek [trans: diminutive of Sławomir] Idziak who thought that Véronique absolutely should return home, to her father. And then we found the tree, which grew there by chance, and we thought she should touch it.

TS: The Tree of Life?

KK: Be my guest, I have no objections against such an interpretation, but it has never crossed our mind.

KP: It's great that you noticed one thing about which no one has said or written anything so far. That in the last scene the music, which stopped in the concert, continues. It was obvious already when writing the script that this is how it had to be, if we were to utilize music at all. Yet, that pause that occurred was to be broken by Véronique's fulfillment through love. But that fulfillment through love hasn't worked out, so that's why the girl salvages herself by escaping; she has a chance to save herself, to escape a kind of captivity.

KK: She salvaged herself by an experience of love, not through love.

KP: Everything is open for her; this music can flow. Véronique is experienced, she's understood, she still has a chance.

KK: I think this tree is a very simple thing. That's something that *was* when she was little, it *was* when her mum was little, and that's something that *will be* when her daughter is little. That tree *is*, it exists. Something constant, reliable. Art is not reliable. You never know how it will end. Véronique's fate attests to that. Love gets realized or it doesn't. That man will either be worth that love, or he won't be worth it. There might be someone who would take advantage of feelings, love, naivety. But the tree will always be. That's a place that can be touched with all conviction that when you touch it, the bark will be there, which has more or less the same shape, the same smell, and the same feel as it had twenty years ago, and [as] it will have twenty years from now. That's something abiding, constant, steady. You have to touch it from time to time, from time to time you have to go back to the place where we feel certain that what we see really exists, that it really *is* [original emphasis].

TS: Let's talk about the puppeteer.

KK: Only during shooting did we find out that fulfillment in love would not be possible, that this puppeteer, this particular Alexandre, does not offer a chance for such clear, pure love.

KP: We have to say that, when writing the script, we believed that fulfillment in love is possible. We still believe in it.

TS: Was it an issue with the actor?

KK: Yes, it was a casting issue.

KP: Yet, you know, perhaps that production experience has shown us that it is really difficult, and we believed, when writing the script, that it would go easily.

KK: That really complicated production, all because of an actor. It was to be very clean and simple.

TS: Yet because of this unfulfilled love an interesting topic arises. After all, that puppeteer is also a metaphor for God. And it turns out that God may be malign, cynical. With that ominous eye flash with which the performance ends.

KP: Of course, it was not the case that we wanted to show a great guy with whom a girl falls in love. If there is a person who performs tricks and brings inanimate objects to life and creates such a situation that we start to believe that dolls are alive, then we assign to him certain attributes. . . .

KK: Of a manipulator, for instance

TS: For Krzysztof Kieślowski this film carries with it possibly one more auto-biographical undertone, because it is a film of which one half takes place in Po-land and the other in France. So, you were also making it partly domestically and partly in the West. In recent times, such crossings have been very dramatic and they have been associated with a so-called "decision" [of leaving Poland behind]. A particular reason and particular decision preceded the departure, or rather the refusal to return, of Tarkovsky, and the departure of Polański, Żuławski, Skoli-mowski. In the meantime, you seem to be entering the local system gently and step-by-step.

KP: Before Krzysztof answers, I would like to say something. So for all these film people who have left, some kind of a severance has come automatically, a sense of caesura between this and the other world. I infer it from observing their work. So from the choice to talk about people, and not about systems, not on a macro-scale but on a micro-scale, comes the effect, then, that when we think of the French and Polish Véroniques, we don't see any differences, apart from their circumstances. And this is an attempt at an authentic forging of certain connec-tions—through art, through creation—between the West and the East (to use slogans), or between one place and another. We think this is the only way, the only direction to develop certain connections, [by] showing through film what connects us and not what divides us. The films that will be shot next year—we are just about to finish writing their scripts—are located in three different European countries and concern people in different situations, but with a common core.

TS: In Poland it is commonly believed—and that has been suggested by Wajda—that we must show what is ours, our own, the national, and only then will it be noticed in the wide world.

KP: In every, or almost every, review of *Véronique* in our press there is an implied accusation that we are not interested in Polish issues, political issues. Yes, we are not interested in that political way of thinking. At least not today.

KK: You know, it's the type of feeling that really works perfectly well in Poland. Nothing in Poland works well: phones, buses, hospital, but that works faultlessly.

We have an entrenched conviction, and we feel very good with it, that we are the most important in the world, and that nothing interests anyone as much as our own fate. I understood a very long time ago that it's a deep fallacy, that people in the world could not care less about Poles. People in the world care nothing at all about Polish history, Polish suffering, and our struggles with Polishness, our heroism and so on. [They] don't care because all the people in the world have their own troubles and problems. So the only chance to talk, to communicate, is not to find what is Polish, but to find in Poles that which concerns all people in the world, and to find in the people in the world that which concerns Poles. It doesn't mean that Wajda is not right. Wajda is right for himself, and I am right for myself, and it doesn't imply a conflict; on the contrary, I think these rights can coexist perfectly together.

KP: What's more, I think Poles now need the way of seeing people and of describing the Polish world that we are attempting to realize for better or worse.

KK: Yes, we need to see Poles as normal people who have the same problems as everybody else.

KP: It doesn't mean flattening the description, reducing it to somebody going shopping and somebody else going away for the weekend. In my opinion, the generation who are now eighteen to twenty-five years old think this way and can hardly accept that other way of thinking about Poland. At the beginning, Krzysztof talked about the unity of the eighties in the framework of the so-called Cinema of Moral Concern. In the meantime, owing to that traditional perspective of the forty-five-to-sixty-year-old generation of seeing matters concerning Poland and Poles, an inter-generational gap is probably emerging. It is not a positive phenomenon. Right now, I cannot see this intergenerational unity.

TS: Yesterday, within a panel debate titled *A Longing for Meaning* that accompanied this year's festival in Mannheim, Krzysztof Kieślowski spoke about a dramatic cultural crisis in our times, about the death of the cinema of grand masters. As a viewer I am also suffering because of it. To me, however, it seems that you belong to this generation that is attempting to fan the barely smoldering ember of auteur cinema.

KK: You know, we cannot be compared [to them]. . . . Unfortunately, that's how it is. . . . We have to state it clearly. . . . It doesn't at all mean that we have to put the camera away in a box; no, we have to keep trying, but with a sense of humility, a consciousness of where we really are with our talents, our capabilities, our wisdom, in relation to people who were already able to articulate it fifteen years ago. We are very, very behind.

TS: And don't you think—and you might be on that trail—that the overcoming of that cultural crisis, a rebirth of film as art, the return of a thinking viewer to the cinema, that all this can be achieved through inspiration from the sacred [sphere]. You are circling around that mystery, searching for the absolute, and your films may facilitate meeting with God, as long as the Church doesn't get in the way.

KK: But it is the Church that does a lot to get in the way. It is again another of our very Polish problems, because after all we are the most Catholic country in the world and we have the most institutionalized Church. Moreover, Krzysztof proved to me once—and it's a holy truth—that it's difficult to ask the Church to act differently. The Church has to act according to its doctrine, it has to demand of people that they behave according to that doctrine. Unfortunately in Poland all the powers, all the lobby groups, all the authorities have fallen.

KP: Or, they are falling.

KK: There remains one well organized institution: that is the Church. In my opinion it's the Church's misfortune and our misfortune, the Polish misfortune.

KP: I don't have to admit here how I'm connected with Christianity, but the Church has entered a vacuum—and this is after all a powerful human organization—and it might not be able to find its place in it, moving around in it not always in the most fortunate of ways. And that's dangerous. After all, if there are people who are searching for God in different ways, or are trying to touch the absolute in a different way, that's magnificent. Then we live in a different [better] world, don't we? Let them talk about God: if they do, they will find their way to Him. Most important is that they always have someone to talk to, that it's accepted that they want to talk.

Beautiful Slogans and Mystery

Hiroshi Takahashi / 1993

From *Kino* 9 (1993): 11–13. Reprinted by permission.

This is a translation of an abbreviated Polish version of the interview conducted by Hiroshi Takahashi for Japanese magazine Switch, *with the assistance of Ewa Misiewicz.*

Hiroshi Takahashi: I have found the text that's sung in *The Double Life of Véronique*. It's a fragment of Dante's *Paradise IV*; a careful viewer can see it as a metaphor for Véronique's fate. What was the origin of the idea of using the *Divine Comedy*?

Krzysztof Kieślowski: The composer came up with it. The idea was to offer poetry that no one would understand (in the film it is sung in old Italian; not even Italians can understand it). For the composer it was a sort of challenge. . . .

HT: Although the name of Van den Budenmayer is fictitious, I've found it in music catalogues and on the CD with the film music.

KK: Van den Budenmayer, it's an old story. I needed classical music for *Decalogue* 9, but I wanted the film's composer, Zbigniew Preisner, to write it. And he created this stylized music. Later, it was necessary for the film's characters to mention the name of that classical composer. I like Holland, so I thought that he could be a Dutch composer from the turn of the seventeenth and eighteenth centuries. I went to the Dutch Embassy and asked for the names of people from that period. From a considerable list I chose the name Van den Budenmayer. But later it started to catch on in a somewhat amusing way; suddenly the British Institute of Music asked for the details of that composer for a new music encyclopedia. They wrote that they understood that I would like to keep the discovery secret, but they asked if I would reveal at least a few details. The correspondence went on for a few months. Germans, very meticulous in those matters, also started to take an interest in Van den Budenmayer. So we also made up his biography. At this moment, he already has a date of birth, death, consecutive opus numbers. . . .

In *Blue*, music plays an even more important, more dramatic role. Van den

Budenmayer appears again, this time as a character who inspires a contemporary French composer writing music for the celebration of Europe's unification. We'll see if Zbyszek [trans: diminutive of Zbigniew] Preisner will meet the challenge and write music about which people will say: yes, it could be performed at the unification of Europe, an event that happens only once in twenty centuries. Van den Budenmayer will definitely be the inspiration for that music.

HT: How well does a finished film fulfill your expectations and intentions contained in the script?

KK: You never get what you expect. Because I like charts, I calculated that if you get some 35 per cent of what you wanted, then you can be more or less content—not pleased, but content. The number of compromises, obstacles that you meet on the way, is so big, that this 30 to 35 per cent is perhaps all you can achieve.

HT: It seems to me that in film narration you are interested more in a single event than in the consequences of events that make up a storyline?

KK: Cinema is storytelling. You cannot escape that and shouldn't. People want to listen to stories, gossip, chat, to say what's happened to them. They tell one another about their dreams, childhood, or what will be. It's natural. . . .

HT: In *Chance* you were telling three stories concurrently; ten in *The Decalogue*, two in *The Double Life of Véronique*, three in *Three Colors*. Why do you have the need to multiply stories? Isn't one enough for you?

KK: If you tell two or three stories that run concurrently or independently of one another, it energizes people's imagination, their natural longing for connotations, for searching for connections with what's unsaid.

In *Three Colors* I tell three different stories, completely distinct. But there are some hidden connections in them to be read by viewers who like the cinema, intellectual games. At the story level, they will be very simple tales. At a higher level, riddles, puzzles. There is in people a natural need to find out what's next. "What is behind this wall?" I always tell simple stories, but at the same time I make an effort to have them contain some other interpretive possibility, something different from the storyline that I'm telling . . .

Whatever the film's fabric—documentary, which is part of real life, or fiction feature—the level of telling stories always exists. I'll return to what I was saying about the desire to unveil the mystery: everybody carries their own mystery and everybody would like to look inside everyone else's mystery. One mystery is certainly death. We want to know, what is it like? What will happen afterwards? What were we before we were born? That kind of curiosity is in my opinion the main drive for attending the cinema, reading books.

HT: Your cooperation with Krzysztof Piesiewicz has been going on for a long time. What is the method of your collaboration on a script?

KK: Our relations are complicated; after all we've been working together already for ten years. Generally, script work looks like this: we discuss some possibility, then I write it up, and he reads it. We discuss. I keep writing, and he reads again. Then we change what I've written. Then I write again, and he reads, and again. . . .

HT: You don't swap the roles?

KK: No, we only change the script. And then during shooting, I change whatever can still be changed.

HT: Do you change a lot?

KK: A lot. Krzysztof Piesiewicz is absent during shooting, but I try to show him all the edit versions. We discuss them together, then I sit at the editing table, cutting, watching. After that, we have screenings together and we again converse.

HT: You edit in person?

KK: I work with an editor, but I don't miss a day, a scene, a cut. Editing I like most out of all the stages of production. In truth, I shoot films to edit them.

HT: You often use the term "observer," also talking about yourself. What does that term mean to you?

KK: An observer is a person who walks the streets and observes.

HT: Is he part of a street crowd or rather does he look from aside?

KK: In fact, I always stay aside, but I think that what's most important to see is not far, but rather—deep. It's the question of the degree of attention of the observer.

Everything is inside. That something cannot be photographed or filmed. You can only try to come near it. . . .

HT: Your protagonists often observe the world through a window. It's associated with the transcendental atmosphere of your films. On which side of the window do you place yourself?

KK: Yes, I like windows and I keep making scenes in which people look through them. I think it's a safe spot. I've taken the position of an observer from documentary film: in it a camera is a window that separates me from reality, despite being in its midst. I am safe with the camera, as if behind glass. Often I've been accused of it, and perhaps deservedly . . . that I separate myself from events, that it is my . . .

HT: Distance?

KK: Yes, I keep a distance. . . .

HT: We are approaching the one hundredth anniversary of the cinema's begin-ning. What does it mean to you?

KK: I think this anniversary comes at the wrong time. Cinema is a marriage that's collapsing just now. For the centenary, one would want some hope for [further] development, new energy, some technical breakthrough as at the time of the in-troduction of sound, color. But there is no such thing; today's cinema seems to be quite stable in a bad sense of this word. And we won't find in the next few years any new means of expression; there will be no new idea of the cinema. Unless great talents appear, auteurs of the standard of Chaplin, Fellini, or Bergman.

HT: Can you imagine working in electronic media, in high-definition television—what would you do if they stopped producing movies on [celluloid] film stock?

KK: No, I won't dabble in that. I will die if need be. I know it's the cinema's future, but it no longer concerns me. . . .

HT: You've said in some interview that as a child you used to watch films in a summer cinema, sitting on the roof? Why? Were you interested in observing the audience?

KK: Yet from that roof I didn't see the full screen, only the bottom right corner. The reason I sat on the roof was very simple: I had no money. . . .

HT: Who are the viewers for you?

KK: They're all these people who feel like thinking about something. . . . It doesn't mean that my viewers are better than others. You also can't say that they are mainly workers or mostly students, or doctors. . . . Sensitive people exist in all classes, all professions, all ages; young ones as much as older ones. Also old folk.

HT: What meaning does the characters' language have for you? To what extent does it define the reality in which the protagonists move?

KK: Even Jesus Christ speaks English in Scorsese. I don't employ such measures, because I think that people have their own personalities, their own world, and they come with all that to the film shoot. The French with their French, Poles with Polish. I detest situations when a German, a Frenchman, and an English woman act in a film and all pretend they are Americans. That's why the first of *Three Col-ors*, which is clearly a French film, will be acted in French; a Polish film—in Polish; the third one, Swiss—in French.

HT: *Three Colors* is, as we know, an allusion to the French Revolution's slogans: Liberty, Equality, and Fraternity. These titles also carry something ironic with them.

KK: I try to pose the question whether those who took on these slogans and fought for them had enough imagination to know what they really meant. Are they compatible with human nature? Because maybe they're only beautiful words. . . . What do they mean from the perspective of an ordinary person's life? Do we really want to be free, or do we only talk about it? Of course, we all want to have the freedom to travel and money for the ticket. But I think that we are predisposed to seek our own captivity; without it we feel bad. Because liberty may also mean loneliness, sacrifice.

The same with equality. I have never yet met a person who would really want to be equal with others. Of course, we are all equal in death, but everyone would like to die more comfortably, suffer less than others. The same concerns fraternity, which is the most humanitarian of the three slogans, but doesn't it perhaps serve to disguise our egoism? Doesn't it stem from the need to shape oneself into a person of a great heart, of grand generosity? Maybe that need of creation is stronger than the authentic need of fraternity?

The Key to Sensitivity

Tadeusz Sobolewski / 1993

From *Kino* 9 (1993): 13–14. Reprinted by permission.

This interview was conducted in Geneva in a van at the shoot of Three Colors: Red *by renowned Polish film critic Tadeusz Sobolewski, whose memory of the meeting is inseparable from a Marlboro packet and clouds of cigarette smoke that accompanied it throughout.*

Tadeusz Sobolewski: Don't you think that mass culture currently gives the young generation less than what it gave us? Around 1968, this culture was talking about freedom: the Beatles, *Hair*. . . .

Krzysztof Kieślowski: Mass culture has never mattered to me. And in 1968? Then there was Karel Gott![1] It was worse than counter-revolution, as Karabasz used to say, and he was right. There were the Beatles, of course, but in the cultural sphere Karel Gott mattered most.

1968? I remember very well. It was not a year that would connect for me in any way with the sphere of freedom. With politics, certainly. And that is, as you know, a negation of freedom. I was into it [politics] at that time. In the Film School I allowed myself to be pulled into the absurdity of activism. I say absurdity, because in reality it turned against what mattered to us.

TS: There was a counterculture. Hippies.

KK: You can become a hippy today as well. Where we've been shooting, near Geneva, the homeless live. By choice. They don't have their own apartments, they don't have money. They could have them, if they wanted to, but they've decided to be homeless. I see no difference between them and those rebels.

TS: Maybe it is them publishing the anarchist leaflet that was planted yesterday during the shoot at the bar "Chez Joseph"; it's called *Guano Sauvage*; it's against the authority of money, and for drugs. But it doesn't have the power that the counterculture of the sixties had; it means little and it breaks down nothing.

KK: One can speak of a difference in [the types of] hope. Here you are right.

TS: The others believed (or maybe we believed?) that the world would change.
KK: In the meantime, the regime has collapsed and the world has not changed; or if so, then for the worse. Because hope has to do with youth. You have it until a certain age. If you managed to live in the times in which that hope is not killed regularly every few years, you can hold on to it for longer. Today's twenty-three-year-olds have the same hope we had at their age. The question is how fast time will take it away from them. From us it was taken away regularly. I was fifteen years old in 1956 and understood consciously, felt consciously, that what was hope then was being hidden, as the Germans put it, under a tablecloth, and if someone wants to use big words, one can say: it was killed, wasted. I was aware of that. What happened next, we all know, is not worth recounting, because you simply get bored with all these Polish dates.

TS: But youth culture, the culture of rebellion, was offering hope, even in that regime.
KK: I just wouldn't agree that it was on a mass scale. Mass culture is not a culture of rebellion—it's a culture of consensus. Mass culture has never contributed anything apart from leisure, which is in fact very useful. If rebellion is on a mass scale, then only in the sense that the student community (and so not everyone), which is a small percentage of society, can be referred to as such.

TS: In that case, in what circles did your first films belong? They were in their way popular, and at the same time rebellious.
KK: They had such a small audience that it's difficult to characterize them as "mass." Were they a rebellion? To some degree, certainly, yes. But it was a clearly political rebellion, and not a rebellion against a stagnated culture. There are a series of misunderstandings about it, mainly because of Kałużyński.[2] I, as I've said, did not contest, as part of a generation, against culture, nor against history. I've never been against Wajda,[3] against Brandys,[4] nor Dygat.[5] I've always thought they created fantastic things, from which we should draw as much as possible; preserve, not destroy.

TS: Today there is no new Dygat. There are no native literary idols.
KK: There are none because there is a crisis, as much in the banking sphere as in the cultural sphere; maybe even deeper in the latter. And this is so because a certain ideology that could have continued living—so it seemed—for some turned out to be a criminal ideology, and for others, a gigantic historical mistake. Let's say: criminal mistake, if we consider how many people lost their sense, and how

many—lives. And a new ideology has not been invented yet, because they are not born that often. Maybe fortunately.

TS: Do you have a sense that your daughter's generation has lost something that the previous generation had?
KK: Not only have they lost [it], but most likely they've never had that sense of unity that we used to have once. The social bond, although I detest the words social, communal, society. Yet I simply confirm the fact: that feeling existed once and that feeling is no longer. All you need to do is to look around Geneva.

TS: I have just seen in a parking lot a car all pasted with stickers: "Solidarity," "Chile," "Nicaragua," "Venceremos," and so on. It stood like a phantom of another era. Like its caricature. Because there are no new slogans about Yugoslavia, about Nagorno-Karabakh. International solidarity doesn't mean anything anymore. It's not on anymore. Marin Karmitz, who remembers 1968 very well, in a conversation with me wonders why there are no war films in Yugoslavia. In the past, he says, the cinema was able to anticipate events: the Parisian May was prophesied by Godard.
KK: It all has to do with the fall of ideology. Then, for instance, almost at the same time as the events [were taking place], they created films about Algeria, but they made them in the name of something. There are no films about Yugoslavia, because no one knows in the name of what they should be made. In the name of what higher goal? Because a straight statement that there is barbarianism happening, that it is inhuman, not humanitarian, is too weak a goal, too obvious. On the other hand, journalism, television, manipulating the facts causes a general desensitization of [public] opinion. We all know that and nothing comes out of that.

TS: The ideas of liberty, equality, and fraternity were partisan-ized a long time ago, hijacked by groups fighting one another.
KK: These slogans divide, not bring together. Each side of the conflict—and hundreds of those are tearing the world apart today—would say that it is fighting for freedom, that it wants equality and brotherhood.

TS: Do you mean to say by that that one cannot make a righteous political film using humanitarian slogans?
KK: It's perhaps a question of finding the right language, reaching to that sphere of sensitivity that is not yet battered, not covered in a plastic, insensitive layer. That sphere most certainly exists in people. The question [is] how to reach it?

TS: In fact, what sphere do you want to reach with your films?

KK: The sphere of sensitivity, but not the "social" or "political," simply the subconscious layer of experience, which people are often ashamed to admit.

TS: I have recently seen Peter Handke's article about the pleasure of returning home from the cinema in the sixties, when the film seen would follow us through the town. I have to say that *A Short Film about Killing* still follows me along the Krakowskie Przedmieście,[6] although it's difficult to refer to it as "pleasure," even though there is no longer a fence next to the Bristol [Hotel], and the corner café in the Europejski [Hotel] is more elegant. Do contemporary young people also have their own films that would follow them? In any case it's a phenomenon incomparably more rare now than then.

KK: It's only a question of finding the right key. There is a door. There is a lock. It's about opening this door. I say that in all my pessimism. But I really think that this door exists and you can open it and that behind this door there is something. . . . And I think that if, in this all-encompassing crisis of culture, you spoke with any serious writer or poet, each would say the same. The only question that follows us today is: where is this key?

Notes

1. Karel Gott is a Czech Schlager singer popular in the Eastern Bloc.

2. Zygmunt Kałużyński (1918–2004) is a well-known Polish cultural critic and scholar.

3. Andrzej Wajda (1926–) is one of the most-known Polish film directors, instrumental in Polish cinema movements such as the Polish School and Cinema of Moral Concern.

4. Kazimierz Brandys (1918–2000) is a highly respected Polish émigré writer and screenwriter.

5. Stanisław Dygat (1914–1978) is an important Polish writer.

6. One of the main streets of Warsaw, close to the Old Town.

Behind the Curtain

Tadeusz Sobolewski / 1993

From *Kino* 9 (1993): 15–16. Reprinted by permission.

Like the previous interview, this one was conducted in Geneva in a smoke-filled van at the shoot of Three Colors: Red, *though the focus here is on details of that film that Sobolewski has observed in production.*

Tadeusz Sobolewski: I have watched the scene in Valentine's room. I was amazed by the care for the tiniest details of the picture, even those that have no bearing on the plot. There was something disinterested in it, as if it were about capturing the moment when reality assumed a perfect shape.

Krzysztof Kieślowski: The world consists of details. Our care for details, still not greater in *Red* than, for instance, in *Blue*, stems from the fundamental assumption: we want to be the authors of chance. And it's not so much about these details, about what book is on the shelf, but about the way of telling, signaling connections between people, in space and time. But first, a viewer has to believe in the photographed world.

TS: When, in the theatre in Lausanne during a take, a beam fell down suddenly with a great bang, Trintignant and Irène Jacob kept on saying their dialogue. The take was used. That scene brought to my mind the famous hammer from *Hospital*, which broke during a take, during an operation. It was such an unprovoked accident, incorporated later into the whole, which "made" the scene, and in a sense "made" that film, since I've remembered it already for twenty years.

KK: Yes, we kept the scene in the theatre with the falling of the beam. It's functioned well. Even though later, it was difficult to achieve in close-ups of the actors the same effect of fright as the first time when it was really happening. If I came up with something like that during writing, most likely we would have deleted it as showy, but because it happened by itself and the actors felt good with it, we've left it.

TS: Production of *Red* was like peeping behind the curtain of reality, forging the rules of the game, assuming the role of fate or chance. Is it about achieving a degree of perfection of the depicted world, like in a documentary, when the whole of reality is acting?

KK: Life is disorderly, but sometimes it happens that we come across an internal fusion that consolidates, makes it into a whole, a world reflected in a drop of water. And suddenly, in one piece of time, you see an awful lot of life and you understand a lot despite it being about a seemingly unimportant trifle.

In documentary something like this has happened to me a few times. Now, because I'm not making documentaries, because the documentary genre has died, unfortunately, I am trying to create such situations in acted films, to build such credibility. At the same time, I'm avoiding the fundamental trouble that one has with a documentary: that there are in it real people who cannot take the mask off. A good actor, even in a mask, is still himself, simultaneously being someone else.

TS: I think immediately about *The Photograph*, this little-known television reportage from 1969, where you flag a documentary maker's drama of interfering in somebody else's life.

KK: When I photographed that, I didn't yet know that I was touching on such fundamental matters.

TS: I remember a scene when the protagonist returns home after work and a film crew takes him by surprise. You show him the photograph in which he recognizes himself from years ago. His reaction is moving but achieved really by force, through surprise. Maybe that's why I thought now about that [reportage] because the Judge from *Red*, eavesdropping on other people's telephone conversations, has something of an artist, of a director in him. He wants to influence others' fate; he intervenes as if he himself were Providence.

KK: The Judge from *Red* lives in the past. He's a man who's been late for life, even though if there were a right word [to describe it], one should say that he comes to life too late. He has missed out on a person he could love.

TS: And now he is trying to fix it by directing other people's fates?

KK: He fixes it for others, but maybe also for himself. For his hypothetical self. A foundation we established when writing this script involved introducing contemporary flashbacks.

TS: What does that mean?

KK: A normal flashback concerns the past tense. Here it happens in the present tense, as a variant of fate. The Judge talks about himself through pictures, through action (very subtle), which takes place in the present.

TS: I was not able to apprehend that intention from the script, printed in *Film na świecie*. Only here, on the set in Geneva I've seen what it's about. Unlike with *White*, which has a graceful, comedic, easy-to-tell story, in *Red*, the story stems really from the form. This film is a type of game, which takes place at many levels. Behind the film we see, there hides another film, inside, which must still be deciphered.

KK: It's always like this, that underneath there is a second film, a third, and a fourth. There are things that a viewer will not manage to register. But it doesn't matter. They are necessary. If out of one thousand, forty come to be associated for someone with something and will constitute the basis for an understanding of the film, that's plenty.

TS: Is there still progress in cinema? Can the boundaries of film expression still be moved?

KK: Each film is such an attempt. The road matters, not the destination. This is how it is in this film: I'm telling a story, which you say is unclear in the script, because it's not known what goals its particular elements serve. For me it's obvious what they do. And if I could make it into a short story or a novel, it would turn out that in literature the story of the Judge can be told precisely and with all the intended meanings. In cinema, you could also tell it more verbatim, using a voiceover monologue and various brutal measures, pointing with your finger to what the viewer should pay attention to. But we want to narrate that film discretely, associating small details or unobvious temporal connections with one another.

It's a story of a certain possibility, about how a life could proceed differently if it started forty years later, or somebody else's life forty years earlier. Can it be told this way? I don't know.

The conditions are advantageous: I have [a] good production [team], excellent actors, excellent DOP. Wonderful technique. So if this story cannot be told, then it may mean two things: either that altogether we don't have enough talent, or that the cinema is too primitive an instrument.

TS: What significance does the reality in which these stories happen carry for them? What is Switzerland to *Red*?

KK: Switzerland is the type of red knife you can see in a bar's window. Reality exists only fragmentarily, on the edges of a frame, in the background. The world is diverse, but people everywhere are the same.

TS: There are moments in this film when the cinema talks as if about itself. When the camera races following a falling book that you cannot see, following a ball in a bowling alley, whose seeing is it? Who is looking at it? The cinema itself?

KK: Maybe there is somebody who sees it all, who is a technocrane, a handheld camera, a steadicam, and he looks from each point. I think we are not acting as cinema, but as that somebody.

TS: In a conversation for *Kino* in 1990 you spoke of the absence of a normal moment. That you are waiting for such a moment. Has it come?

KK: In Poland?

TS: In life.

KK: It will never come. And I don't think it has to come. You just have to wait for it and pursue it. You can come into money, to own a car, your own house. But that real moment you will never reach. That's just what's really most interesting in life. That you won't reach [it].

TS: But there are still enlightening moments of seeing a whole. Isn't it these that this film talks about?

KK: It rather talks about life possibly going differently if it were not for something, some time. If it were not for a trifle . . . if it were not for some word said and then forgotten, but remembered by the person to whom it was spoken . . . if it were not for some gesture, facial expression . . . and then something gives way. Nobody knows why, but after all the cause does exist, really lies somewhere. And we simply want to find it.

Blue Lollipop

Tadeusz Sobolewski / 1993

From *Tygodnik Powszechny* 43 (1993): 9. Reprinted by permission.

This interview was conducted on October 2, 1993, and was originally intended for a Catholic publication, hence the many references to religious symbolism.

Tadeusz Sobolewski: We are talking soon after recording a television program that also showed your documentaries from the seventies, and a fragment of *Camera Buff*, the part about a midget worker who says he is "pleased with life." That scene has always made an impression on me. It goes beyond the Cinema of Moral Concern. Your films from those years contain, of course, an understanding of the system, but also something more: an awareness that we are limited. Mortal. Our flight is always a flight in captivity; that's how I read a scene from *Blue*, where people throw themselves into a precipice tied to a rope. Doesn't it symbolize all our limitations, which on the one hand constrain us, and on the other allow us to live?

Krzysztof Kieślowski: Death, as an inevitable prospect, has always been present in my films. Despite what they say, I haven't changed much in all these years. Yes, I use different means of storytelling, I have at my disposal—owing to the French producer—continuously better technology (especially sound). But using new tools I still talk about the same thing.

TS: Only the reach of reception is different. The films from the seventies, even though they concerned ordinary people, were elitist. These newest, made in France, are in fact a mass spectacle.

KK: Yes, it's a risk to make very personal films at the same time as counting on them filling up the cinemas.

TS: But isn't it that the intended mass [appeal] of these films demands the use of stronger means? Stepping on the gas? Employing pathos?

KK: Somebody has already written that *Blue* was made especially for the festival in Venice. It's a false lead. Equally plausible would be saying that Piesiewicz and I wrote the script for *Blue* so the film wins in Venice and helps Piesiewicz in the election to the Senate (which he didn't win)! Only, could we have anticipated when writing in 1989–90, that in three years President Wałęsa would dissolve Parliament?

To return to your question; it is not the case that I employ powerful effects to attract the audience. The subject matter calls for it. In the next films of the *Three Colors* series there are no effects as powerful or as jarring.

Blue is told in a clearly subjective way. We wanted to show what the world looked like from the perspective of a woman who has lost her loved ones. What is important to her? How does she react to the world? What does she look at? In this editing room where we are talking, there are hundreds, if not thousands, of details, at which we could look and to which we could assign some meaning. What you choose out of a thousand details will say a lot about you, who you are, where you come from, how you've grown up, what books you've read.

TS: That's a psychological truth: a person weighed down by a disaster establishes a strong connection with objects. The world recedes, people become strangers. This comes out very well in *Blue*. In this film, objects play yet another role. I would say—quasi-sacral. I see the scene when Julie puts her daughter's lollipop in her mouth as an attempt at [holy] communion. Unsuccessful. Why is this woman doing it? What does it mean?

KK: You are finding something in this film that perhaps exists in it, although our intentions were different. I will tell you now how. We took a long time to think about the scene you are talking about, to convey to the viewer that the blue lollipop that Julie finds at the bottom of her handbag in the twentieth minute of the film is one of the two lollipops she bought for her child before the trip, and which we saw in the opening scene. The whole film is built based on this principle of such associations.

Yet the woman's hopeless gesture does not stem from her will to experience a [holy] communion. It was rather an act of destruction. Julie wants to destroy a memory. Many women in her situation hold on to mementos. Others, to forget, try to experience something powerful; drugs or sex come into play. She does not do that. At the first instance, she feels like jumping out of the window. But her courage fails her. Or maybe it's not courage failing her, maybe her convictions do not allow her to do that? In any case, she tries twice, and each time it does not work out.

Julie is, of course, inconsistent, like everyone. She throws out all the mementos, but she leaves the lamp. When she returns home from hospital, the gardener assures her that he has thrown out everything from the child's room as she has asked, but it turns out that he hasn't looked at the ceiling; he's forgotten the ceiling lamp. Julie, when she notices it, wants to tear it down, she rips at it, but she manages to tear off only a couple of beads, those shiny crystals, which she squeezes in her hand for a long time.

I will tell [you] an anecdote from the shoot. We were trying to shoot the scene with the lollipop in a few takes. We had to have many lollipops for that. And because you always try to save in film, we had ordered only fifteen. Juliette had eaten a few during rehearsals. Then we made a few trials and we were still not happy with the way she was unwrapping that lollipop, how she was reacting to it. Until it turned out that there was only one left; the last chance to shoot. We put that lollipop in [her] handbag, we covered it with notebooks, puff-boxes, lipsticks, all those odds and ends that women have in their handbags. We set up the camera, she emptied out the contents; the lollipop fell out—she takes it into her hand and sees it is broken. Juliette Binoche then did this kind of a gesture: with a sigh she pulled her head back. . . . It was the completely private gesture of an actress who had noticed that she had no prop anymore. But in that several-second part of a take we found everything that we wanted to achieve.

TS: She acted a sense of loss. And, in fact, I've called it "a communion," an attempt to establish communication, to reconcile with fate, no matter how ineffective. Julie's estrangement brings out all the more the sacramental sense of that action, although nothing gets fulfilled here, everything screams of emptiness. You reject such interpretations?

KK: No, I only reject it if someone says: you wanted to put a symbol in this film. Then I answer: I didn't want it to be a symbol. I reject inaccurate interpretations of intentions. But I don't reject most extreme interpretations. If someone finds a symbol in art, then it is there, independently of the author's intentions.

TS: In *Decalogue 1*, in *Decalogue 8*, to some extent in *Blue*—in those films that touch on the issues of faith—next to an agnostic protagonist, there always stands another person, a believer. These films in a way remove the distance between them, showing it as insignificant. For your protagonist, religion is enslavement, accepting something that you really do not believe. But on the other hand, you keep questioning the possibility of freedom, you reduce to the minimum the option of choice. Hence the perennial trouble with reading these films, with people of contrary worldviews adopting them as theirs.

KK: Religion is enslavement in an obvious way. It's that type of enslavement that you take on voluntarily, and even desire. However, faith for me is a chance for freedom. Faith, in its very essence, is separate from institutionalized religions.

TS: Do you see in them a threat of totalitarianism?

KK: In religion, where we deal with voluntary enslavement, that threat always exists. And with faith, no.

Faith is freedom, because it means freedom of choice, it is a constant choice. Religion, however, takes that possibility away, it tells you very clearly: you will live this and that way, do this and that, this and that day you will be in the church, and you will not eat meat on this and that day.

Faith does not say anything like that. It does not concern itself with the sphere of duties. Faith is your own attitude, or your own notion of that someone whom we call God (someone once said that if he didn't exist, he would have had to be invented) and who exists in each one of us. Because otherwise we could not make sense of our lives. To amass goods, to bear to the world new generations so they again amass goods: this is not enough [for anyone] to make any sense.

TS: The discord or confluence of religion and faith, religion and freedom, that is a task for philosophy, theology. But each of us has his own private experiences and own traumas. I would like to ask you privately, not philosophically: do you have a personal grievance with religion? With Polish Catholicism?

KK: I don't have a complex about religion (and even if I did, I am hiding it carefully under a layer of external aversion). But I have an aversion to the Church as an institution for many reasons, about which I wouldn't like to speak here in detail, because it would be indiscreet and disloyal, even if I really feel that I have suffered harm or injustices. And not in childhood, but as a grown-up.

I have to say that in recent years that resentment has been increasing. And recent events in Poland have confirmed my fears. I could put together, off the top of my head, a list of people I would consider personally responsible for SLD's[1] electoral win. It's obvious that the Polish social democrats have won the election not because they are better, but because the right [wing] is so bad, so stupid, rapacious. I repeat: there is no credit to social democrats for winning the election. It is the right's fault. They often say that it's a result of the economic situation. I don't believe [it]. It's a result of the politics of the people associated with the Church and of the Church itself for allowing that.

TS: A mistake.

KK: Not necessarily. It might turn out from the perspective of what is to come that the Church after all did the right thing. I am talking about something else: about the personal responsibility of specific people, driven by the rapacious desire to organize our lives according to their own expectations. It should not have been done, in a country freed after forty-five years from the authorities, telling people at each step how to live. People were not able to accept such coercion for a second time, from different authorities, even if [this time] our own.

That's why they voted against the institution that at the state level wants to put up a moral barrage, barriers. The result of the election is a defeat of that type of thinking. It was lost by all those who were unleashing a campaign of hatred, contrary to the human feeling of unity, solidarity.

TS: And what will happen next?
KK: Alternate swings of the pendulum. I dream of the time when this political pendulum starts to calm down, and at last it stops. In the middle.

TS: Let's not forget that the clock of history has already stopped once in our lifetime. In the People's Republic, life was as if nothing were ever to change. But it's interesting that in those times, somewhere in the lower social layers, there was possible a form of freedom (see: Białoszewski).[2] Was it a slave's freedom? I think it was something more: it was possible to preserve dignity, like your midget-worker.
KK: Yes, of course.

TS: You have never succumbed to any utopian belief in the possibility of organizing an ideal world?
KK: No, never. I've managed to avoid it.

Notes

1. Democratic Left Alliance (Polish: Sojusz Lewicy Demokratycznej), a major center-left political party with roots in the pre-1989 communist system.

2. Although politically independent and unconventional, Miron Białoszewski (1922–1983) was already a well-acclaimed Polish poet during his lifetime and was seen by some as the most significant literary figure of postwar Poland.

No End to the Enigma

Jonathan Romney / 1993

Like many newspaper "interviews" (of which we have included relatively few in this volume), this one is essentially a mix of profile, film critique, and interview proper, revealing more than anything Romney's wariness about Krzysztof Kieślowski's vaunted status.

Introducing a Krzysztof Kieślowski film on television a few years ago, Lindsay Anderson commented that what he most associated with Polish cinema was a quality of seriousness. No one, he added, better exemplified this seriousness than Kieślowski. Some people consider Kieślowski to be the finest film director currently working in Europe; that he's among the most serious there can be no doubt.

His seriousness has an allure that can keep an audience in awestruck thrall—which is not always the best critical response a filmmaker could wish for. His films are sparing with their humor and their moral gravity is of the sort that brooks no argument. Kieślowski favors the large themes. His acclaimed series of television films, *The Decalogue* (1988), illustrated the Ten Commandments; his last feature, *The Double Life of Véronique*, addressed life, death, and the elusive nature of identity. His new trilogy, *Three Colors* (*Blue* is released today with *White* and *Red* to follow), takes on the values of Liberty, Equality, and Fraternity.

For devotees of the art-house tradition at its most somber, Kieślowski belongs in the lineage of Bergman and Tarkovsky, who figure in his own pantheon. He is another of those northern directors whose austerity suggests an uncompromising vision with transcendental import. A former documentarist, he made films in the 1970s and 1980s that dealt directly with the hard political realities of everyday life in Poland, notably *Blind Chance* and *No End*. But it was the *Decalogue*'s more abstract moral concern that put him on the world map as an object of auteur adulation.

Fans of the *Decalogue* tend to be so reverent that it is hard not to wonder whether there isn't less to these dramas than meets the eye. Visually prosaic, the series had enough elusive symbolism and gravitas of pacing to make it more resonant than its anecdotal nature seemed to allow for. *The Double Life of Véronique*, on the other hand, was extremely stylized, Sławomir Idziak's baroque photography bringing an eerie depth to an already elliptical story (Idziak achieves similar wonders in *Blue*).

Kieślowski is anxious to play down the mystery quotient of his work, but he's not inclined to give too much away. "My part of the work is to make the film. Your part is to find something in the film, or perhaps not. For me it's always important to hear viewers' interpretations. They turn out to be very different to my intentions. I don't hide my intentions. I speak about them—but not about my interpretations."

In fairness, Kieślowski cannot be accused of cultivating a gnomic air, but his tendency to reduce questions to commonsense basics only fuels the mystique. Interviewing him through an interpreter, you get a sense of somehow skirting the heart of the matter, and his Polish intonations—a drawl with peculiar dying cadences—contrive to make him sound either dismissive or excessively self-deprecating.

On his relationship with his audience, Kieślowski manages to suggest that he's at once out to make his meaning crystal clear, and the exact opposite. "Whatever stage I'm at with a film, whether I'm writing the script or editing, I always look at it from the point of view of the viewer—what he's expecting, the way he'd like me to entrap him and the way he'd like to be released from the trap, when he wants to be surprised, when he wants to laugh, when he wants to cry. You could describe my job as a game with the viewer—to give him what he wants but at the same time covertly to slip in something that he might not be expecting."

That covert something is, one imagines, the sense of the transcendental. "People are looking for this," he agrees, "but it's not because of a particular director or film. I think they need something like that, because what they have isn't enough. What they already have isn't explained to them—the sense of getting up in the morning, the sense of its history, sometimes of religion or of politics, a sense of the terrible.

"The Stalinists used to get up in the morning to kill their opponents and pull their fingernails out—we're always looking for some meaning in life. Throughout history and even now, there are lots of us trying to find out a sense of why we're here, but nobody ever has."

The vagueness and open-endedness of his narratives suggest that Kieślowski is something of an old-school existentialist. Things simply happen, who knows why, and people just have to react to them. In his notes for *Blue*, he makes it clear that the theme of freedom is meant in a non-political sense: "We're talking about individual freedom, a profound freedom, freedom of life."

It's debatable, though, how far-reaching Kieślowski's films really are as moral inquiries. In the *Decalogue*, the detached style gets us close to the characters' anxieties, but ultimately shrugs them off as unknowable. In *Véronique* and in *Blue*, he goes even further—the elaborate camera work and unworldly beauty of Irène Jacob and Juliette Binoche make his heroines all but opaque.

Conversely, there's often an over-statement that seems intrusive; in *A Short Film about Killing* (from the *Decalogue*), the argument against capital punishment comes across as incongruously rhetorical.

As a moral observer, Kieślowski again keeps his options open. "I do think people are good. It's just situations that put them into terrible predicaments, although of course human beings like to create their own situations." He explains that the young murderer of the *Decalogue*, who kills a taxi driver for no apparent reason, is basically good; if his sister hadn't been run over by a tractor, things might have been different. "It's important to get to the roots of things—the moment when something actually started happening."

This approach is illustrated at the start of *Blue*. The story is about to begin with a car crash; Kieślowski gives us advance notice by showing a close-up of an oil drip. But, he stresses, this is just chance: it's futile to look for a greater why.

"Every day thousands of people die in car accidents. Sometimes it's slippery, sometimes somebody falls asleep, perhaps a screw comes undone. I'm not for investigating accidents, I'm just saying there was an accident, a man and a girl died, and then I start thinking what's going to happen with the woman who's left behind."

Kieślowski's films seem to invoke metaphysical imponderables while at the same time shrugging them off. But when things resist explanation, meaning is invested in the image itself. What really makes Kieślowski's films—which, arguably, he pulls off with complete success only in *Véronique*—are those images that don't easily translate into words. It happens when Irène Jacob's face breaks out into a radiant grin as rain falls on it, or when we're given a luminously bloated glass globe to contemplate at leisure.

When the images do fit concepts, then beware. Kieślowski has a tendency to overburden objects with glaring symbolism: candle wax drips like tears on the face of the Virgin; a wasp struggles out of a glass just as a dying man rallies round; a devil's-head car ornament signals doom. And yet Kieślowski has insisted, "I don't film metaphors. . . . For me a bottle of milk is a bottle of milk." In *Blue*, he explains, "Juliette Binoche's face is reflected upside down in a spoon. Spoons reflect images upside down."

This denial of meaning seems disingenuous. *Véronique*, for example, was remarkable for the way Kieślowski turned funding circumstances to his advantage. Working with French co-production money, he devised a story about a girl who dies in Poland and her double who goes on living in France. Clearly his symbolic farewell to Poland? "It wasn't my intention for it to be a symbol of anything. A girl dies in Poland, that's all."

The fact that he has been working in France, Kieślowski claims, is strictly a matter of funding, even though his new trilogy refers to the tricolor flag and a set of values dear to the Gallic heart. "These concepts touch on everybody, not just France. If you ask Arafat's warriors what they're fighting for, they'll say exactly the same—liberty, equality, fraternity. Ask the Bosnians or the Serbs, they'll say the same. The concepts themselves are just pretexts to make films."

Nevertheless, the three concepts have provided him with some philosophical grist. "They're impossible to attain from the point of view of individuals. Politically, perhaps—apart from equality, of course. You can say, I want to be free, but how do you free yourself from your own feelings, your own memories, your own desires? Perhaps we can't function without them—which automatically means we aren't free, we're prisoners of our own emotions."

As yet, it's hard to evaluate *Blue*, which has left many viewers feeling dissatisfied, especially in the light of a cryptic, portentous closing sequence. Perhaps Kieślowski would advise skeptics to wait and see how the rest of the trilogy develops? "Absolutely no. I'd say, don't buy any more tickets."

Glowing in the Dark

Tony Rayns / 1994

From *Sight and Sound* 4, no. 6 (June 1994): 8–10. Reprinted by permission.

This interview was originally included in a larger critical article defending Kieślowski and the Three Colors *trilogy, but was conducted before Rayns had seen the final film,* Red. *He frames the interview by noting that many critics and journalists were interpreting Kieślowski's public statements (about his retirement, for instance) and interview answers as cynical and sarcastic, but that he believes that this is a mishearing of Kieślowski's irony, "a key weapon in the armory of all East European intellectuals in the communist years."*

Tony Rayns: Why a trilogy? Why isn't one film enough?

Krzysztof Kieślowski: Because it makes everything more interesting. Differing points of view are inherently more interesting than one point of view. Since I don't have any answers but do know how to pose questions, it suits me to leave the door open to varying possibilities. I realized this some years ago. I don't want to pose as a relativist, because I'm not one, but I have to admit that there's an element of relativism in play here.

TR: Is *White* in some sense a parody of the other films in the trilogy, in the way that *Decalogue 10* parodied aspects of that series?

KK: You could see it that way. But I think *Red* is different in tone. It's hard to put a handle on it.

TR: Isn't the "liberté-égalité-fraternité" theme a pretext, just as the Ten Commandments were for *Decalogue*?

KK: Yes, exclusively that.

TR: So you don't lie awake at night worrying about such themes?

KK: No, but I did spend a lot of time thinking about them.

TR: How seriously do you discuss these things with your co-writer Krzysztof Piesiewicz?

KK: We crack a lot of jokes. We talk about cars, about women. The conclusion we came to about equality is that nobody really wants it. Karol in *White* doesn't want equality, he wants to be *better* than others.

TR: Did anyone pressure you to make the three parts of the trilogy in different countries?

KK: No, I did it this way because I wanted to. The issues these films raise are deeply rooted in European traditions, so it was natural to spread them around Europe. The production company helped us decide where to shoot, but nobody forced us.

TR: This isn't a case like *The Double Life of Véronique*, where there's a material relationship between the financing and the structure of the story?

KK: Actually, that film didn't need to be a co-production between Poland and France. You could imagine it done with one girl living in Kraków and the other in Gdańsk. I didn't frame the story of *Véronique* that way because of the financial background to the production; the subject itself was something close to my heart.

TR: But the way you finally made the film did reflect the financing?

KK: For sure. But this trilogy is a rather different case. I don't think these storylines are as original as the one in *Véronique*, and anyway, these are mainly French films.

TR: You have a strong sense of humor, but there isn't much evidence of it in serious films like *Véronique* and *Blue*.

KK: It's true that I have a certain sense of . . . irony. Sometimes you have to laugh, but I think it's worth trying to be serious from time to time. It's difficult to do both at the same time, but I hope that *White* strikes the odd lyrical note. For example, the character Mikołaj, who wants to die—he's kind of serious.

TR: What's the song Karol plays on the comb in the Métro?

KK: A pre-war Polish song, every Pole knows it. It's stupid and sentimental; we sing it when we drink. It goes: "This is our last Sunday, tomorrow we part forever. . . ." We become very sentimental when we drink.

TR: *White* offers a fairly scathing picture of post-communist Poland.

KK: Only in the background. But yes, that's the way it is now—unfortunately.

TR: You still live in Poland?

KK: Yes. I see it with a certain bitterness. I'm not against Polish entrepreneurialism, but people now care for nothing but money. I don't know what happened to us.

TR: Do people in Poland resent the fact that you're working abroad?

KK: Patriots do, yes. Normal people, I hope don't.

TR: Who are these patriots? Do they have any power?

KK: Nationalists, fascists, call them what you like. They're a crazy minority, but they shout loudly enough to be heard. They have newspapers, and access to television.

TR: Last year in Poland, I found a widespread desire to come to terms with the past—for example, the treatment of the Jews. But the election result suggested a nostalgia for the "security" of the communist period. . . .

KK: What you say is evident, but I don't think it's just. For me, it wasn't that the Left won, it was that the Right lost. That's not the same thing. There's no nostalgia for the Left. After forty-five years of being told what was good and what was bad, Polish people have had enough of it. They don't want someone else telling them the same story, even if the meanings are reversed. What happened was that they threw out the Right and the Church.

TR: Do you see a way forward for Poland?

KK: I think we have to die first, all of us. Eventually there will be new people with new ideas. It's not just a generational change, it's a matter of changing a way of thinking that has been inculcated for forty-five years. I can't see it taking less than two generations. Decades of Marxist education have left Poland unable to think in normal human terms. We can only think in terms of Left and Right.

TR: You've said you won't make any more films. So how come I've seen the outline for a film you've written for the BFI's "Century of Cinema" series?

KK: That's just a short film for television. I promised to do it some time ago, so it's just a matter of fulfilling a promise. But the financial side of it hasn't been sorted out yet; I hope they won't find the money, so I won't be obliged to do it.

TR: Why do you want to stop making films?

KK: I don't have enough patience for it any more. I didn't realize it, but it suddenly dawned on me: I've run out of patience. And patience is a fundamental requirement in this line of work.

TR: Does the situation in Poland have anything to do with it?

KK: No, I've just become old. I want to live normally. I've had no normal life for the past twenty years, and I want to go back to having one.

TR: Are you rich? Don't you need to work?

KK: Not that rich, but I don't need many things. I have enough to live . . . peacefully.

TR: How will you fill your days?

KK: There are many books I haven't read. Or books that I've read four times and want to read three times more.

TR: You'll be missed.

KK: Don't worry, someone else will come along.

Kieślowski: The End

Katherine Monk / 1994

From *Vancouver Sun*, October 8, 1994. Reprinted by permission.

This interview took place while Kieślowski was attending the Vancouver International Film Festival, at which Three Colors: Red *was voted "Most Popular Film." The festival also included a tribute to his work, including screenings of all of the* Decalogue.

Krzysztof Kieślowski sits in a sun-drenched room high above Vancouver's skyline, smoking cigarettes, composed, relaxed, and entirely certain that he will never make another movie.

At fifty-three, and at the very pinnacle of his filmmaking career that has included accolades and trophies from around the world for such films as *The Double Life of Véronique, Camera Buff, Decalogue,* and now his final trilogy, *Blue, White,* and *Red,* Kieślowski would seem to be slapping fate squarely in the face.

Directors work entire lifetimes to achieve the kind of success he has just recently grasped. Why, oh why, desert your muses now that they have shown you the way?

Perhaps because Kieślowski believes the pursuit is hollow. Perhaps the muses have led him astray. Perhaps the kind-faced man with long, bushy eyebrows sees nothing but a hall of mirrors: self-reflection everywhere, but nothing he can touch.

"I don't really see the point in talking about it," he says early on in the rare one-on-one interview during the Vancouver International Film Festival. "This is a very complex and yet very simple decision, but one that is finally very private."

Private, perhaps, but not hidden. Kieślowski's search for meaning is an integral part of every movie he has ever made—from *Decalogue*'s reinterpretation of the Ten Commandments to *Camera Buff*'s revision of personal autonomy. Yet nowhere in his twenty-five-year filmmaking career has his quest been more evident than the Tricolor trilogy—a re-evaluation of the ideals behind the French flag: liberty, equality, fraternity.

In *Blue* (liberty), Juliette Binoche plays a woman grieving the loss of her family

143

in a car crash. Kieślowski's question to the viewer is "can one fall in love again, and isn't love just a trap limiting our own freedom? What means more to us: freedom or love?"

In *White* (equality), Kieślowski takes us on a black humor–filled trip to his home country through the Chaplinesque tale of Karol Karol—a hairdresser who returns to Poland in a suitcase to make his fortune. The only problem is that the woman he loves still lives in France. He does bring the two together, but only through the bars of a prison cell. Again—love is a trap, even though it's the only thing that gives life meaning.

In *Red* (fraternity), Kieślowski pulls the stitches together. "I have the feeling that I am a part of something very important," the lead character Valentine says to a retired judge. But neither Valentine, nor the old judge who eavesdrops on his neighbor's phone conversations, has any idea as to what that meaning is. Yes, love is the meaning (as suggested even in the name of Valentine). Love can even save. But again, love remains intangible.

Sooner or later, it seems, the entire circle repeats itself—over and over and over. And that's where the pattern, and the resulting frustration, inherent in Kieślowski's work begins to take shape.

"I have made the same movie over and over and I still haven't found that level of meaning of which you are speaking. I'm still not satisfied. I haven't found what I am looking for.

"But I'm not complaining. The levels of meaning that I have resolved are present in the films—and I think they speak for themselves," Kieślowski says, pulling a hefty drag off his king-size smoke.

"The fact that I am leaving film has no particular meaning—except for me. I tell stories for a purpose. And if that purpose is anything, it is to tell people that there are other elements in life that we are often too busy to address. I'm saying one doesn't have to make movies to search for meaning; one simply has to live."

More precisely, to live and to love.

"Yes, love is what makes us meaningful and that's why I made these films—to say that. But love is a very complex thing. It has its black side and its very bright and beautiful side. But love is never obvious. It's often hidden deep inside us. That's essentially what the trilogy is about: the ways love is finally revealed."

And the fact that love is revealed at all—the fact that order seems to exist—some would suggest that would indicate a presence of a higher consciousness.

"You're asking me if God exists or not, but every person must find his or her own answer. Perhaps God sleeps for a long time. I think there is an example of an order that we try to achieve, but with great difficulty. I simply make movies and I tell stories, this has nothing to do with God. I am not creating the world. . . . I am creating a drop of water in which the people who surround me are reflected. These are two very different things."

But in the process, Kieślowski has apparently surrendered himself to an internal split: the tangible and the intangible; the real and the reflected with an unbridgeable gap in between.

"We will always yearn for what we do not have, and most of us have no idea what it is that we want."

But surely, there must be a way of finding peace in the moment and being satisfied with what we are, as we exist. What about integration?

"While I believe that is the key to happiness: to take pleasure in the things we have around us, I do not believe that is truly possible because we always want more."

Can't we forgive ourselves and accept what we are?

"I don't think forgiveness is honest. That's a religious sentiment that doesn't really hold true when you look at our society," Kieślowski says in an even-paced, staccato Polish.

"Kafka," Kieślowski begins, "understood that justice—and the resulting concept of forgiveness—is entirely without meaning. We always feel as though we are misjudged and misunderstood. People make mistakes that they cannot take back. They must live with these mistakes for the rest of their lives. . . . We see justice as this big building, this big promise, but we can never get in.

"America seems obsessed with this concrete notion of justice. Every time one turns on the television—there it is, some promise, some belief that people expect to be realized. None of that is important in the direct sense, what is important is our feeling of helplessness in the face of justice."

Kieślowski acknowledges it was these sentiments that shaped the character of the eavesdropping, reclusive judge in *Red*—a character that could be seen as Kieślowski's own celluloid reflection.

"This bitter man is me, but so is Karol Karol and so, for that matter is Valentine. I love all my characters equally."

Each character, then, is a piece in the big Kieślowski puzzle—and that puzzle is a reflection of your own struggle for meaning?

"Yes, of course."

But now that you are no longer interested in being a filmmaker, what happens to your struggle to find meaning?

"I have abandoned myself to the black hole. I am not afraid of what will happen. Life will continue and the search will also continue, but now it will take place in a private sphere instead of a public one, where I will be surrounded by the people whom I love, and the people who love me."

Colors of Life Interest Filmmaker

John Griffin / 1994

Material republished with the express permission of: *Montreal Gazette*, a division of Postmedia Network Inc., October 22, 1994. Reprinted by permission.

This interview was conducted in Montreal as Kieślowski made his way home from the Vancouver International Film Festival. Interestingly, we get a different sense of the reasons for his retirement than in the previous interview with Katherine Monk.

If he were the sort to acknowledge such things, Krzysztof Kieślowski would appreciate the coincidence.

The date for an interview with the esteemed, enigmatic Polish filmmaker had been established weeks in advance.

He would be stopping in town on his way home to Warsaw after a tribute to his work at the Vancouver Film Festival.

He had agreed to talk about his career and—in the most indirect of ways for so anti-commercial an artist—to thrum lightly on the drum for the local release of his acclaimed new film *Trois Couleurs: Rouge*, a film he, at age fifty-four, says will be his last.

On the day of the great event with the master, it transpires a mid-morning press screening has also been independently arranged for Quentin Tarantino's *Pulp Fiction*.

Film buffs will remember that earlier this year, Tarantino's joyously lurid movie about the movies had rudely elbowed Kieślowski's elegant and vastly favored *Rouge* aside to grab the top prize at Cannes.

The jury decision had shocked the faithful at the French seaside town, who responded in predictable Gallic fashion by booing lustily.

Now, our city's critics were trooping out of Tarantino's gangster extravaganza and briskly across town for *sotto voce* audiences with the very man whose movie had been tripped at the post.

Sweetly ironic, yes? A bit of fate to be savored by the man who has fashioned a brilliant career on matters of synchronistic happenstance and old-fashioned fate.

Kieślowski shrugs his shoulders and chuckles, well, enigmatically.

It is an appropriate Kieślowski response, and one he offers often. A "things happen" kind of response, and one that needs no explanation from the director's translator, factotum, and friend Stan Latek.

Kieślowski has no opinion about *Pulp Fiction*, its relative merits *vis à vis Rouge*, or its role in the American pop culture that is eroding his old-guard European values.

"I haven't seen this film," he says simply, and leaves the rest of that meaning hanging in the air.

As for the competitive nature of film festivals like Cannes, the master observes "they're like a circus."

"I can't decide whether I'm in the ring or watching it from the stands. I don't like it, but what can you do?"

Pulp Fiction is one of the few subjects Kieślowski hasn't considered in a twenty-nine-year career that has minutely examined modern morality.

It is a chequered career—one that began with documentaries, included a 1981 feature called *Blind Chance* that was banned in communist Poland for five years, and hit high gear with such applauded work as *Decalogue*, the ten-hour 1988 TV project based on the Ten Commandments—and two expanded *Decalogue* episodes, *A Short Film about Killing*, and *A Short Film about Love*.

More recently, Kieślowski has ascended toward the throne of European cinema with the 1991 international hit *La Double Vie de Véronique*, and the recently completed *Trois Couleurs* trilogy, *Bleu*, *Blanc*, and *Rouge*—based on the French republican cornerstones of liberty, equality, and fraternity.

His has been a prodigious, ferocious output—Latek will argue it's seventeen films in five years, though Kieślowski claims those numbers are inflated.

Regardless, the filmmaker has created more work of a higher standard in a shorter period of time than anyone else in feature film.

When he says he's tired, it's understandable.

When he says he wants to return to his single-storey country home in Poland and watch a smaller world go round, that's understandable, too.

But when he says he will quit making films—that *Rouge* is his last statement—it doesn't sit at all well with his many fans (and probably not too comfortably with those who've depended on him for a living all these years, either).

Kieślowski is pulling the plug because he can. "Everyone envies me. I'm in a luxury situation. I don't have to plan any more."

Under cross-examination, he will allow it's good to be quitting the scene at the top of his game.

"It's the very best moment to leave. Otherwise someone will pull the plug for me.

"I will go to the countryside. Afterwards, I may go someplace else. I want to live as simply as possible. That is my desire.

"People may think about me for some time. Then they will forget."

But he's also plainly unhappy with the state of the world, though he admits, "I expect too much."

The *Trois Couleurs* series has addressed the question of a unified Europe, a situation he fears will dilute the cultures of the individual member states.

He worries about technology: all-pervasive.

The current generation: too soft.

He worries about what will happen to those growing up with the current radical change in the old communist bloc.

He rails softly against the marketplace—where films are made solely for bottom-line considerations and culture is reduced to terms of black and white.

In this condemnation he does not point the finger exclusively at the United States.

"Young Europeans want to see things in simple terms now. They do not want colors in shades that are not black and white."

These other shades, of course, are the colors of Kieślowski's creations.

Yes, my films are enigmatic, he admits. But so is life.

Yes, fate plays a part. There is a greater pattern to existence, he allows.

"But in this pattern we can move freely. We're not only moved by fate, or coincidence, but by our own will."

Finally, though, Kieślowski says: "The subject of my films is love. The lack of love. The need for love. That's the only subject for me."

And that may ultimately explain his decision to quit now. There's just not enough love going around.

Auteur of His Own Destruction

Simon Hattenstone / 1994

From the *Guardian*, November 8, 1994. Copyright Guardian News & Media Ltd 1994. Reprinted by permission.

Once again in this interview, the focus is on Kieślowski's retirement, though Hattenstone frames a discussion of that decision in relation to Kieślowski's whole life and filmmaking career.

Krzysztof Kieślowski is in top form, full of beans, raring to go. He sits in a pool of cigarette smoke, inhales with relish, and scrubs out his past. "It's enough. It's with pleasure that I'm putting filmmaking aside. I never enjoyed making films. I didn't like the whole film world, an invented, unreal world whose values are completely different to those I'm used to. Basic values. It's not an honorable profession."

What is an honorable profession? "Making shoes, that's honorable. Something which is useful." So he's going back to Poland to make shoes? "No, unfortunately, I don't know how to. I am trained as a filmmaker. There is nothing else I can do."

After the *Decalogue*, *The Double Life of Véronique* and the *Blue, White*, and *Red* trilogy, all written with Krzystztof Piesiewicz, at fifty-two he is widely regarded as Europe's top filmmaker. Has he at least enjoyed the critical acclaim? "It's not interesting to achieve; the ways of achievement are interesting." Ah, he's quitting because he has achieved so much that making films is no longer a challenge? "No, I haven't achieved in films and I never will, and therefore I think you have to find the right moment and back away." After a few minutes, I begin to feel I'm interviewing Beckett's Vladimir, or a Rubik's Cube.

He says life is made up of contradictions, and a good film—he cites Fellini's *La Strada*—manages to describe the world as it is while also creating its own world. By that measure, he has made some truly wonderful films. His greatest, for me, is the *Decalogue*, a series of ten films loosely and agnostically based on the Ten Commandments. Writhing in pessimism and humanism, they camouflage their big themes—chance and fate, right and wrong, connecting and not connecting, belonging and not belonging—in little, elliptical stories that more than anything

149

convey the unknowability of life. An envelope remains sealed and life turns one way. If it had been opened . . .

The philosopher Walter Benjamin once demonstrated the power of story-telling stripped of psychology. Kieślowski's films—especially up to and including the *Decalogue*—illustrate this perfectly. Whereas most Hollywood movies make explicit the motivation behind every action, he simply allows things to happen. In his film *No End*, a woman stares across a bar at a young man whose hands remind her of her recently dead husband. He walks over, buys her a drink, and offers her money for sex. She is not a prostitute—has probably never even considered it—but she accepts. The scene takes seconds, with barely a word and no explanation. Kieślowski not only leaves us to interpret the films, he leaves us to complete them. As Stanley Kubrick says in his foreword to the screenplay of the *Decalogue*: "You never see the ideas coming and don't realize until much later how profoundly they have reached your heart."

After spending most of the last few years filming in France and Switzerland, Kieślowski is now back in Poland with his family, intent on re-establishing the basic values. Is it an easier country to live in nowadays? "No, things have changed for the worse. That's why former Eastern Bloc countries are electing communists again. We are missing them and longing for the times we cursed before." Surely Kieślowski, who spent so many years as an underground cultural activist making politically unacceptable documentaries about what life was really like for Poland's Mr. and Mrs. Normal, is not wishing himself back into the not-so-old days. "Quite the contrary. I hated the communists and still hate them. But I do long for various friendships and ties that used to exist and don't anymore. The camaraderie of old times has gone."

Although he speaks good English, he prefers to use an interpreter. His sentences quietly bleed into each other and are almost over before they have begun. Sometimes it is hard to work out whether he has spoken or just taken another drag of cigarette. When his extraordinary cross-hatched eyebrows—they should, by rights, carry Ordnance Survey coordinates—dance up and down his forehead it generally means he is talking.

In *White*, Kieślowski caricatured the black-market, barrow-boy capitalism of the new Poland where anything from death to respect to love could be bought. It sounds hideous and extreme, but is it so different from England or America? Is it not the Utopian free market? His eyebrows start dancing. "In England you still think about tomorrow whereas in Poland we just think about today or this evening." In a recent television documentary, he said that people don't want a better common future, they just want a little more for themselves; people don't want equality, they want to be a little more equal than their neighbors. It sounded as if he approved. "No, it's extremely egoistic, very short term. Poland has been through so much in the past, and it has ruined us."

Kieślowski was brought up in a tiny isolated town "where politics didn't penetrate." His mother was a clerk, his father permanently sick with TB, the biggest local event was a neighbor painting his house, and all he knew was the rush of freedom. "There was no sense of being repressed. If I wanted to play football, I played football. If I wanted to go looking for mushrooms, I went looking for mushrooms."

Despite his own contented childhood, the children of his films have a heaviness, a precocious sadness; they may not be able to articulate the worries around them, but they sense them even more acutely than the adults. Why? "Because children do know more than adults; when they grow up they forget. Children know more because they think with their instinct, not their reason. They carry the burden of what awaits them."

He says that ambition rather than a love of cinema led him to films. And while in the early days the state may not have given him moral support at least it gave financial support. "You couldn't make the films you wanted to, of course. We had to look for substitutes. It was a challenge to create something that would not be understood by the censors but would be understood by the people. It was quite straightforward because we all had the same attitude to the political system, the same way of thinking."

Necessity forced him into the implicit and elliptical. After the early documentaries he turned away from politics, saying he wasn't interested. And it is true that most of his films are not political in the polemical sense. But the suffocating bureaucracy, the silent scream, the bilious damp of everyday life have never better been portrayed than in *No End* or the *Decalogue*.

Kieślowski has no time for formal religion, but there has always been a spiritual, metaphysical quality to his work. In the *Decalogue* it was brilliantly rooted in naturalism: a woman demands of a doctor if her husband will live or die—although he is, in effect, asked to play God, the allegory is not forced upon us, it is merely there if we wish to see it. In the more recent films, most of them made outside Poland, the symbolism has become slightly contrived and clumsy (the telephone voyeur of *Red* also manipulates, also plays God, but his symbolic presence crushes his real self).

Kieślowski's films have always been complex and stylish, but whereas they once appeared simple and artless, the cleverness now envelops us. In *A Short Story about Killing* [sic], he used a filter to paint Poland the color of bronchial phlegm. Of course it was not naturalistic, but somehow it appeared to be, it felt right. The Trilogy has also been shot through filters, but now it is merely a clever cinematic game; Peter Greenaway meets French art-house. At its worst, with de-signer locations married to Irene Jacob's perfect face, *Red* looks like a Volkswagen commercial for the existential professional woman.

If I am being harsh on the later films, it is only disappointment. In fact, they have thoroughly divided critics. Rather than being marred by this self-conscious artistry, many have argued that it is only in The Trilogy he has perfected his art.

Does Kieślowski see a difference between the Polish and French work? "No, I don't think so. Of course the conditions of production are better with more money and of course the world in France is much prettier, more colorful than Poland. But the people are the same—equally hopeless, they can't cope with life and they suffer in love the same way. They die, they get born."

There he goes again, like a downbeat Beckett. Are people really born astride the grave? "Yes, of course we are. I don't need to be Samuel Beckett to think that one up." He breaks out into one of his lovely, shy smiles, before returning to monotone moroseness.

He says in retirement he would most like to find peace, with the people he loves, but that again this is a contradiction. Does he think he will be happy? "No, I doubt it." Has he ever been happy making films? "No, but I've got everything that should make me happy. From time to time one ought to look objectively at life. When you achieve something, you don't actually realize you've achieved anything. It's only afterwards when you've lost it that you realize you've lost it." Is that why he is quitting? To realize his achievement? "Possibly. Maybe that is it."

Past, Present . . . Future?

Kristine McKenna / 1995

Kristine McKenna had interviewed Kieślowski, along with Irène Jacob, in 1991 when he first became widely known in the United States because of the release there of The Double Life of Véronique. *This, her second interview, was reprinted in a collection of her interviews* Book of Changes, *in 2001, with a different opening, a few small omissions, and changes of punctuation. This is the original* LA Times *version.*

With the success of Polish director Krzysztof Kieślowski's *Red*, American movie-goers have been introduced to a filmmaker long acknowledged throughout Europe as one of the late twentieth century's great geniuses of cinema. The third segment in a trilogy examining the principles represented by the colors of the French flag (liberty, equality, and fraternity), *Red*, which was preceded last year by the release of *Blue* and *White*, is quintessential Kieślowski.

Depicting life as a series of moral conflicts capable of producing moments of transcendence, his films couch complex philosophical questions in simple fables set among the European middle class. His greatest work, and the one he'll no doubt be remembered for, is the *Decalogue*, a dauntingly ambitious ten-film cycle exploring the Ten Commandments and how they can be seen operating today in the lives of tenants of a Warsaw apartment complex.

The *Decalogue* premiered on Polish television in 1988 but is embroiled in a legal fight that prevents its commercial release in the United States. The few who manage to see it don't forget it. "Filmmaking simply doesn't get any better than this," said *Times* film critic Kenneth Turan after attending a screening held last year as part of the American Film Institute Film Festival. Fans of this magnificent work were, needless to say, saddened by Kieślowski's vow that *Red* will be his final film.

The director—subject of a recently published autobiography, *Kieślowski on Kieślowski*, written with Danusia Stok—was born in Warsaw in 1941 and grew up amid the rubble of World War II under Poland's oppressive post-Stalinist regime.

After an aborted career as a firefighter, he enrolled at the Łódź Film School and graduated with a degree in 1969, the same year he married his wife, Marysia [Maria] Kieślowska, with whom he has a daughter.

After devoting the next seven years to documentaries chronicling Polish life, he released his debut feature, *The Scar*, in 1976, then completed three more features before embarking on the *Decalogue* in 1984.

Briefly in Los Angeles to attend the ceremony for the LA Film Critics Awards, which honored *Red* as this past year's best foreign film, Kieślowski greets a visitor in his Hollywood hotel room with the apologetic confession "I'm sorry—I'm a smoker," as he proceeds to light up. "The last of the Mohicans," one jokes in response, to which Kieślowski replies: "But the last will be the first—that's from the Bible. I did the *Decalogue*, you know." Following are Kieślowski's thoughts on God, guilt, politics, and living in the real world.

Kristine McKenna: Did you read the Bible in preparing to make the *Decalogue*?
Krzysztof Kieślowski: Naturally, I read it, but I'd read it prior to that — I was raised in a Catholic country.

KM: Did Catholicism mean anything to you?
KK: Yes, it did—as for whether it still does, all I'll say is that I still live in a Catholic country. During the years of communism in Poland, many people turned to the church as an antidote to communism, and the church became identified with the struggle for freedom. My solution when martial law came to Poland in 1981, however, was to sleep. I slept for almost an entire year. It was the only way to cope.

KM: Do you believe in God?
KK: Something exists over there. Is that something benevolent, malevolent, or indifferent? Let's just say something's been asleep for a long time, and maybe one day it will wake up.

KM: Other than the Catholic Church, what played a role in shaping your sense of morality?
KK: I wouldn't say Catholicism was important to me in that regard. It had more to do with the fact that early on I became independent in my thinking. My parents weren't intellectuals—my father was an engineer and my mother was a clerk—so I attribute my ability to take a broader view of life to luck, and to the fact that I worked hard for this. Of course, life is simpler when one has a narrow focus but it's not as interesting, and one of the main reasons we're here is to live interesting lives. It takes courage to be curious about life, but I think people are courageous.

KM: In your book, you express the belief that people are basically good; on what evidence do you base this belief?

KK: I draw this conclusion because I don't meet bad people. Yes, people behave selfishly, with cowardice and stupidity, but they do so because they find themselves in situations where they have no other option. They create traps for themselves and there's no escape. People don't want to be dishonest—life forces them into it.

KM: That suggests you don't believe there are absolutes of good and evil, that those things are always relative and in a state of flux. Is that your belief?

KK: No, I don't believe in relativism. There are absolutes of good and evil.

KM: Is the human race evolving over the centuries?

KK: In the technological realm, yes, but as to whether man has a more refined sense of morality today than he had two centuries ago, obviously not. If you look at the Greeks, you see the same questions and problems we struggle with today, and no philosopher or artist has been able to answer these questions. These questions are only answered by religion, but the answers religion offers are merely theoretical. So the questions remain unanswered.

KM: Who's your favorite philosopher?

KK: At the moment I'm reading Kierkegaard and I find him exciting and provocative, but I can't say he's my favorite. I much prefer Kant.

(Nineteenth-century Danish philosopher Søren Kierkegaard is considered one of the founders of Existentialism and believed that religious faith is irrational. Immanuel Kant, an eighteenth-century German philosopher who concerned himself with ethics, aesthetics, and the nature and limits of human knowledge, believed it was man's duty to live morally.)

KM: Have you ever had a religious experience?

KK: Yes, the first time I went to confession. The thing that was transcendent about it was the feeling of being relieved of guilt. Unfortunately, it never worked for me that way again, so now dealing with guilt is difficult.

KM: Is everyone afflicted with guilt?

KK: Some people aren't afflicted with *feelings* of guilt, but we are all guilty.

KM: You once said, "Although justice and equality sound exciting, it's simply not possible, because I've never met anybody who wanted to be equal. Everybody wants to be a little *more* equal in everything—to have a better car, more money, a slightly better house." One could make the case that not everyone is driven by greed and egotistical needs.

KK: It's a proven fact that it's human nature to want to be better than others, and that eliminates the possibility of equality—it's pure logic. You may not want to be better than I am, but I imagine you do want to be better than your colleagues. And there's another aspect to this that's even more significant: You want to be better than *you* are.

KM: Does romantic love bring out the best or the worst in people?

KK: Love always has two faces: the horrible and the beautiful. The beautiful face creates an impulse to share something profound, while the horrible face creates jealousy, which can degenerate into hatred. This is the same all over the world— we're all neurotic about love because it's a very egotistical experience.

KM: What are you incapable of being sensible about?

KK: Politics. Yes, I left Poland because of the political situation there and moved to Paris, but I returned, and that decision could be described as less than sensible. Why did I return? Because it's my country. Ideally, we'd all feel ourselves citizens of the world, but life doesn't work that way. I came to understand this not long ago one evening in Paris. I was standing on a balcony and two people were quarreling in the street below. A woman was crying, a man was hitting a boy, and though I understood the words, I couldn't understand what it was about. I realized that were I watching a similar scene take place in Poland, I would've understood, and that's when I knew I should live in Poland.

KM: Ideally, how should films function in the culture? What should they do?

KK: Film is often just business—I understand that, and it's not something I concern myself with. But if film aspires to be part of culture, it should do the things great literature, music, and art do: elevate the spirit, help us understand ourselves and the life around us, and give people the feeling they are not alone. Loneliness is one of the central problems culture must address.

KM: Does film shape the culture or simply reflect it as it already exists?

KK: It does both, but it should shape—the question, of course, is whether it shapes it positively or negatively. Films like *La Strada* and *Citizen Kane* were positive forces because they gave a feeling of community, but there are many other films that shape destructively.

KM: Do movies create false expectations of life?

KK: No. Movies photograph the false expectations.

KM: What aspect of filmmaking was the most enjoyable for you?

KK: Although I love actors and actresses, there was only one part of filmmaking I liked, and that was editing. The stress of shooting is over and I find myself in a room with all this film that holds countless possibilities. The aspects of filmmaking that were most unpleasant were location scouting and promotion, although doing promotion can be interesting in that in speaking to critics and journalists, I learn interpretations of my films that had never occurred to me. Film has a life of its own and can take on meanings the director didn't consciously put there, and this is a very magical and wonderful thing. The parts of promotion I don't like are the festivals, TV lights, and crowds of people.

KM: Have your feelings changed about your decision to no longer make films?

KK: No. This isn't to suggest I feel I "completed" my work as a filmmaker—such a thing is impossible. Rather, I choose not to make movies because I want to live.

One lives in a fictional world when making movies, and I have nothing against this because it's very beautiful to live in fiction. When you make movies, everything is fiction—the script, the shooting; it's all illusory, and it fills your life to the point that you start to take fiction for real life. I was having a hard time seeing the difference between fiction and reality, and that's why I decided to stop. I think it's important to understand that difference because maybe real life is more important than the fictive life we create.

KM: Having put film behind you, what's a typical day like for you?

KK: I don't have a typical day, but if I were at my country house, which is where I most like to be, I wake in the morning and there is snow on the ground, so I turn on the snow-clearing machine so I can move my car. (Kieślowski's country home, which he built himself, is in northeast Poland.) Then I warm up the soup my wife prepared and left in the fridge, do a bit of writing, then I go to bed. That may sound boring measured against the turbulent life of a filmmaker, but I yearn to be bored.

KM: How did you feel about the academy's decision not to allow *Red* to compete in this year's Oscar race? (Submitted as a Swiss film, *Red* was disqualified from competition on the grounds that too few of the people in creative control of the film were of Swiss descent.)

KK: I found it confusing. Last year *Blue* wasn't allowed to compete on the basis of language—the question of creative control wasn't an issue last year. This year they won't allow *Red* to compete on the basis of creative control, but language isn't an issue. I don't know if *Red* deserves to win an Oscar, or even deserves to be nominated, but I do think it deserves to be treated with equality, and the rules seem peculiarly flexible.

KM: You've commented that one of the questions you hoped to raise with your recent trilogy was: Exactly what is freedom for the individual? Do you have an answer to that question?

KK: Freedom as an abstract idea is a trap because it directs you toward solitude, and solitude and loneliness is hell. The acceptance of one's own limits is a kind of freedom, because if we can accept ourselves as we really are with all our faults, it helps us accept life with all its difficulties. This kind of acceptance is very difficult to achieve, of course.

KM: What's the most one can hope for in life?

KK: I can only speak for myself, but what I hope for is peace. This is something we all experience in fleeting moments, but ultimately it's not achievable. It wouldn't be interesting to achieve it, though, because it's the pursuit of it that has meaning.

The Same Questions

Tadeusz Sobolewski / 1995

From *Film*, May 1995, 68–69. Reprinted by permission.

The renowned film critic conducted this interview for the "People" section of this popular but now defunct film magazine in Poland.

Tadeusz Sobolewski: You have kept your promise: you are not making films. But how do you live? Judging by today's schedule (plenty of meetings, an interview for Canal Plus), you are not less busy than a year ago.

Krzysztof Kieślowski: It's the leftovers. Normally, I am not so very busy and I hope that I will very soon not be. How do I live? I live a life. I walk on the ground. Does anything ensue from that? Not much, but I didn't associate big hopes with my decision. I simply don't have to shower to go to a shoot; I take a shower to live the day. Today it seems more worthy. Whether it's more interesting, I don't know.

TS: Yet your older films are living a second life. Especially the documentaries. There are retrospectives in Montreal, Copenhagen, even in Warsaw's Iluzjon.[1] A lot of people are impressed with *Talking Heads*, a short, forgotten film from 1980, which is important in your filmography.

KK: I liked it.

TS: You ask random people, from a one-year-old child to an old-lady centenarian, two questions: who are you? And what do you want? Your contemporary, born in 1941, answers this way: "It appears to me that I have everything that a normal, average person should have. Maybe it is all quite good, but something is missing. I don't know what I would like to change, but I would like for things to be different." Is that also your answer? How would you answer that question today?

KK: I don't know. I have received more from life than I expected and probably more than I am worth; however, I could not say that I have everything. The second question—what do I want?—I'd also maybe answer differently. I know exactly what I want. Something unattainable that's expressed in the title of one of the first feature fiction films I made: calmness.[2]

TS: *Talking Heads* has a paradoxical meaning: in a way there is no hope; at the same time one cannot live without hope. It is also a film about there being no answer to the most important questions, although everybody searches for that answer.

KK: When you ask what is two times two, and it turns out it's four, it's perhaps interesting as a fact, but the truly exciting questions are those to which there are no answers. There are a few, maybe a dozen or so, questions like that and they accompany us from childhood to death.

TS: Don't you have the impression that many questions by which we lived, by which Polish cinema lived, have simply petered away?

KK: Krzysztof Zanussi has recently written an article about questions disappearing from contemporary culture. I disagree. People are not ceasing to ask questions. Besides, Zanussi, with whom I've spoken after that article was published, was himself asking whether it is the case that people, when they watch the comic-strip cinema, are looking for answers to the same questions we were looking for in Dostoyevsky or Proust?

TS: *Forrest Gump*, this year's big hit, is an example of the philosophy of popular cinema. "Life is like a box of chocolates, you never know what you're going to get," says Forrest to his Mum. That's a parody of philosophy. In Zemeckis all the questions are silenced. The viewer feels a different type of satisfaction: just like bumpkin Forrest, we don't understand life, but we also don't have to understand it. Maybe I'm dumb, but I'm certainly worthy!

KK: [That statement] already contains a question: why do I live? Who am I? I haven't seen *Forrest Gump*, but I think it's a pretty clever film that answers some human need.

TS: Are you in touch with the young?

KK: I am trying to be as much as possible. At Łódź [Film] School, [among] other places. If I commit my time to one thing, that would be it.

TS: Don't you feel distanced from them?

KK: I have never felt that.

TS: But they belong to a different era, they live really in a different country than the one in which we lived in our youth. They don't feel the wall of the [political] system, in the shadow of which we grew up.

KK: There is always some wall. In those times, because of political and censorship considerations, we used to stop in front of that wall, trying to bypass it. They have a chance to jump over it.

TS: We recently watched new films by Ken Loach, the director to whom you are often compared, to whom you would be prepared to—as you've written—"serve coffee on the shoot." He hasn't changed. He keeps making films critical of English reality, he bangs his head against the wall, he practices some sort of "Czech cinema," or "Cinema of Moral Concern." What do you say to that?

KK: I look with admiration at someone who has enough energy to describe the world that's dear to him, who loves people struggling in life, not having enough money, people with a sense of impermanence, who lose meaning under the pressure of everyday problems, so they can suddenly find it again, as happens in Loach, following some dramatic event. If one applied stringent moral criteria, one could say that he hasn't betrayed the simple man, as I have, for instance.

TS: You have that feeling?

KK: I don't. But they sometimes accuse me of making French films, too aestheticized, too beautiful, invented. In my opinion they are neither particularly French, nor invented; however, if they make this accusation, there must be something to it.

TS: Those films contain "bothersome questions," but they are packaged very elegantly.

KK: What you refer to as the elegance of form is only a fulfillment of dramaturgic rules.

TS: Let me rephrase it: the form of these films suggests something different to what they contain; it makes you think of an easier cinema that gives symbolic answers. In the meantime, the viewer is left with the huge unknown. It seems to me that your films express a longing for a world that would make sense as a whole, but this "whole cannot put itself together," in Tadeusz Różewicz's words.[3] I am intentionally bringing up the name of the poet who announced "the death of poetry" because I think that you have something in common. You have also found yourself in the situation of an artist who "subsided into silence," which doesn't imply—as can be seen in [the case of] Różewicz—an absence of creativity. Besides an artist's silence can also be meaningful.

KK: Różewicz is close to me, in drama and in poetry. He is close in his way of thinking, his rationalism and pessimism. But I was not announcing "the death of the cinema." The reasons for my decisions are very mundane. I am not expressing myself at that level of generalization. Yes, from time to time, I do repeat provocatively in interviews that documentary film, the genre, which I liked a lot, has died. It has been replaced by television forms: reportage, talk-shows.

TS: *89mm from Europe* by Marcel Łoziński, a film nominated for an Oscar [in 1993], is a classical documentary of the type that was made in the seventies.
KK: Marcel Łoziński belongs to those few dinosaurs who in a beautiful way cultivate the genre that doesn't exist anymore, thus contradicting my thesis. And thank God. In fact, it's Łoziński who accuses me of having "betrayed" the coarse, simple world for cellophane tinsel. And I value the censure of people whom I trust.

TS: On the other hand, the same Łoziński in his newest film *Anything May Happen* poses questions about the meaning of life: using a child character, he ponders on the origin of hope in people, how faith emerges. In one word, that social activist, ironist, investigator of manipulation, as if following your trail, enters the field of philosophy, religion. It would be interesting to expand on this comparison of two nominated Polish directors, but we have no room [for that]. So I will only ask about your last visit to the States, for the occasion of the Oscars.
KK: I don't like America, so I try to spend as little [time] there [as possible].

TS: But American critics like your films.
KK: But I am not saying that I don't like Americans. I don't like America, just like I don't like Russia, even though I like Russians.

TS: What in America annoys you most?
KK: During the Oscar ceremony, I noticed people with a tag "seat filler." When somebody gets up from their seat to go to the bathroom, or for a cigarette, like me for instance, immediately a "seat filler" appears and sits where I was sitting a moment ago, so on television it looks like all the seats are taken. Observing that, I thought about those crowds we constantly watch on television screens, when they protest for this or that. How many among them are "seat fillers," and how many are really advocating something; are they for or against abortion, for or against war? For a brief moment there, in America, I saw the ubiquity of manipulation and I asked myself the question: where is the truth?

TS: And what happens with those independent ones who don't belong to the world of "seat fillers" and artificial applause—aren't they, on the other hand, packed away in some safe drawer? We watch with admiration Loach's films, but doesn't he sit in a cage with the tag "unyielding Ken Loach"? His protest doesn't mean the same thing as it did in the sixties and seventies, does it?

KK: Then, he belonged to a certain movement. Today, he is a rogue. Most likely he is more right than before. Maybe that's why he is a rogue. But a normal world still exists, besides that of "seat fillers." Everywhere you can meet people who refuse to be manipulated.

Notes

1. *Iluzjon* is associated with the Museum of Film Art in Warsaw.

2. Krzysztof Kieślowski refers here to his film *The Calm* as well as his quest for the big calm, an ultimate peace of mind.

3. Tadeusz Różewicz (b. 1918) is a poet, writer, and playwright in the highest tradition of the theatre of the absurd.

The Inner Life Is the Only Thing That Interests Me

Paul Coates / 1995

From *Lucid Dreams: The Films of Krzysztof Kieślowski*, ed. Paul Coates (Trowbridge: Flicks Books, 1999). Reprinted by permission.

This interview was conducted in Warsaw, in October 1995, but was not published until 1999. English translation is by Paul Coates.

Paul Coates: I would like to begin with a question that concerns your position in the cinematic tradition. You were once described as continuing the line of Munk in Polish cinema. Do you consider this an appropriate, or the best, way of describing your work, or are there other possible models you would prefer?

Krzysztof Kieślowski: I do not engage in classifications of this kind, particularly not theoretical classifications, for an objective view is impossible. Everyone who does so has a more objective view than I do, and regardless of whether he does so badly or well, from his own point of view he is right. If there is a tradition that could be subdivided, in the most crass and idiotic manner, into, let us say, the romantic tradition of Wajda and the more rational one of Munk—

PC: As has been done traditionally . . .

KK: . . . then I suppose that obviously I stand more in the rational than the romantic one. But I don't think that my films are devoid of romanticism, perhaps not in the sense that is traditional in Polish Romanticism, which is more historical and more closely linked to social movements. My own romanticism is probably more human and personal, more concerned with the fate of the individual, but I think there is a considerable amount of it in these films. So I don't think one can clearly say "I am closest to this one." At least I can't personally.

PC: Moving on to a different context, that of world and auteur cinema. There is a scene in *Three Colors: White* in which a poster for *Le Mépris* [*Contempt*, 1963] is shown next to Dominique's window, recalling the practices of the Nouvelle Vague of which *Contempt* itself was an expression—the use of posters to pay homage or signal thematic links. Does this mean that you situate yourself in a Nouvelle Vague tradition, and perhaps even render homage to Godard, a director who is not much liked in Poland?

KK: The answer to that happens to be very simple. I very much like and value Godard's early films and would gladly pay them some kind of homage. Not the later ones, for they are alien to me and I think that unfortunately they are to the public as well. And it isn't a question of whether or not he's liked in Poland—I think he's hardly known. Very few of his films have been screened in Poland, which is the main reason for saying he's little known. Of course, I know the early films and would gladly pay homage to them. The poster from *Contempt* found its way there completely accidentally. I had absolutely no intention of putting up a poster from Godard or *Contempt* or anything that would make any kind of allusion. I wanted to put up a contemporary poster with an actress considered beautiful and sexy— someone like Kim Basinger—and it was a matter of complete indifference to me who it was. But that turned out to be tremendously expensive. So the producer suggested putting up one of his own posters, and since he'd distributed *Contempt* it didn't cost a thing. So we used that. The reasons were purely financial and had nothing to do with homage or love, and absolutely nothing to do with any distaste for anything either.

PC: Would you consider that accidental solution perhaps a better one?

KK: No, the solution was a worse one, only cheaper. It wasn't a matter of principle, and I gladly oblige the producer where non-essentials are concerned and the result will be that the film is cheaper.

PC: When discussing *Byłem żołnierzem* [*I Was a Soldier*, 1970]—which is the first of your documentaries I saw and, to my mind, a shattering film—you said among other things that what interested you most were the soldiers' dreams. Do you see dreams as a leitmotif of your films—in the sense of a utopia, a window onto something else?

KK: Obviously that has been of interest to me all along. It's less a question of dreams as such than of dreams as one expression of people's inner lives. Dreams are the classic expression of inner life: they belong to a single person and, as you well know, a dream is one of the few things that cannot be narrated. Not even the greatest literature has done them justice—not to mention the cinema, which has never done so.

PC: Not even Surrealism?

KK: Not even Surrealism has done dreams justice—no one has. Not even literature, which is far less literal, less real, and allows a far greater margin of interpretive freedom. So they are typical of something one person is unable to share with another. It often happens that we tell someone a dream, or someone tells us one, out of a desire to share our experience. At the same time, dreams are extraordinary because they cannot be shared, for the feeling of helplessness or fear or happiness within the dream only concerns ourselves and cannot be shared in any way. There is no known way of sharing it with anyone. It is a classic element of inner life. And since the inner life—unlike public life—is the only thing that interests me, dreams obviously continue to do so, and you are doubtless right to say that dreams are reflected in various ways in many, many of the films.

PC: You once remarked in an interview that you prefer not to spell things out in full, and prefer to leave the viewer the option of taking something away from the cinema, so the film is not expended when the lights come up. Does that have any connection with your recent tendency to make films in cycles, and do you now only want to make films in cycles?

KK: No, I think I have long believed that the viewer can become a partner. From the very outset it always seemed to me—and I once said as much to a Polish essay [sic] and am reproached for it to this day—that I make films for myself. I meant that I make films for people like me, people who are open to sitting down and having a chat, reflecting together, sharing. In other words, I think that, if I share the film with the viewer, the viewer will share its reception with me—which means that there is a certain balance and justice about the matter. I tell him a story and expect him not only to hear it out, but also to enter into some kind of a relationship with it. And, in order for him to be able to do so, the story I tell him must leave him a certain amount of space and freedom to interpret or take it—or certain parts of it—one way or another. I've always thought this and still do today. It has nothing to do with the cycles, which were simply practical. There came a point at which I found it interesting and practical for production reasons. And obviously it is probably linked to a biological feature or trait of mine, which is that I like and want to do a lot and do it quickly in order to have peace and quiet afterwards. But, although I imagine I'll have peace and quiet afterwards, of course I never do, for there is something else that needs to be done. For instance, when making the *Decalogue* (1988), I thought: I'll make ten films and then I'll have peace and quiet and won't have to do anything for five, six, or seven years. Meanwhile, it obviously isn't like that at all. There is certainly a kind of psychic need within me to do as much as possible.

PC: The issue of "pessimism" has often been raised in connection with your films.

You remarked once, *à propos* the ending of *Three Colors: Red* (1994), that the fact that you had learned how to make a film with an optimistic ending did not mean you had become an optimist. Would you accept Gramsci's famous formula of optimism of the will, pessimism of the intellect?

KK: I agree completely with Gramsci. There definitely is something of the sort. One could enlarge upon it and speak not only of pessimism of the intellect, but also regarding the sphere for which feelings are responsible, the domain of sensibility. I would be pessimistic with regard to that too. But I agree completely where optimism of the will is concerned.

PC: The motif of cold has appeared from time to time in your films in connection with art—for instance, in *Camera Buff* (1979), Irenka accuses Filip of having become cold, and in *The Double Life of Véronique* (1991), Alexandre betrays Véronique by using her life as material. The theme also appears in other great artists of this century—Thomas Mann, for instance, or Bergman. Various critiques of your own work, particularly towards the end of the 1980s, even speak of vivisection. Do you think that such a connection necessarily exists? And is that the reason why you do not accept the word "artist" as a description of yourself?

KK: I do not consider myself to be an artist at all. As you know, I have never said I was an artist, since I think that word has to be reserved for certain special people and events of which—one has to admit—there have been fewer and fewer in recent decades. There are fewer and fewer people worthy of the name. That is also why I do not use the word of myself.

PC: But neither did Bergman—he described himself as an artisan working on a cathedral.

KK: I use the word "artisan" too. I've always viewed film as artisanal, and every film as something produced in a single edition. That is a feature both of artworks and artisanal work. There is only one Notre Dame Cathedral, but every piece of artisanal work is unique too, for that is what underlies the craftsman's feel for it as he produces it. It requires a certain feel for it, for giving something of oneself. An artisan is not just someone who works with his hands but someone who imparts to the work he is producing something of his own heart or intellect, as Gramsci would have it. It has nothing to do with coldness. Coldness or cynicism . . .

PC: They're not the same thing—

KK: They're not the same at all, but coldness, cynicism, distance—all these things have a common identity somewhere. And this is very characteristic of our era. I have the impression that we are increasingly cold and cynical towards one another and create ever-greater distances. I even have the impression that I can remember a time when it was warmer, and that over the fifty years of my life I have been watching it grow colder around each and every one of us. We treat others more coolly and they do the same to us. I think this is a trend we are witnessing and that everything in the world changes at some point. It can easily be observed and so it obviously finds its way into the films I have made, for I have tried to depict the times in which we live.

PC: I would like to revert to the documentaries and gradually work through various films from your career. Traditionally documentary has been considered an "educational" form. Does the fact that you have ceased making documentaries have something to do with a shift to a more agnostic position?

KK: No. In Poland the documentary does not have an educational tradition—so much so that in Poland there has been a very clear institutional and milieu-based distinction between the educational film and the documentary, which need not have any ambitions to teach. During the period of Communism there were two production studios—the Wytwórnia Filmów Oświatowych [Educational Film Studio] in Łódź and the Documentary Film Studio in Warsaw—so there was an institutional separation. And on top of that there were completely different sections for documentarists and educational film directors within the Association of Polish Filmmakers. Thus, postwar Poland saw the creation of a tradition in which the documentary did not have to educate at all, but concerned itself rather with description. That is, it was concerned to answer the question "what is the world like?" rather than "what ought it to look like, or how good it would be if it looked this way?" No one imposed an educational function upon documentarists. The public made no such demand nor, in fact, did the authorities, who provided the money. Obviously, the authorities wanted one to describe the world as better than it was, and that was why they had censorship and various other instruments. But that doesn't mean they required any educational function of us.

PC: Documentaries mostly tend to be short, although perhaps that tradition has altered somewhat in recent years, with the films of Lanzmann, Ophüls, and so on. Did you ever consider this a fundamental problem with the way in which this form is used and did you ever aspire to making longer documentaries, even especially long ones, in the manner of Lanzmann?

KK: Of course, I did have ambitions of that kind and even made some long films and wanted to make some—as you put it—exceptionally long ones. That wasn't possible, but I did want to do that, and I made several documentaries of over an hour and fifteen minutes. That possibility existed. Of course, there was always the problem of how to distribute them, except that—unlike today, when the costs have to be met—at that time they didn't, so one could go ahead and freely make films which didn't have to cover their costs. It was a completely different way of thinking, and Western viewers or readers find it terribly hard to understand that there was a time in Poland, under Communism, when film—which is now a product, and also an element in an economic game—was not and did not have to be a product. I could make a documentary that lasted an hour and twenty minutes and was not screened anywhere, and this was not held against me at all. Of course, I was criticized on the grounds that these films were not particularly pro-government, and perhaps even opposed to the authorities, but not because they didn't pay their way. Incidentally, despite everything, the films I made *did* make money, for they were sold abroad and shown many times within Poland. I never had the problem of feeling that I owed the state any money. I made a few films like that. One was called *Życiorys* [*Curriculum Vitae*, 1975], another *Pierwsza miłość* [*First Love*, 1974], and yet another *Nie wiem* [*I Don't Know*, 1977]. These films lasted about an hour. I probably even made one that was even longer, I'm not sure which, but I probably did.

PC: I would like to move on to *Blizna* [*The Scar*, 1976], since, in your interview with Danusia Stok, which is well-known to English readers, you described this film as "Socialist realism *à rebours*." I do not think you have been completely fair to your own film. Would you like to say a bit more about it?
KK: I simply didn't like this film and never have done—neither when I made it nor today.

PC: Why?
KK: It seems to me—to start with—that it was based on a script with a completely false concept. And it is probably so badly directed that I don't think it could appeal to anyone for any reason. I personally dislike it so it's hard for me to have a better attitude to it. Muddled, messy, badly made, badly acted, badly edited, overlong, and, in general, I don't know if it's any good for anything to anyone.

PC: Did you deliberately begin making "short films"—to use a title that was later to have its own career—because of certain criticisms leveled at your earlier films (for instance, *Bez końca* [*No End*, 1984], which immediately preceded the change), charges of incoherence and containing too much material?
KK: Those criticisms are accurate and correct. These films really are too long and do not cohere; they really do fall apart. Of course, some of them may contain an idea that holds them together, but it is harder to discern one in the others. That is true. In using the title "short," I did not deliberately set out to embark on a new

path. To tell the truth, the idea of calling these films "short films" came to me when they were already finished, when the first had already been edited.

PC: Was this a kind of substitute title, like *The Double Life of Véronique*, with which you have expressed dissatisfaction?

KK: No, it wasn't. These films didn't have any titles at all, since we thought we'd call them, for example, *Decalogue 5*, and that would be that. Later, when making the film version I already knew, of course, that I would have to find a title, but I never found one I seriously considered. I remember that we were at the stage of completing the editing of the film about killing. I went to the post office to post a letter somewhere and on my way back, just as I was leaving the post office, the idea "a short film about killing" came to me. I thought it was a good idea, because it was true: it really was about killing, really was short, and was a film. I thought it was a good title because it would then make it possible to call the next film, which we had finished shooting and were starting to edit, *Krótki film o miłości* [*A Short Film about Love*, 1988]. And this would create a sort of cycle, as you put it. For quite apart from the fact that the *Decalogue* is a television cycle, within it there emerged an additional tiny film cycle made up of two films. At one point, there was even a plan to make a feature out of another one of the films in the *Decalogue*, and to shoot extra material for it.

PC: Which one would that have been?

KK: Zanussi, who heads our production unit, wanted to do this with *Decalogue 9*. One could calmly have added some incidents, shot them and made a feature that would simply have been called *A Short Film about Jealousy*.

PC: Would that have been due to the fact that *Decalogue 9* and *A Short Film about Love* have often been linked, since there are certain obvious connections?

KK: Yes, there are obvious connections. I don't know whether the film would have been about love or about jealousy—it would have been a film about two sides of the same feeling, the same coin. So they would naturally have to have been connected in some way. For Zanussi, it was rather a question of it being a story that was very attractive and told briskly, and that it could be turned into a feature with only a small injection of finance. And in connection with that there began to be talk of the money's importance, and that some money could perhaps be made on it. But to tell the truth I didn't have the strength to set about it. I no longer wanted to.

PC: You had no desire to do it?

KK: I did not have any strong desire. This was after producing those ten films, after over a year's shooting with editing at the same time: it was all too much. I suppose that, had I been fresher and more relaxed, I would have decided to do it. But since I was already really all-in I simply felt I didn't want to.

PC: Since the *Decalogue*, words such as "mystery" and "mysticism" begin to appear in articles about your films, and you yourself have often used the word "mystery" to designate a certain value. Would you like to define it more precisely? Does it have a certain religious undertone, for instance?

KK: No, there are no religious undertones. I think it has very clear existential connotations—that it is purely and simply the mystery we actually face every day. The mystery of life, of death, of what follows death, what preceded life: the general mystery of our presence in the world at this particular time, in this particular social, political, personal, and familial context, and any other context you might think of. Strictly speaking, every question contains a mystery. And it doesn't seem to me to be an issue whether or not we succeed in deciphering it, since obviously we won't. Since this is how I think about life—both my own, and life in general—this way of thinking obviously must be inherent in my films, since I don't just pursue directing as a profession, but make my own films with my own stories. This is the heart of the matter. Of course, within the framework of the film, the story one tells, what appears on the screen, these mysteries often involve very small things or things that are inexplicable, things the heroes do not want to explain, or things about the heroes I do not want to explain myself. They are often very tiny, insignificant things. But I think that there is a point at which all these trifling matters, all these little mysteries, come together like droplets of mercury to form a larger question about the meaning of life, about our presence here, what in fact went before and what will come after, whether there is someone who controls all this, or whether it all depends on our own reason or on someone or something else. That mystery is there all the time. Of course, it has certain religious connotations, but those connotations fundamentally arise out of the existential questions, rather than the other way around.

PC: Although it is only with the *Decalogue* that the word begins to appear in your own interviews and in essays about your films, would you see any continuity with your earlier films here?

KK: Definitely. You mentioned *I Was a Soldier*: after all, the dreams of people who lost their sight during the war, what they imagine, is, in fact, a mystery. Perhaps—no one can know, but perhaps—it is thanks to their having dreams (and, as some of them said, even in color) that they are able to live through each successive day. That is a mystery. This mystery has always been a part of my films because I have always tried to get close to people, whether the film is a documentary or fiction—to get close to the heroes. If one is close to the heroes that mystery is bound to come out, for it really does exist.

PC: I would like to take this question a step further. Since this religio-mystical, mysterious element appears most clearly in the films you have co-written with Krzysztof Piesiewicz, although it seems to me less in the films themselves than in the scripts (for instance, in the script for *Three Colors: Red*, Valentine crosses herself on entering the church, and this is absent from the film, while the priest who appears at the end of the script to *Decalogue 8* isn't in the film, and so on), can one say that your contribution to this collaboration is more agnostic than that of Piesiewicz?

KK: I don't know. I don't think one can say that. I think that the priest, or the need for belief, for example, appears tremendously clearly in *Przypadek* [*Blind Chance*, 1981], if you've seen it.

PC: Yes, I have.

KK: In the second section, the hero has a clear need to discover some sort of meaning in life and belief. I'm not certain whether a priest appears there, and that's not terribly important, but perhaps the most religious scene in all the films I've made occurs in *Blind Chance*, when the hero kneels during baptism and prays "O God, I have been baptized, I ask only one thing of you: be there. I ask only that: be there." This is perhaps the most religious scene in all my films and I wrote its script by myself. So I do not think that there was a difference between Krzysztof Piesiewicz and myself concerning belief, God, and the meaning of belief, which affected my view of these things in any way. Overall, I have done perhaps two religious scenes—that is, two scenes about belief. One, in *Blind Chance*, about the need for belief, and the other, which is also about the need for belief—through negation—when the hero overturns the altar in *Decalogue 1*. In one, it is a matter of a screenplay I wrote myself; in the other, of one I co-wrote with Piesiewicz. Valentine does not cross herself in the church for the simple reason that we thought it took up too much time. That church interior was not so attractive that it was worth saying much about it, although doubtless if I had thought about Valentine's attitude she ought to have crossed herself—except that we did not even shoot this, for it would definitely have gone on too long. In *Decalogue 8*, we cut out an element we had already shot, because it was too obvious.

PC: With regard to *Three Colors* (1993–1994), did you ever consider giving these films different titles—for instance, *Liberté*, *Egalité*, and *Fraternité*?

KK: No, I never considered titles of that kind, just as I never considered naming the parts of the *Decalogue* after the commandments—particularly since in the

case of the *Decalogue*, as you know, there is the problem of the different number-
ing in the translations into different languages. That would have been meaning-
less. But it wasn't for that reason that I didn't name the parts of the *Decalogue*
after the commandments, or call *Three Colors: Blue* (1993) "Liberty," but because it
seems to me to be a question of the partnership with the viewer, the possibility
of opening a dialogue. The moment something is named, the possibility of free
interpretation is cut off. The moment you leave something unnamed, and leave
the place of the name open, that place can be filled by anyone in the cinema, everyone who has bought a ticket. If *I* fill that space, it cannot be filled by the viewer.
It's very simple, logical.

PC: So you would consider the name of a color more open than that of a concept?
KK: Quite definitely, since, although people may know that to some extent I
am referring to freedom, if I don't name it outright then everyone can imagine
equally well that the question at issue is the negation of whatever is, or could be,
contained in the title. Logic dictates that it is definitely more open. It is simple
logic, and not my own intentions, that causes this to be more open than naming
it outright as "freedom."

PC: But in various cultures, and perhaps even most of them, colors have certain
conventional associations—for instance, blue with cold, depression and so on.
KK: You could say so, but it is not necessarily the case—it depends.

PC: At least within our culture . . .
KK: It depends which cultures. Even within ours—"ours" being the so-called
West European culture—there are massive differences.

PC: For instance, "I am blue today," as one could say in English.
KK: Which means "sad," of course. But on the other hand in Spain—or perhaps
Portugal, I'm not sure—it's quite the reverse: their age-old traditions identify
blue with something vital and full of energy. I can't quite recall the examples,
but I've met numerous people from various parts of the world—and even from
our cultural sphere—who have explained that there are vastly different relations
with these colors. In Greece, too—which unfortunately I won't be visiting in two
days' time—the relationship with the color is completely different. How strange!
It is not necessarily the case that our area classifies a single color unambiguously.
But the fact that in English—or, in fact, in American—blue is associated with
sadness, as in "the blues," does not mean that it is associated with freedom. Freedom has nothing whatsoever in common with sadness or cold—one could say,
quite the reverse. Actually, freedom ought to be in red, since if we really wished

to reflect on what is associated with liberty, what color flag, it would be with revolution, blood, and so on. But I term it "blue" for the simple reason that on the French flag—and the film's finances came from France—blue is the first color. If a different country had provided the finance—Germany, for instance—and I had made it as a German film, then yellow would have taken the place of blue and one would have had "yellow, red, and black." It really is not important. However, the very fact that it has this name means that it is open to possible interpretations, as is shown by our current discussion; that it can be associated with the meanings this color has in our culture and with other meanings in other cultures; that "blue" need not mean "freedom" at all, but actually be its complete opposite; and that it can be freedom, too—for why shouldn't it? Consequently, as I've said, it is logically far more open. Of course, I considered other titles and, to tell the truth, I even think it would be better if one could find different titles for these films—not "liberty," "equality," and "brotherhood," but completely different ones. I stopped puzzling over this when the producer said he liked it. I told him that I didn't like the fact that, in a certain sense, *Three Colors* falls under a particular Godardian tradition of the title. But he told me that he liked that a lot. And, since he was quite definite, I realized that there could be two opinions on this matter and gave up my search for a title. What is more I knew what terrible problems I have finding titles, and, since he liked it, I left it at that.

PC: Within the first two films at least you allude to their possible titles, since the word *liberté* appears in one shot as Julie climbs the steps of the Palais de justice, and the next film reveals the next word, *égalité*—but one never sees *fraternité*. Is this just because that story is set in Geneva and does not involve Paris?
KK: Precisely for that reason. If it had had some link with Paris we would definitely have repeated this joke—for it is anecdotal and has nothing to do with the heart of the matter—for a third time, but we didn't succeed. And unfortunately there is no such inscription on Geneva's Palais de Justice.

PC: So although you value surprise very highly—it is a word that appears often in your interviews, and you like the documentary because not everything is predictable, worked out in advance—you did not do this in order to surprise those viewers who expected that word to appear?
KK: No, for you know hardly anyone notices those words. Those sort of things are for very sophisticated and attentive viewers.

PC: But critics kept on writing about the concepts that were linked to the colors.
KK: And they were right to do so. Debates and meditations about what these words actually mean seem appropriate to me, for we often use words whose

meanings we have forgotten. They become merely symbols of certain events and so become detached from reality, life, the concrete. They become symbols or metaphors, things that seem self-evident. However, as soon as we cease to consider them self-evident and begin to reflect again on the meanings of these words, and our relationship to those meanings, the word acquires a concrete context, that of a person's life. I think it is time to ponder the actual meaning of everything within our tradition—I mean the Judaeo-Christian, West European tradition that shapes us. We have to reflect not only on where we find ourselves, but also on the meaning of these words that have shaped us throughout history, through eras, years, wars, revolutions, and generations. These things are where we come from—the first, second, and tenth commandments, but also "liberty, equality and brotherhood"—and we are as we are today because once upon a time somebody gave his head for these three words, allowed himself to be crucified for these ten commandments. All these things have a certain significance for modern life and our relationship with the world and each other. They all build and shape us. So the question arises—where are they located within us, what is our real attitude to them? I think the question is worth revisiting because, if we fail to understand where we came from and what we are made of, we cannot understand who we are, what we are doing on this earth, where we are headed. Of course, I do not advocate any historicist way of thinking or situating the present in the context of history, but I do not think one should overlook where a person is coming from.

PC: Do you have any intention of making historical films?
KK: No, that doesn't interest me at all.

PC: You have often spoken very warmly of actors, and one can see the effect in the strength of the performances in your films. I wonder, did you find any difficulties—or even find it frustrating—working with actors who use languages you do not know and dialogue that lacks colloquial contact with your everyday reality here?
KK: No, overall I did not find that uncomfortable. It was simply unimportant, since I think people make themselves understood independently of language. It really isn't that important. Of course, it is very important to make oneself understood on a basic level, but once you reach a level even a little bit above the basic it is not language that determines whether or not we understand one another.

PC: It has been said on occasions that your films have become increasingly elliptical. One example of this particularly interests me—and how you would read it and react to my own reaction to it. I am thinking of the ending of *Three Colors: White*, and how it should be read—for criticism of the film concerned the ending in particular, which, for me, seemed to interweave three of your earlier films: the short films about love and killing, and also *No End*, since Karol is now "dead" and officially a ghost. How do you feel this ending ought to be read?

KK: For me, it's a very simple ending to the story.

PC: But the story continues in *Three Colors: Red*.

KK: It simply means that the story ends well. The fact that the hero goes to some prison to get in touch with the heroine, who is up there behind bars at some window, and yet nevertheless they make contact—that simply means that the story ends well, that there is—so to speak—a "happy end." Of course, this "happy end" was incomparably more developed in the script, and was later cut down considerably. A whole block of the story was cut out.

PC: Why?

KK: Mainly because it wasn't done too well and was simply rather messy—we failed to do things precisely and that prolonged the film terribly and added nothing essential, since for me the essential thing was a kind of "happy end," and the fact that between these two people, who hated each other and ought to have hated each other—her hating him and him hating her for humiliating him—love won out over hatred. And I thought that if we succeeded in saying that it would be enough. I agree with those criticisms that say the ending is not clear, but nevertheless I did not think it worthwhile burdening the viewer with a long story—for it went on for at least another ten minutes that in effect said the same thing. It might perhaps have been clearer, but it would have been more of the same. For I am terribly afraid of overextending a film. The viewer has a certain amount of staying power, but, although he is capable of sitting through tremendously attractive chases, escapes, and shootouts—particularly when they are expensive and the money can be seen on the screen—he is not able to bear stories that are far subtler, far less dramatic and action-packed. So to save him from leaving the cinema—and myself from having him leave—I prefer to shorten the story.

PC: Yet, it seems to me that the tendency of auteur cinema is rather going in the opposite direction, that we are seeing more and more films that last two and a half hours.

KK: Yes. I very much fear that these films will have fewer and fewer viewers. More money is needed to make a two-and-a-half-hour film than an hour-and-a-half one, so far more viewers are needed to cover its costs. I don't know how things will be in the future. I know that today my colleagues in various countries—Angelopoulos, for instance—are making very protracted stories.

PC: But Angelopoulos has always made very long films.

KK: He always has. But who is going to watch these two-and-a-half-hour films today, with life's current tempo? I am afraid that there won't be enough people to make a second film possible.

PC: But *Pulp Fiction* (1994) lasts that long.

KK: But *Pulp Fiction* is a classic example of the action film. Of course, one can say it is an auteur film by Tarantino, since he wrote it himself, but it is a film that situates itself on the side of commercial films, action films, films of brutality and violence, rather than the side of reflection and certain subtle, dimly apprehended feelings, the side usually occupied by the auteur film. I am simply afraid of longer films.

PC: Music has been foregrounded increasingly in your recent films, particularly in *The Double Life of Véronique* and *Three Colors: White*. Zbigniew Preisner himself has said that his film music is not "serious music." How would you relate this view to the compositions of Julie—or her husband, it is not clear—in *Three Colors: Blue*? How are we to take the symphony—as a masterpiece, or ironically?

KK: I think that symphony might have sounded worthy, if only. . . . Do not forget that we wrote the script in 1990, when the unification of Europe was planned for the middle of 1992. As you know, every fourth year works are commissioned for the Olympics from the most distinguished composers. Europe would unify for the first time in history, and so it would require exceptional scene-setting. And then one could say that all sorts of elevated tones and exceptionally weighty words—to put it positively—or bombast—to put it negatively—would sound and be in accord with the ceremony of European unification. Since, as we know, Europe did not unite and will not—certainly not in the way some Euro-optimists imagine—it clearly has to be taken ironically as a program. It is rather as if we had planned to celebrate a name-day or birthday, had ordered an enormous cake with a large number of candles, and had taken exceptional care to make sure that it looked right, tasted right—except that when the birthday came the person celebrating it doesn't, for he has other business elsewhere. At that moment the cake becomes ironic, bitterly ironic in relation to what had been supposed to happen. It is exactly the same with this work, which is just such a cake. Except that the person for whom it was meant did not come.

PC: Does that mean that the words that accompany that music are also to be taken ironically?

KK: No, the words remain relevant anyway, except that they sound differently depending on whether a marriage takes place or not. It is rather as if what you had prepared was not a cake but the music we are discussing for a wedding at which a certain beautiful woman is to marry a handsome and worthy man. To mark the occasion someone composes a song that speaks of the love that binds, and the wedding approaches. So far, so good. But in the meantime either the man or the woman backs out, and the song is left standing. Does it lose its value? No. There is only a certain kind of bitterness over the disappointment, for we had expected more of our marriage candidates—we had expected them to unite. But they do not. Are they unworthy of this love? Perhaps, since they do not unite. Perhaps they do not feel it in a way that would take them to the altar. It's very simple. One does not have to treat this as something that loses its value, for it doesn't in the least. The same words will be just as much to the point for the next couple that comes to the church and unites as they were for the couple that didn't. They remain just as valid. It could be that one day our heroes—the man and the woman—will find their other halves, she her man and he his woman, and the words will again be just as valid and appropriate as they would have been had they been united. But they continue to be valid—for the French, the English, the Germans, the Spanish, the Portuguese. They did not unite but the words retain their validity. These words about love continue to be just as valid.

Fragments of the Meeting at the Ósmego Dnia Theatre

Marek Hendrykowski and Mikołaj Jazdon / 1996

Interview conducted February, 24, 1996, at Ósmego Dnia Theater, Poznań. Published by permission.

This is a translation of Professor Marek Hendrykowski and Mikołaj Jazdon's edited transcript of a recording of the last public meeting with Krzysztof Kieślowski. The occasion was a retrospective of Kieślowski's films organized by Teatr Ósmego Dnia in Poznań. At first, Kieślowski refused the invitation due to physical exhaustion. He appeared last minute in the dark theatre overflowing with viewers standing in doorways and laying on the floor in front of the screen. The question-and-answer session following the screening was conducted by Professor Hendrykowski.

Krzysztof Kieślowski: Marcel Łoziński spoke so fondly of you that I finally set out to visit you here, even though I am not really in the best shape. In fact, I should not really be moving around, but they told me that I must come to Poznań because there are an awful lot of interesting and bright young people here.

It's probably easiest if you throw out a topic, something that interests you. . . . I don't think there's a need to limit anything in any way: not to a documentary, nor to film in general. We can talk about life, because that's also a curious business. Perhaps more curious than films.

Marek Hendrykowski: If every one of us asked only one question, we would have to cancel your [return] ticket [to leave] tomorrow.

KK: [Smiling] No, there's also the question of how long I would talk, and I am not very talkative, so please. . . .

Voice from the audience: Which of your films is closest to you, closest to what you wanted to communicate?

KK: I have never managed to make a film the way I really wanted. In a few films

I achieved it 35 percent. For instance, *Personnel* is one such film. Also *Red*, *The Double Life of Veronique*, maybe *Blind Chance*. . . . Among the documentaries, I like *Hospital*, *First Love*, *From a Night Porter's Point of View*. In the film about the porter there is truth, but it is manipulated; that is, in a sense, I provoked it. His reactions are real, but I triggered these reactions. Of course, we can say that we know such people, they are around us and, in their potential, they are extremely dangerous. However, one has to remember that this is a real living man. He exists in reality, is called Marian Osuch, lives in Warsaw in Bemowo. I did not want to harm him and I still don't want to. I wanted to harm the phenomenon, which one may call Fascism, or, if you will, something else. It may be called Zhirinovskyism[1]; it's all the same.

Maria Blimel: And how did you find the subject for that film?
KK: The People's Printing Co-op [Ludowa Spółdzielnia Wydawnicza] used to publish a collection of diaries every year, which was called *Diaries of My Life*. Among these appeared a text by a guy from Łódź, who was a porter. In it, he presented very clearly his view of the world: that is, orderliness is needed, everything should be arranged to keep up appearances, and all this riff raff should be eliminated as soon as possible. I read this diary and I saw that I really wanted to make a film about such a guy, because then there were an awful lot of them. It [these attitudes] went on from March 1968[2] and these attitudes were a continuous leitmotif, they would resurface on different occasions.

I sent my assistant to meet the guy in Łódź, but unfortunately he turned out to be unsuitable. He had no front teeth at all and he lisped, so it was impossible to understand what he was saying. He didn't fit the bill for film. I instructed my assistant to look for a similar guy. And he was simply walking into Warsaw factories and asking if they might have such a porter who liked orderliness everywhere, who wanted to put everything to rights. Listen, in every factory there was a guy like that! The only problem was with making a choice. Of course, I wanted it to be a guard from the Central Committee [KC], for instance, but that was indeed impossible. I chose the most "picturesque" one.

Marcin Kęszycki: And has the night porter seen the film about himself?
KK: Yes, and he was delighted. He befriended us. After that film, we came to Kracow to shoot *Camera Buff*. One day, I am in a room. Suddenly, someone knocks. I open the door: Marian stands there. I say: "What happened, for God's sake? What are you doing here?" "I quit everything, damn it! I will act in your film!" And, if you see *Camera Buff*, Marian is really there, he plays the porter. At the end, there is this scene: Stuhr comes running and jumps over the chain at the porter's booth, and Marian screams after him: "Not over the chain! Not over the chain!"

Voice from the audience: Why did you give up making documentary films?

KK: There were plenty of reasons. Responsibility for the person one photographs. Another reason, much more important for me, lies in that what really most interests me must not, should not, be filmed. There are, of course, different views about this, but I simply object to barging in with a camera on people's feelings, passions, and emotions. A few times in my life, I managed to film emotions and I was very happy to have found myself there with a camera. I remember well a scene from *First Love*: a boy, after his daughter was born, simply burst out crying. After that, I thought, do I have a right to film this, or not? Certainly, he would have also burst out crying if I was not there. I came to the conclusion that I must not be there with a camera. This is the main reason why I stopped making documentary films. I saw that it was better to hire actors and buy glycerin at the drugstore, squeeze a few drops into their eyes, let them cry. And with them this would be fair—they're carrying out their vocation—and I have a right to demand it from them.

Mikołaj Jazdon: While watching *Personnel*, I was under the impression that the film was shot like a documentary. It seemed to me that the tailors who appeared in it were provoked with questions from the actors, and a camera was simply spying on them. Was that indeed the case?

KK: It was precisely that way. The film was thought out that way. Shooting documentary films, at some point I realized that what was most bewildering—various states, moods, some silly chitchat—I had to cut out from the film because this was what its construction demanded. Following from that I thought that I would construct *Personnel* so that what I had always deleted from a documentary, because it was not necessary, would this time constitute the substance of the film. A few times we laid low in a way that allowed us to photograph something that I simply loved. If you go to any office or government office, for instance, to pay taxes, you will see old women sitting there, calculating something and gossiping: "Have you been to see Jadźka?" "Nah, because, you know, she is feeling terrible," and so on. They bring in doughnuts and they munch away. Of course, they don't offer them to anyone else, but they devour them all themselves. It is something simply amazing to see. I love these scenes from life. It seems to me that Karabasz had the same type of attitude towards it, yet he somehow saw more the gracious side. And I see the doughnuts.

We filmed *Personnel* at the Opera in Wrocław. It had the most interesting costume workshop in Poland, because I had seen them all, including the one here in Poznań. Throughout the whole production of that film, they [the tailors] were making costumes that were assigned to them by their stage producer, and apart from that, they were the background for my friends' acting. Most roles were played not by actors, but directors: Juliusz Machulski was the main character. Tomasz Zygadło also acted in it, and Tomasz Lengren. It was very easy to tell the real tailors from the fake ones. For a long time, no rushes were being returned, because something was out of order at the film lab, then suddenly a great chunk came back. It turned out that all the non-tailors had tape-measures around their necks! Of course, a real tailor doesn't wear a tape-measure; it's only that we imagine him this way.

Voice from the audience: Does your giving up filmmaking mean that you have already achieved some goal?

KK: I stopped making films for many reasons, and I suppose one of them is fatigue. I made an awful lot of films in not too long a time, perhaps too many. . . . There was in it, undoubtedly, much bitterness that I had stretched myself and never achieved even close to what I wanted. But besides that, I had started to live in a world of fiction, imaginary and artificial. I had stopped participating in real life, and had started in the life which I had made up earlier myself, or with my friend Piesiewicz. And because it rolled over from one film to another, practically without a break, so I actually stopped feeling that I was in touch with the world. I had chased myself into some unreal world, away from people close to me, because fictitious problems started to be incredibly important to me: whether one can do this or that, test this or that person in that moment. Real things ceased to matter, because the imagined ones took their place. Then I simply thought, that's enough of that.

Voice from the audience: What has replaced directing for you?

KK: Life, ordinary life. I have many debts in relation to people, to my family, debts to friends. And soon after I started to pay off these debts, suddenly it turned out I had to flit around hospitals again. I have debts that have to do with not seeing people, not exchanging thoughts for many years, so many things have gone by. . . . You don't know this yet, because you are too young, but later it really is awfully difficult to go back. If you feel some closeness with someone, you must share with this someone everything that is, good and bad, because if you don't do it a big chasm develops, and it is practically impossible to go back. And I am now desperately trying to go back to the people towards whom I feel an enormous indebtedness.

Voice from the audience: I would like to ask how important your daughter is in your life and whether she influenced your film heroines.

KK: Film heroines? I don't suppose so. This is generally a sphere that has to remain hidden always, the sphere of what carries from the private realm into film.

One must not reveal it and perhaps one should not snoop into it. Marta is very important to me and I can give you a very simple and clear example. Recently I became seriously ill with heart disease, and before then I used to smoke a lot of cigarettes. The doctors said that really I must not smoke anymore, but why would I care what they say? . . . However, my daughter came and said, "Daddy, when you asked me not to smoke, did I smoke?" I said, "No." "So I ask you not to smoke." And really I have not smoked a cigarette for over half a year, and this is more or less the type of relationship we have.

Voice from the audience: Don't you think that ending *Blue* with *Hymn to Love* is too literal?

KK: Note that this hymn came into being two thousand years ago; it is the only part of the Bible that contains no mention of God or religion, only love. I would probably still today insist on this *Hymn to Love*. I think it is something quite incredible and it testifies very clearly to our human condition; this faith in, need for, and necessity of love as a propelling motor of our life. And if someone could formulate it two thousand years ago and today we also relate to it, and we say that love is also most important to us, so I think I would still insist on it, just because it has held for so long. If it were Shakespeare, maybe I would hesitate, but because it is one of the oldest sources in existence, I think it says an awful lot about us; we haven't changed at all. Of course, we have cameras, computers, while they had none, they couldn't even write; however, love was most important to them, just like it is for us.

Voice from the audience: What interested you most in this vocation soon after graduating from film school?

KK: At the beginning, it seemed to me that one had to describe the world. It came out of the fact that the world was not being described at all. And when I finished it seemed that a camera was such an excellent tool to describe the world. I made a film about a milk bar. Old ladies come and eat dumplings off other people's plates, and at the front of the bar sits a violinist who saws away at the Polish national anthem, weirdly off key. It seemed to me awfully meaningful. I filmed it all and showed it to Karabasz, and he said, "You know, even if Eisenstein came here, he could not edit anything out of it." And he was right, because all that I described was in there. There were old ladies. There were dumplings. There was the violinist, and there was the Polish anthem. However, there was no deeper thought developing out of it. There was only the sense that we are hereby describing what some milk bar looks like; that is, we are with that singular old lady with the dumplings; there is no other meaning; it does not express a kind of universal suffering.

Voice from the audience: Does that mean that for you there was nothing beautiful in old ladies?

KK: There was something beautiful to me. It was happening in Łódź. In Łódź these old ladies eat other people's dumplings even now. Recently, I went, I looked, they're still there. Different old ladies, different dumplings, but acting in the same way, precisely. Later I wanted to be closer and closer to people. They interested me more and more as individuals, not only because they were eating off someone's plate, but also [because I wanted to know] why they were eating, how did they come to be eating like this, what happened before.

Voice from the audience: Did you manage that?

KK: You know, not entirely, no. . . . It never works out entirely, but it is not interesting for it to work out. What's interesting is to keep going. Of course, one has to have a goal, but reaching it is not really a concern. It is the road that's really interesting. I think that's just the way we are. We know where the goal is and reaching it is not really as interesting as the path. That's very curious. I think it's the same with films, just like with anything else, with writing books, making dumplings to be eaten off other people's plates by old ladies. Yes. . . . It is perhaps like that with everything. . . .

Notes

1. Vladimir Volfovich Zhirinovsky (born 1946) is a founder and leader of the Liberal Democratic Party of Russia, with a strong media presence for his provocative and confrontational statements.

2. The end of the diary series falls on a period of wide-scale repressions in Poland. For more detail, see the Chronology in this volume.

Transcript of a Conversation for Polish Television

Grażyna Torbicka and Tadeusz Sobolewski / 1996

From *Reżyser* 65 (March 1997): 4–8. Reprinted by permission.

This interview was conducted by Grażyna Torbicka and Tadeusz Sobolewski in 1996 for Channel 2 of Polish TV, not long before Krzysztof Kieślowski died. The following transcript is based on the original archival recording of the conversation.

Grażyna Torbicka: Good evening, Ladies and Gentlemen. The guest of the following edition of *I Love Cinema* is Krzysztof Kieślowski.
Krzysztof Kieślowski: Good evening to all.

GT: I would like to welcome you very warmly and thank you for accepting our invitation and Tadeusz Sobolewski for agreeing to be the co-host of the program.

At many film festivals, Krzysztof Kieślowski's documentary films are reviewed. Today, we would like to remind you about three films: *Railway Station, Seven Women of Different Ages*, and *Talking Heads*.
Tadeusz Sobolewski: I've had the following adventure with your films: recently, a young girl came from France to Poland to write something about Polish documentary. She knew nothing about Polish cinema, she knew only two names: Kieślowski and Wajda. I showed her your films and it turned out that I didn't have to explain anything, that she'd understood everything. These films function beyond that era, beyond politics. They are separate. For me they are really like a kind of poem written in prose. Maybe to start with, using these three films, let's define their genre, documentary film, a genre that doesn't exist today. Today a documentary is reportage, and your films are definitely not reportage.
KK: No . . . in a way they are reportage. Today the reportage is much longer and made more sloppily . . . but the genre exists: it's not really clear why a few strange mammoths remain in the world and still practice this genre. There is an American, Wiseman, there is our friend in Finland, Jarmo Jaskaalainen, who in

fact graduated from Łódź [Film] School. In Poland, there are at least a few documentary filmmakers, certainly Marcel Łoziński and his son Paweł. These films are still being made. It's simply a recording of what's happening around us, with a very clear personal attitude to what is being recorded. Reportage should also have a personal attitude. Yet if a camera stands in the Parliament and presents us with very serious agricultural problems for half an hour, then it's very difficult to have a personal attitude to it. Besides starting to feel resentful towards that talkativeness.

GT: You've said that these films are now sloppy—
KK: Yes.

GT: —that what characterised the films you used to make and the school you grew out from—
KK: — yes, yes, films we used to make in those times were done scrupulously. You know, we were shooting for months. . . .

GT: What was that scrupulousness about?
KK: First, we took a long time for preparation. Then shooting would take a day or a year. Then we would edit for three or four months. And there was no electronic editing: each cut had to be made by hand. With fingers. And when you do something with your fingers, you have a good look, because this (he demonstrates with a gesture) engages these fingers. Takes have to be cut out, put together, glued, and checked to see if they've stuck. In short, it requires some effort. You want this effort to pay off. For it to pay off on the screen, to show some result from that effort. So, you try to think a little about what you want to express and why the hell you want to bother yourself with it.

GT: Exactly. "You need to know what you want to say." I've wondered many times watching your films to what degree, starting another documentary, you remain faithful to what has been your intention at the start. Have the stories that emerged during this "shaping with fingers" turned out to be more important . . . ?
KK: It varies, you know. . . . Very often these films have stemmed from some kind of . . . a general thought, general observation, general need, or also from feeling that it's worth it, saying something on that topic just then. *Talking Heads* was, for instance, a classical journalistic film. [To TS] I'm even surprised that you say that it works to some degree today, because it seems to me that it is a typical portrayal of the seventies, the last year of that decade, 1979. . . .

TS: Just before the August [of 1980].[1]

KK: Yes. It shows the state of mind of Poles just before that August. I thought that I had to put it together because then—not everybody remembers that, but this is how it really was—people did not talk about the reality, did they? You would not read, not see on television what it was like. So I thought to myself that maybe it was worth telling. What is in the heads of people at the end of the seventies? What are they really thinking? What do they want? And from that stemmed two simple questions: who are you? What do you want? And several hundred, several dozen, and then—as we've said: "necessarily hand-picked from all those"—thirty or forty people answer these questions. They answer the questions honestly and out of that there comes—I think—a portrayal of the state of mind of the country at that time. [To TS] So I am surprised when you say that it is current, because today the portrayal of minds would be completely different. . . . It would be. It would be if one made it. . . .

TS: People keep asking those very questions all the time. It's characteristic of this film that all of them, those dozens of talking heads, unite in a way into one head, because each of us could give many of these answers. . . . It is a philosophizing film.

KK: No. No, they don't give answers. . . . I treat this film as a journalistic film; for me it is a film very clearly situated at the end of the seventies. What did people really want then? Of course, they needed a place to live, a little bit better living conditions, but really everyone wanted freedom. And they spoke of freedom, of democracy. . . . These were the words then . . . a little bit as if taken out of a strange dictionary, weren't they? Because then democracy was kind of spoken about, but it was a socialist democracy. They spoke about ordinary democracy, they wanted ordinary democracy.

TS: Especially people born in the thirties, the twenties—
KK: —who remembered the so-called "pre-war" period, yes. But the young also. They also wanted it. There was only one guy who said he had everything he wanted. It was a drunkard. To the question "who are you?" he says: "I am a drunk and I drink." "And what do you want?" "I don't want anything. Everything is alright." And this is also quite typical, that really at some point in life, in some kind of a state, it is very easy to fulfil your needs. If only . . . [he shows with a hand gesture "having a drink"] suffices.

TS: This is your second-last [documentary] film; the last one is *Railway Station*. But films of the type of *From the City of Łódź*, *Refrain*, films from the beginning of the decade show different people. I would refer to them as "films about supplicants." About people on one side of the counter, glad that they manage to get anything done. We look at it today with fascination, because that type of person doesn't really exist anymore. We were all supplicants; I also used to be pleased easily. . . . We were supplicants in that state and you made films about us.

KK: Yes, that's true, I've made many films like that, yet those films about supplicants—it's a good term!—are films we are not going to be watching today, because today we focus on films with a little bit broader horizons, less blunt, less literary, less everyday—

GT: —those that the girl who has come from abroad understood perfectly.

TS: *Seven Women of Different Ages*—it's a film about an artist, in a sense it is a film about you.

KK: No, no, it's not a film about me, not at all—

TS: —about everyone—

KK: —OK, if it is about everyone of us, then in the same way it is a film about you.

GT: But Tadeusz has said, about every artist, right?

KK: No, no, let's leave these artists completely out of it. No. It is a film about life being simply very short and being only a moment. That it seems to us we have so much time, that we can still do a bunch of stuff, that after all everything is ahead of us, that we will still achieve so much, and in reality it is only a tiny moment. . . .

GT: It's a film about that fleeting moment. That's, after all, what characterizes your documentary films, and not only that. That struggle with time. . . . Here you mark time using consecutive days of the week; they are a synonym of the years, flowing by unbelievably fast, like days of the week—

KK: —years, tens of years. Yes, yes. Life, which passes like that [he gestures with a hand]. So I often keep turning back to time. Time is significant. In a documentary, it helps to organize the film.

GT: But it's difficult to organize that passage of time, especially in a documentary film.

KK: No, it doesn't make a difference if it's a documentary or feature fiction film. If it interests me, if I think that for some reason it has to be told, then it's not at all difficult. You simply have to invent it. . . .

GT: One other thing fascinates me, that is, in your films we watch people whom we think are not aware of being watched by a camera. Did you spend a lot of time with them? Did they get used to the camera, or was it for some other reason? *Hospital* is such a film.

KK: Each of these films is made differently. *Hospital* came out of a feeling that despite all the difficulties, despite shortages of everything around, there are in Poland some groups of people who desire something and get it. I've looked for their exemplars for a long time. . . . I don't know whether it's right to talk about *Hospital*, which we will not be showing to you today; I don't know if it's worth it. . . . If need be, you can always cut it out later. Around then, the Polish netball team won the Olympic gold medal, so I thought that maybe we needed to make a film about people like that; people who want something in a group and achieve it, although there is absolutely no reason for them to achieve anything. For instance, I searched for mountain rescuers or mining rescuers who managed to reach a guy buried underground; it was damn difficult to reach him; they reach him after one week, and he is alive. Then there was a certain miner; his surname was Friday; he drank his own urine to survive. In all that mess that surrounded us, amidst all that feeling of impossibility, it seemed to me that it was worth it to talk about what sometimes could be done. I didn't make a film about mountain rescuers, because it was extremely difficult to photograph. I didn't make a film about net-ballers, because it seemed to me that a few of these netballers . . . I couldn't iden-tify with; in short. I didn't make a film about many other groups of people who came to mind, but it required time to get to know these people, didn't it? To find out that it's difficult to make a film about miners, you have to go there. And wait until there is an accident, and you have to go to that mine with the rescuers and see how it can possibly be photographed. It took a year. After a year, I thought that it should be doctors. Later I thought that it should be surgeons. Then that it should be tough surgeons. That is, the guys [real] to the bone, working with something very definite. Then we had to find these doctors. And I found them—exactly the way I wanted them—in the hospital in Barska [Street]. For me it was about people who not only desire something, but who also know how to deal with people around them. When I understood that it's doctors, I knew that it would have to be doctors who have a heart for patients. And a true heart, not for show for television because it [the TV crew] has just shown up. I stayed there . . . how long? A good few months. They were on night duty once a week. We spent a few months there to see if these people have a little bit of heart and never mind that there is no cotton wool, there is no power, there is no equipment, there is no . . . even hammers break on the screen.

TS: The famous hammer . . .

KK: The famous hammer, yes. And despite all that, they put these broken pa-tients together. And people simply feel better than before, than when they came there. That's an illustration of the thesis that despite everything, groups of people exist who can achieve something if they really want it. In those times it seemed obvious to me that it would take so much time to shoot something.

TS: Your subject matter was people together, either as supplicants, or as people who are doing well and stand united, because then central propaganda still existed, there was a wall between the people and the authorities, and this made it easier to reach a [real] person, to identify with that person, right?
KK: Yes.

TS: Because we were united, weren't we?
KK: Yes, yes, of course.

TS: The same thing exists today, the same need, but there is no longer that main cause which was then fuelled by propaganda. . . . You were making films without [propaganda].
KK: Yes, that's true.

TS: Is it the end of a genre? You've stopped, many people have stopped, practicing it. . . .
KK: You know, it's not about people no longer practicing it. People no longer practice it because other people no longer need it. If they needed [it], then this genre would still exist, that's very simple. If people ski, then they produce skis, build ski-lifts for skiing down the hill; the same is the case with documentary film. If it were needed, it would exist. But it is probably not needed.

TS: But at the moment it is needed.
KK: No.

GT: Then I cannot agree with you. Recently we watched a documentary film, based on your idea, which was made by Paweł Łoziński.
TS: 100 Years [of Polish] Cinema.
KK: Yes, I've seen it.

GT: It's a film that, in my opinion, has done more on the occasion of a hundred years of cinema than any other program presented that year on television.
KK: What you are saying interests, or rather, surprises me, because I've also watched that film with pleasure. I liked the way it was made and I remember that my daughter watched it as well; naturally, she is from a much younger generation but it interested her as well; yet I haven't heard any, really even the tiniest

murmur that this film has made any impression on anyone, apart from doing so for me and for my daughter. And also my wife. Now I know that it also did for you and Tadeusz. But I am so surprised that no one expresses it. Nowhere.

GT: Here we come to the point when one has to say that documentary is after all an art that people don't reject, really being quite in need of it, but—I have to say it—that the media [do reject].
KK: It's nice that you say that, and not me, who comes here as an outsider—

TS: Did you want to say [the same]—?
KK: No, I didn't feel like saying it, I listened to what you were saying. I was curious what you would finish with. . . .

GT: Is it only our fault, or that of some artists, who used to fight in a way with that propaganda, but today don't want to fight—?
KK: Against what?

GT: For a stronger presence of the arts and culture. . . .
KK: I think that you're confusing things, that it's not really like this. You can, of course, fight against something that is a type of institution, regardless of whether that institution is called censorship or propaganda or communism, it doesn't matter. Of course, you can fight against that in ways. But what right do I, or anybody else, have to fight against people's tastes or needs? To fight . . . Maybe we should rouse the others, with that I'd say I'd agree. . . .

GT: In fact, maybe I've used the wrong word, maybe that's it; we should arouse, attract attention, knock on the door—
KK: What door? I don't know where the door is. I really don't know.

TS: Wim Wenders has been to this studio and he's said that to him all films are documentaries. Even when he watches Hitchcock's film, for him it is also a documentary about San Francisco. About tramways in San Francisco. I don't know, perhaps there is something deep in that? Do you have a similar feeling? Because they keep talking about feature fiction, documentary, genre divisions. And you think about the cinema in general, don't you?
KK: It's not us who are concerned with categories. It's you [speaking to both TS and GT], and [other] critics, you make compartments, various shelves, and you put on them various people's names, genres, subgenres—you do it all and it is, in a sense, helpful; we know what the difference between a documentary and a feature film is. Although I like Wenders a lot and we are friends, I still don't think

at all that a feature fiction film is a documentary, because it's not. A feature fiction film is a recorded fiction. Everything that is recorded in a feature fiction film is precisely fiction, even if it's really happened. Because it fulfills the requirements of fictitious storytelling.

TS: Yes, yet with you, I think, there was a smooth transition from documentary to fiction. Not only because films of the type of *The Scar* or *The Calm* had documentary elements, but because films such as *Seven Women of Different Ages* were in fact telling life stories, weren't they? Later you told the story of two Véroniques, and before you'd told a story of seven women. In summary.
KK: Yes, one is connected with the other. Only *Véronique* was a classical fiction film and in it we recorded fiction and nothing else, apart from the way people looked at that time, which is all that's really documentary [about it] to some degree. . . .

TS: But the pleasure of watching those films and the effect they evoke, also an emotional effect, are similar.
KK: Yes.

TS: When I watch *Seven Women of Different Ages* today, I think about my issues, all sorts of them, human. . . .
KK: I agree.

TS: And I don't think about the documentary fabric. . . . I only appreciate the art, the way in which that fabric was transformed into something more.
KK: That's true.

GT: And why does it happen that in many cases if a director starts with a documentary film—often with a short film—and then moves on to feature fiction film, he very rarely creates simultaneously documentaries and fiction features. Even less likely does he return to documentary; most often he abandons it altogether.
KK: Yes.

GT: Why?
KK: Usually, there is no time. Feature fiction, if someone really concerns themselves with it, absorbs a huge amount of time and a huge amount of energy. You really need to devote a lot of time and a huge amount of patience to record in a documentary one true human gesture that means something. Or a tear, or a little bit of suffering, or true happiness. To record that, you need a lot, a huge amount of time and patience. And making feature fiction films you don't have time. And,

independently of other things, I have to admit I have also lost patience. That means that [instead of] waiting for a tear, I preferred to fabricate it with glycerin's help, put it in an actor's or an actress's eye, let her cry already so it can be recorded so that we can move onto the next thing. . . .

TS: In a feature fiction film a director is the master of 90 percent of what's happening. In a documentary it is not so. You once said that this incident happened in relation to the film *Railway Station*: the film you shot was appropriated by the police and you felt ill at ease.

KK: Yes, that's true. . . . It's a part of a greater whole. For very many reasons, I had a feeling that I should move out of documentary. And so really the story with *Railway Station*, which I also don't like, which is a failed film—

TS: Today it is very impressive—

KK: —because we didn't achieve in this film what we wanted to achieve, but that's not significant. The story, anecdote, associated with that film really was the last drop in the glass, or the bucket, whatever the saying, for me. I understood that I didn't want to make documentary films any more. The idea of *Railway Station* was such that it was going to be a type of a poppy-seed strudel cut across. That's how we wanted to show a railway station: to see what's happening at the same time on different levels. A type of a cake cut in half—it's best to think about a strudel, because you can then see its layers. One of these layers was a place where people put suitcases in the luggage and bag lockers. They had just introduced it then and so it was interesting because we didn't know at all how to work it. These lockers had combination locks; you had to set up that combination; nobody knew how to do it. We stood there with a camera, covered it with some cloth or coat and we tried to record how people approached these combinations, didn't know how to open them, didn't know how to close them, didn't know how to use them. They would read the instructions with astonishment, seeing that they were to lock it using not the key, as they had always been used to doing, but all of a sudden using some combination. So we were shooting there a whole night. In the morning we came to the studio, sometime around 4 or 5 AM, and there the police were waiting for us, and they arrested [trans: Kieślowski's own rather peculiar word choice, rather than the expected "confiscated"] the entire film. And they didn't want to say why. Later it turned out that that night they discovered that some girl had murdered her mother and cut her into pieces, put her in suitcases in the lockers at the railway station. They knew it somehow; somebody probably must have reported that it had happened that night at the railway station. They hoped that we accidentally recorded the moment when that girl was putting the suitcases into the lockers.

TS: In a way you would have worked for them. . . .

KK: Well, not in a way, we were simply, really—apart from the fact that we didn't take money for the job—collaborators of the police, in this case of the criminal police, who were looking for the murderer. But I didn't want to be the police's collaborator. I wanted to collaborate with neither political nor even criminal police. I didn't want to look for murderers. I wanted to do something else in life.

TS: No matter in what cause?

KK: Completely independently of it. I understand that the police have to find the murderers, that's alright, but it is not my vocation to concern myself with providing evidence in that case. And I never really in my entire life wanted to do it. Then I understood that it was one more proof that filmed material could be manipulated. In some way it may serve goals completely different from those for which we turn the camera on. Then I thought I would no longer do it.

TS: This is a very powerful film. It's a metaphor for a state that doesn't serve the people. That's how it's read and that's how it was read by the French girl I spoke about at the beginning. That the whole of this railway station is inconvenient for people. People go to the ticket counters, the ticket counters are closed; here it's lunch break; here some cleaning equipment is moving, tearing women's stocking; all that is not serving the people; and on top of it they are under surveillance by cameras that follow them. You can see in it the TV news, which already today looks exotic, because it is some kind of . . . a ritualized speech.

KK: Well, it is everything for us, Tadzio [trans: diminutive of Tadeusz], for our generation, Grażyna doesn't remember those times anymore, we still know them well. . . .

GT: But I do remember them. . . .

KK: I am trying to be charming.

GT: I see. I wonder if when you were a student, or soon after graduation, you believed at any time that you could influence reality by showing it?

KK: You know, when I understood that I could influence it, I escaped. Because I didn't want to deal with it at all, I wanted to concern myself with describing. Describing aimed at description. Yes. To preserve, to describe, to tell other people how things are. After all not everyone can spend a night, for instance, in hospital, and it won't cross everybody's mind that Monday, Tuesday, or Wednesday are days of the week that mark some milestones in the life of a ballerina. Yes. To describe in order to have it described. To show to people who haven't seen it, or who cannot see it, or for whom it will not cross their minds that it could be interesting. And nothing more.

GT: Thank you very much for talking with us. Tadeusz, have you got anything else?

TS: [Looking at KK] You have a concluding smile. Can we use you if you still have a moment?

I keep thinking about these "films about supplicants." To what extent did we have a feeling at the time—I'm asking you that, but I could equally well ask my-self—that the reality in which we lived was abnormal?

KK: If you asked yourself, what would you answer?

TS: That I had that feeling. At the same time I didn't know what normality was like.

KK: It seemed to me that all that was unruly was quite natural. Or—if you will—normal. Just because it was normal, it required recording, required some description.

TS: Which didn't exist.

KK: Which didn't exist, because—as you remember we've spoken about it—that world was not [supposed] to be described. Kornhauser and Zagajewski have written a theoretical book on that subject.

TS: *The Undescribed World.*

KK: *The Undescribed World* in Krakow in 1976. We, who as filmmakers were really mainly revolving around Warsaw, more or less at the same time, understood that the world, the reality in Poland, is not described at all. It is not described by literature, not to mention television or newspapers. It's not described by the theatre; painters are not describing it, apart from Wróblewski perhaps, because there was a trend to paint figuratively rather than to report on what's happening around. Kornhauser and Zagajewski were close to me then; in fact still today they are people who are close to me; they formulated it theoretically, and we had made at the time at least a dozen odd films that were a precise practical realization of that book. That's somehow interesting. But I am getting at reality not having been described. And that the description in itself constituted something worthy, because nothing was described. That's what I thought.

TS: But it was an interesting world. This Łódź, where you were studying, was an amazing world, the Polish bush, wasn't it? Were you as students distant from that strange world?

KK: We loved it, Tadzio. We loved that city, we loved those people. You know, I think that without that feeling you cannot make films at all. Without some sense of proximity, empathy. Or compassion. After all, listen, it was my world, I was simply describing my world. Today we talk about it as if it were something invented, and it was not invented! It's something that by the nature of things surrounded me; it was my place, my world. The world that was very close to me, that I understood, and the world I thought it normal to describe and talk about, since I lived in it. This was Łódź, then there was Warsaw, of course, because I moved out of Łódź since I preferred to live in Warsaw. In fact, I've made almost all the films in Warsaw, apart from a few, but if I travelled out of Warsaw, it was also to places that were mine! They were not other people's places. It's not the way the BBC today makes fantastic films: they go deep inside a volcano in them, or underwater with sharks . . . and they describe something—

TS: —which is interesting.
KK: I thought then that my world was interesting. And that the problem of my world was about it not being described and that it should be described.

GT: Describing your first years at the Film School and the beginning of your studies, you say you had a provincialism complex. I have to admit I don't quite understand why.
KK: I don't remember having said that, but it's possible I did because . . . I did have a provincialism complex.

GT: Even though you were from Warsaw?
KK: No, I was not from Warsaw, you see. I lived in Warsaw, but really all my life I spent in various small towns, tiny ones. For family reasons. I kept moving to places that were utterly provincial. When today I juxtapose that experience with that of people of my age who grew up in Warsaw, in a big city, I see that we lived in completely different worlds. Completely different. With different value systems also. In which different things mattered.

GT: Maybe also with a different sense of observation?
KK: You know, as a child or a young man, I didn't have a feeling that I was observing something. I no longer remember on what occasion we've spoken about it, I don't even remember with whom, but we suddenly understood that we really lived in completely different worlds.

TS: The center and . . . what's outside the center.
KK: Yes, you know . . . I don't feel like going back to that.

TS: I think that I am watching the world in your films from the seventies as my own and as very foreign. I would like it to be one world, I would like to touch it. . . . I can't.

KK: Yes.

TS: And when we say that only, well, Antarctica would engage us, maybe the interior of a volcano, maybe sharks, then I think to myself: what's happened so that what's most interesting in a way is outside the field of view. You say that those documentaries are not needed. They are. Wenders, to whom I keep returning, had to go to Lisbon to find the city of his childhood, although he is not at all from Lisbon. But he found there something similar. Old-fashioned, small, as if from the sixties. So—we are searching.

KK: Yes, we are searching, because we are already beginning to reach that age when everything that has been is beautiful and great . . . we will never go back to it. That is why, I think. Wenders says so because he is of that age. It's also amusing, you see: because I am now a little bit unwell, I am staying at home, reading, surfing TV channels and watching various things. How rarely and at the same time with what pleasure one returns to—rarely, because the television makes it impossible for us—those films from the sixties, seventies, feature fiction films. Let's agree with Wenders that they are also documentaries.

TS: Yes, yes.

KK: Once, two, or three days ago, they screened a film here. . . . Listen, I was sitting with my wife and we were simply delighted. We laughed out loud, which happens rarely in front of the television, because people laugh in the cinema loudly, and in front of television it happens rarely, even though they often tell them: "laugh here!" and from off-screen comes an audience's laughter. I was laughing at Bareja's film *What Will You Do When You Catch Me* (1978).

TS: Of course! I was doing the same with my wife.

KK: What a moronic film! It really is a moronic storyline, a moronic fiction feature film, an idiotic film that has such charm!

TS: What a great documentary!

KK: And it has such a great deal of grace from those times! Not only does it remind us of them, but it is so ours, so much our own. . . . It really was like that, even though then it was a completely absurdly invented film. So for a moment I agree with Wenders that there really is something to it, that this recorded, photographed picture stays somewhere; somewhere later it fulfills the function of registering its own Time.

GT: I have another question. Why, do you think, screenings of your documentary films at film festivals attract so much interest?
KK: I don't know. I was simply in fashion for some time.

GT: I know that after such screenings there are seminars with you and those films arouse a lot of discussion.
KK: It is really not me who should be questioned on it. I'm not curious about those films, so you have to ask people who are curious about them.

TS: They are looking for the source. Perhaps they are looking for the traces of what in your fiction features . . .
KK: Perhaps, perhaps, but it's professionals. I think that . . . it's just the way it is, that people like to look at old photographs. Recently I also found old albums and saw how my child wanted to look at the photographs from the time she was not yet alive in the world. What did the world of her parents look like? We go back to it; it is also some type of a need in people. How did they live? How did they live by their wits? There is perhaps something important in that desire in young people, who want to find out something about the world that they would otherwise never get to know, because it has passed, because it has finished, because it is no more.

TS: It's a luxurious situation: to enter that world and participate. . . .
KK: Not participate.

TS: These films exist. And it could have been us in them, but it is not. . . .
KK: Yes.
[The voice from the control room: One moment, let's shoot cutaways.]

KK: So can I go now?

Note
1. In August of 1980, a series of strikes in Gdańsk shipyard and the rest of Poland led to the inception of Solidarity (Workers' Union) and more unrest, eventuating in the 1981 martial law.

We Slip from God's Hand

Agata Otrębska and Jacek Błach / 1996

From *Gazeta Wyborcza* 071 (March 23–24, 1996): 8–9 and *Incipit* 2 (April 1996): 3–12. Reprinted by permission.

Krzysztof Kieślowski's last interview was conducted by two high school students, Agata Otrębska and Jacek Błach, four days before his heart operation, which resulted in his death. The full unedited text was published in their school's cultural-literary bimonthly Incipit, *and a heavily edited version appeared earlier in the daily broadsheet* Gazeta Wyborcza. *We have followed the edited version of the interview printed in the* Gazeta Wyborcza *but have re-inserted some parts of the original interview, especially a section about styles of screenwriting.*

Agata Otrębska and Jacek Błach: We are young, so actually it's awkward that we are trying to ask wise questions. What interests us is not always noble, wise, and proper.

Krzysztof Kieślowski: It's better to ask questions that really interest you, and not pretend [to be] somebody else, because people can always sense it later.

AO&JB: What do you think about the young generation? Do you think we differ much from your generation?

KK: Apart from it being younger, it hasn't changed at all.

AO&JB: Don't you feel some kind of responsibility? Many of my friends see you almost as a God, and they treat your films almost like a Bible.

KK: Let's not exaggerate, let's not exaggerate. I don't feel at all responsible for that.

AO&JB: Doesn't it mean anything to you, don't you wonder about it?

KK: It does mean something. I think about it deeply, but it doesn't mean I have a sense of responsibility, because that would be pathetic and untrue.

I was making films to have a conversation with people. Of course, a conversation has a kind of responsibility from each party. But let's not exaggerate. It's only a conversation, an exchange of thoughts or an exchange of impressions, or an exchange of moods. Nothing results from it apart from that those involved may either become wiser or dumber during the conversation. That's all. That's the full extent of responsibility. There is nothing more to it. At least I don't feel that there is.

I know there is that sense that art, culture, are responsible for a nation's condition or a society's standards. But I simply don't accept that; I'm not taking on that degree of responsibility.

AO&JB: So you don't subscribe to the Romantic concept of art.

KK: Romantic in the sense you've just used it now, I don't.

AO&JB: Everyone thinks that youth is impulsive. . . . Even [Czesław] Miłosz has written that he goes on being a child, he maintains this impulsiveness. It seems to me that if you don't have that youthful romanticism in you, there is no point in creating.

KK: I think that it is not so much romanticism, but some kind of idealism and naivety. Because I don't think you are all terribly romantic. I don't know at all if romanticism is the right word to describe what we are talking about. I think it's more naivety associated with youth, curiosity, and some kind of idealism, meaning the trust that things can be better, because that is what idealism is about.

AO&JB: Can't one trip over one's trust and curiosity?

KK: Of course you can trip over [it]. A great many people do. And they remain tripped over. And they stay down. I know a great many people like that.

AO&JB: What helps to raise us up in these cases?

KK: It's best simply not to fall. That is, in all you should . . .

AO&JB: . . . exercise moderation.

KK: Yes, exercise moderation, find the right proportions.

AO&JB: They try very hard to convince us that our magazine [trans: *Incipit*] is not "young" because we are not rebelling at all, we don't have any agenda. . . . But is there a model for rebellion? I think you cannot rebel purely on principle, because you are ordered to.

KK: I think that unfortunately I won't answer many of your questions too clearly, because I simply don't know myself. When I remember myself at your age, I can't say I was particularly rebellious. I rebelled, for instance, against stupidity, but now I rebel against the same stupidity, which is now manifested differently; I now find it somewhere else. But it's the same stupidity. Or thoughtlessness. Or cruelty.

AO&JB: It's perceived differently—in youth as a rebellion, and in adulthood differently.

KK: I feel that I rebel the same way now. Back then I felt that I was rebelling, but it was not rebellion against my parents, because I had no reason to rebel against them, because they were terrific. And I had absolutely no reason to rebel against my teachers, even though obviously they were old farts, just like all teachers are always. But I didn't feel I had to rebel against them, because they were really alright—I've always felt they were giving me something. Since they were giving me something, I saw no reason to rebel against them. But against stupidity, yes, that definitely always.

And, of course, you are probably right that it is called once this, another time that. But, certainly, it's not the case that your generation, actually similarly to mine, is simply a collection of walking (suitably rebellious) ideals. It is not the case at all. But of course a lot of people, in your generation maybe even more than in mine, rebel in an absolutely idiotic, absurd way.

AO&JB: To spite all.

KK: To spite absolutely everything, for rebellion's sake, for the sake of discord itself, for the sake of expressing aggression, which is not in them at all, but they superficially find it in themselves, driven by all kinds of surrounding events, such as mass media. So it's not so great.

AO&JB: But that fight against stupidity—what is it about? Stupidity is a very abstract concept.

KK: It's a very specific concept. Stupidity is something which we keep coming across, and which hugely impedes reasonable functioning. Sensible or romantic [functioning], it's all the same because there is not much difference. Stupidity is not abstract. It is extremely specific.

AO&JB: Is the aim of your films to show stupidity?

KK: No, God forbid. We were talking about rebellion, that's how we started with stupidity. And the goal of a film and of every kind of descriptive cultural form is always the same: telling a story.

AO&JB: I thought otherwise after watching *Blue*: there was little action in it, and more emotions, feelings. . . .

KK: And why should a story be associated with action and not with emotions?

AO&JB: There is a story, so there is action. . . .
KK: [You're referring to] an anecdote, right? A story implies an anecdote, a story implies action? No, a story means a story. There could be nothing happening, and you can still describe that: nothing is happening. It certainly is a film about emotions, for sure. But emotion is also a story. What is a story? It's something that happens in time, right? Events that take place in time. If it concerns an earthquake or a train robbery, or that someone comes in indifferent and leaves with a feeling of hatred to what he's come across, or with a feeling of love, that's a story.

AO&JB: So, film as a description, a type of an observatory. But it seems to me it's difficult to observe yourself; it's easier [to observe] others. How much of you is there in your films?
KK: A lot, but I will never tell anyone that, because it is a thing that belongs to the alchemy of the profession, of each profession of a "storyteller," and you have to keep it to yourself. I think it is not something that can be displayed at the market of vanities, or sold.

AO&JB: In the end, life is not emotions. You say that emotions are so important, but emotions are completely disconnected from biography.
KK: You really keep it deep down somewhere, even if just for simple decorum, or the unwillingness to pull your trousers down in public. No one knows that and no one will ever know that. Even the people closest to me will never know that.

AO&JB: In literature, theatre, in all the arts, we always keep asking the same question. Isn't it fraudulent that all the time we give a different form to the same [matter]?
KK: Firstly, [this is] probably not one question but a few. Secondly, I think there is nothing fraudulent in it because you can say, in the same regard, that life itself is fraudulent, since it has always been about a person being born and then dying at the end. That person would know this or that, would have invented a wheel or not, would know what fire is or not; effectively it is all the same. So, is it a fraud? Every time we are born, we know that we will die; and despite that, it is still a completely singular story. Separate. Completely separate. [One] that has never happened before, and will never happen again.

The same concerns a story that is told. These are stories that could happen sometime. Something often happens that is a cliché, schema, repetition, or a joke about something that has already been; nevertheless each story may be a one-of-a-kind story and may exist only for one reason, that there is a demand for it.

Stories are told only because there are people who feel like listening. Everything is for a need. And regardless of whether we have capitalism or whether we have communism, the truth is that people need something and this something is then produced. In capitalism [it is done] a little bit more slyly.

After all, it was always like that: that somebody told a story and there was a circle of people sitting around. At the beginning they had no fire, then they had fire, but it was still like that. Somebody would tell a story. Later, they started to write the story down, because they invented writing. Then they started to copy it, because they invented print. Then they invented film; soon they will have invented computers. It doesn't matter, it's still telling a story. Why? Because there continue to be these people who sit around and listen. If there were none, nobody would be telling [stories].

AO&JB: You are telling stories, creating films and there are as many interpretations of these films as there are viewers. In one word, don't you think that interpreting, in the long term, makes no sense? Delving into the titles of [your] *Trilogy*, for instance. Is the symbolism of those colors so important?

KK: No, it's not important at all. You know, if someone is amused by it, if it enriches someone, if someone needs it for something, if it helps someone to show off their intelligence, be my guest.

AO&JB: So, how was this title chosen, if it's not significant?

KK: It's not significant at all; however at some stage you have to decide on something. It doesn't matter what. In this case, money played a role. Because the money was French, the flag is French and we thought it somewhat coincidental that those colors of the French flag have to do with Liberty, Equality, and Fraternity. There are three of these, and three of those—it's the motto of the French Revolution; at least this is how it's popularly accepted—so we decided that it's all connected. It appears that there is no connection; for the French it doesn't connote at all. It's another element.

Now: the titles are registered by an institution. Because they were already registered, we didn't feel like changing these titles. We could have changed them, but we didn't feel like it, and the producer didn't feel like it. . . . The producer even thought that there was an advantage to this title. And that's how it has stayed. But it doesn't matter at all. Of course, since we had the title, clearly we tried to relate to this title, meaning to the color, because if the title is *Blue* we thought something had to be done with that color. We had to use it somehow, more or less intelligently, but use it, do something with it.

In fact, it's for the people who like playing with connotations and finding meanings, so they could entertain themselves in the cinema. That's why there are plenty of things in *Blue* that are blue. We established that some things would be blue, but only these and no others, so it became somehow meaningful. Is it significant for the story? No, it's not important for the story, but it is important to people, who are entertained or amused by it.

AO&JB: We would like to believe that somewhere there in physical space the film exists, so we can touch it. This invites the question: do your characters live in your head, or are they only tools to tell stories about humanity?

KK: It's a very strange thing. They are born as tools. Using this person we can tell this story from this and not another perspective, and at some stage, I even know precisely when—about the twenty-fifth page of the script—they start to live their own life. They start to behave in some way. They start to take on particular qualities, behave in a particular way. And later you cannot do everything that you want to do with them. They already have their own life, views, truth, and then you have to follow their train of thought. Of course, I do introduce them to the situations that I need; they cannot act freely.

Every person at some stage of life—be it at eighteen, seventeen, or even sixteen—absorbs something, right? You talk with people, you have your parents, you go to school, you have these and not other teachers, you read these and not other books, you watch these and not other films or theater performances, television, you listen to music, which works for you. You soak [it] up like blotting paper. At some stage, you will be mature, around the twentieth-something year of life. So now, as mature people, can you do everything? No, you can't anymore, because you have these and no other grandparents and great-grandparents. You are all that you have absorbed, that you have read; all of it is you. And at some stage you cannot become different any more.

AO&JB: Would it be better to keep one's neutrality and not absorb anything?

KK: You cannot not absorb anything, because you absorb something every day. This morning you are infused with coffee and a conversation with me. You have already soaked that up, and you can't help it. You can of course not drink coffee or not talk with me, but with somebody else. But then you will absorb somebody else. You will go for a walk, then you will soak up the start of spring, which can already be felt a little bit in the air.

And now take notice how it is: really, there are people that you know are capable of malice. But there are people that you know are not, no matter what. That person may be oppressed, humiliated, destroyed, but he won't betray you. And you know that for certain. Why? Because that person is infused with that and that's the way he is, he can't be different.

It is the same with film characters. That twenty-fifth page of the film is a turning point for the film, an important moment. It is also an important moment in life. From some point on we cannot be any different. We can find ourselves in different situations, on a sinking ship, a falling plane, or in a calm life in the country. But you will already be yourself. In each of these situations.

AO&JB: Is it because your characters can no longer change that your films take place in the so-called no-man's land, as if in a dream?

KK: No, it has nothing to do with it. As a director, I am interested in the things that seem to me more interesting and incomparably more significant than those signs through which, according to you, we understand reality, the world. I am simply not interested in these signs. Emotions interest me; they are much more important, are much hotter and more interesting that whether someone is queuing up for milk, or isn't queuing up for milk, whether he has enough [money] to get this milk, or whether he still has to come up with a little bit more money.

AO&JB: Since we soak all that up, haven't you been tempted to shape somebody's worldview?

KK: I definitely wouldn't want to. I absolutely don't feel like influencing anyone, shaping anyone, pushing anyone in any particular direction. I refuse. And that's perhaps one of many reasons why at some stage I withdrew from documentary film, and now I've withdrawn from making films altogether. But it is impossible because you always influence someone: firstly, you live among some people, the dear and the dearest whom you influence in this or that way; secondly, practicing this particular vocation that I practice. So what I would want is far removed from what I can or must [inevitably do]. It does not connect.

AO&JB: You have influence over a large group of viewers. Isn't creating a type of world that viewers would like to see and to live in deceitful?

KK: Undoubtedly yes, of course. You can put a negative charge to it and say that it is deceitful, and you can put a positive charge to it and say that it's fulfilling demand, right? A kind of reconciliation of your own aspirations with demand [by others].

AO&JB: Aren't you then contradicting yourself?

KK: It's always a question of proportions, with which we started. One has to find a compromise, something that is not yet a departure from a principle, that isn't yet contradicting yourself, and that at the same time is in keeping with what they expect from us.

AO&JB: That could be seen as taking an easy way.

KK: Yes, of course. And that's also true.

AO&JB: You have once said that one cannot film a good word. But after all, you are writing scripts. What are scripts for you? Are they only an auxiliary, or an [independent] piece?

KK: No, not [independent] pieces at all, no, no. A script is purely a technical transcript of a future film. Although it depends on what school it originates in. There are two schools of script writing: one Russian, later Soviet, and another American. The Russian [one] says that the script is a piece of literature, and the Russian scriptwriters write them as they would literature. With descriptions and so on, and so on. The Americans think that a script is purely a technical transcript, so that's why their scripts, if you see them, are "sparsely" written. It is characteristic that Russian scripts are written on every line; there are thirty-five lines on one typed page, and in American [ones] there are twenty or fifteen lines, half of that. So, Americans write only: he came in, sat down, said something, and left. And that's it. Nothing else.

AO&JB: They leave more room to maneuver for the director.

KK: They don't give too much, the Americans. They came up with it so that, once you strip the script of everything descriptive—for instance you should not use adjectives, or use them only sparingly—then you can observe very clearly the dramaturgy. Meaning that you can observe and evaluate if the script is well or badly structured, where there are structural errors, because there is nothing to interfere in that. Dramaturgy is like a skeleton; like a skeleton stripped of life. There is nothing else, just a skeleton, so you can easily see it. Whereas, if you dress that skeleton up in descriptions of nature, descriptions of emotions—for instance that "he left deep in thought, reminiscing on last night" and so on— you can't film it at all. And you can't say what exactly the dramaturgy is [in such descriptions]: in that "deep in thought," or that "reminiscing." There is no more dramaturgy; there is a description.

AO&JB: So you are definitely a "fan" of dramaturgy.

KK: I stand somewhere in the middle. I don't write the type of scripts that Americans do, because that would simply be boring. And besides I always think that actors, the crew, who make films, they also need to understand a little what I am on about, what mood I would like to film. That's why I try not to use adjectives, but also don't write that "he came" in and "he left."

AO&JB: Do the scripts take place NOWHERE [original emphasis]?

KK: It's only supposedly nowhere, but this NOWHERE [original emphasis] consists of quite concrete things: that there are these and not other flowers on the table, or that there is a green and not another color tablecloth. NOWHERE consists also of ten thousand small elements that have to be constructed. I try to write it a little bit into the script. But it doesn't mean that I write it like the Russians. No, no. I have found my own way, which is a compromise between these two methods, and I always strive to be incredibly true to dramaturgy's basic fundamentals that were thought out by the Greeks writing their first tragedies; those are really incredibly precise, and in fact today they are calculated to a script page by specialists.

AO&JB: Do you believe in art for art's sake, shocking someone with form for the sake of the shock itself? Is the viewer important or only what's being created?
KK: There is no film without a viewer. For me there is no film without a viewer. The viewer is most important. Art for art's sake, form for form's sake, astounding with my cleverness or talent do not interest me at all. My goal is to tell a story that would be engaging for people. This doesn't imply action, no. It means it is engaging, because it is somehow close to them.

AO&JB: Why is there so much chance in your films?
KK: No, that's a misunderstanding. The misunderstanding exists because I once shot a film titled *Blind Chance* and since then they started to think that chance is something that powers my films, and perhaps also my life, that I think that chance is most important in the world, and so on. I would not say at all that chance is most important in the world. Not at all. There is precisely as much chance in my films as in others. Not more, nor less.

AO&JB: However the end of *Red* was, I think, an exceptional coincidence.
KK: You are deeply mistaken. Those three films were shot for the very reason that these six people survived a certain accident. That's why. It's not chance. Someone survived, right. Once, a certain Yugoslav stewardess fell out of a plane at five thousand meters, the plane crashed. Everyone died, and she fell into a snowdrift and survived. Sure, we can now wonder if a story of a Yugoslav stewardess interests us. I decided that the story of those six people interested me.

AO&JB: So following the thread backwards.
KK: Yes. What happened at the end of the third film was the beginning of thinking about all [three].

AO&JB: Is all this chance that makes up our life, such as for instance that the book opens on the page that's important to the student, and that coincides with the judge's life. . . .

KK: Surely, you have also had a book open sometime on the right page, and if not, you will. The coincidence with the judge's life is a different issue; it has nothing in common with chance. It's rather a question of whether life can at all repeat itself, and if so, can it repeat itself in a version better than the previous one. Kierkegaard dealt with chance completely in theory, but you can also deal with it in practice. Can it repeat? Maybe so, and if it can repeat, then you can derive conclusions from your actions. Bad or stupid. You don't have to take that step, do you? Now, no one can take the false step, because they don't know how, they don't know about that repetition. If someone knows about that repetition, and that someone obviously has to be above us, then he can say: do not go this way, do not leave through this door, do not get on this bus. Wait for the next one. And this is the very function of the book, or of what repeats from the judge's life. Maybe the judge knows?

AO&JB: So the judge is someone above us?
KK: Maybe he is that someone.

AO&JB: The last scene with a newspaper suggests that he doesn't know after all.
KK: Well, he doesn't know, but you see: I think that if there is someone such as God who has created all this that surrounds us and also us, then we very often slip out of his hand. If you look at the history of the world, our history, then you can clearly see how frequently we slip out [of that Godly hand].

AO&JB: We do slip out [of his view], but in general we often return to the point of origin.
KK: I'm not saying that we don't return, I am only saying that we slip out [of his hands]. It's the same with *Red*. We slip out [of his view] for a moment, we don't know something. Then it turns out that even though he doesn't know about the tragedy and the couple [at first] slip out, they then fulfill his wish and they meet. I don't know how it is precisely, because I'm not dealing with the interpretation of my films, but if this is the case, then I agree.

AO&JB: You are someone who stands above film. If this is the case, does film slip out of your control also?
KK: Of course, it slips out, naturally, very often.

AO&JB: Returning to the person who stands above us: do you believe in God, or only in yourself, or maybe in others, in some idea, goal, fate, luck, anything? Is [God] a generic term?

KK: It's hard to say. I think all this comes together, in constantly shifting, fluid proportions. And generally if life is interesting, it is really because those proportions keep changing, [because] we keep imagining that our fate is most important, or that it is shaped by those among whom we live, by circumstances in which we live, or that somebody directs this fate, or coincidences happen to us and we derive conclusions from them. I think it's fluid, complex, just like a very complicated braid, whose threads disappear from time to time, to re-emerge again after a while.

AO&JB: When you stopped making documentary films and started to create fiction, it was about being able to be less responsible with fiction, that documentary brings more concrete effects?

KK: It is not about the ability to check [the facts] in a documentary; the issue is taking responsibility for influencing them. It is very clear in a documentary. When you have a camera, especially in that political reality that was, you are responsible to a very serious degree for the life of whomever you direct your camera toward. I didn't want that, I escaped that. And secondly, all that appears to me to be most important, most interesting in life, is too intimate to film. You must not film it. At least I am deeply convinced that I must not. It is quite logical. So, I could not make documentary films anymore, because I was under the impression that I would not place the camera in front of what was most important to me. And even if the camera were there, I would not start it. I started it a few times, but I always had the feeling that—although I captured a fantastic moment—I must not do it. I've escaped documentary film.

I started to make fiction feature films; it seemed to me that in terms of responsibility it was much simpler, because what do I really do? I hire actors. They are people who have their vocation, so they practice it well, giving much more than their vocation demands from them. I made those films for many years, and then suddenly I saw that I had removed myself from normal life, in which things matter because the next day depends on them, because people around will judge us based on them. In fact I chose a very comfortable place where everything was invented, where I invented everything myself or with my screenwriter friend; but we invent everything and only what we invent matters. Of course, you have to solve many problems, spend a huge amount of money, make important decisions, but all this money and all these decisions, it is all spent on something invented, a fictitious life. It is a non-existent world, thus not real, where there are big emotions, but they are all untrue emotions. They are invented. And I started to feel that I was in some folly, that I had gotten myself into complete cretinism, that I had started to live a life that was not true.

AO&JB: Didn't you have a sense of power? You were creating a new world. . . .
KK: Ah, yes. The question is whether I enjoyed it or not. It seemed to me so natural, easy. [At first] I thought I could tell myself that it was only during business hours, and then normal life returned. Or that it was for three months, and then there was real life. In the meantime, it turned out that I had gotten myself caught in a spiral; I don't even know where it had come from—to tell the truth, probably from ambition—that I got myself into a spiral of work round the clock; then I suddenly understood, after a long time, but suddenly, that I didn't have a normal life at all. . . .

AO&JB: That it's not clear what is life and what [is] fiction?
KK: It is very clear. There is no more life. There is only fiction. It only matters to make this or that, to send something somewhere or to check some numbers. All of this matters. All of this deals with something that doesn't exist.

AO&JB: You have said that a good word cannot be filmed. But I don't believe that you have not been tempted to film that good word.
KK: No, you know, no. I discovered very early on how primitive an instrument the camera was. Don Quixotism. I am not interested in doing something that I know is impossible.

AO&JB: But at this moment you are diminishing the value of your profession.
KK: I do not diminish it; to the contrary. I respect the essence of this profession, even though I am pleased to leave it. You can say that "primitive" is a pejorative term. That is true, but you can also use words such as "simple" or "literal," and this is no longer pejorative. Yet also no longer interesting. I say [cinema is] "primitive" by comparison to the word, which is incomparably richer.

AO&JB: Since we [are talking about] words, I will ask you perhaps a clichéd question: what books have influenced you most?
KK: I am in the good position of simply reading just for myself. I do not read at all to speak about it publicly. This is mine.

AO&JB: Maybe you could just mention a title?
KK: I am not going to say anything. That is the advantage of my situation, that I don't have to say anything on the topic.

AO&JB: Could you [talk] about the actors. Binoche has left such a great impression on me; how much she could express [just with her] face. What do you think about this actress?

KK: I love my actors a lot, simply [put]. I love actors in general, and amateur [actors] especially; those with whom I work, because I know how much I expect from them. What I get from them cannot be bought. This is a matter of—I don't know—some kind of unity, trust, that we think similarly on this topic and we want to express it. The same applies to Binoche, of course.

AO&JB: It's time for the question on everyone's mind: could you please tell us on what you are working now?

KK: I am going to hospital to have an operation.

AO&JB: But everyone knows that you are writing a new script with Piesiewicz.

KK: Yes, we keep at it (to be precise) because we seem not to be able to finish it. I've already been sick for a long time and I can't commit either enough time or energy to it. I don't have a calm head for that, and probably that's why it is all stuck. We are writing three short treatments. If they come out alright, they will become scripts, and then maybe someone will make films. We'll see.

AO&JB: Let us return to *Three Colors*. *Blue* and *Red* had a particular mood. *White* was somehow jarring.

KK: It is terribly difficult to keep everything in the same mood. After such a somber and sad film as *Blue*, in which pondering on someone's fate, time, a moment was important, it was very good to get away from that and try to live in a more tactile, tangible, live reality, in which things advance through action. I cannot be sitting there all the time with this [long] face. Sometimes you have to look around to see if there is something amusing out there, right?

AO&JB: Can you distance yourself from your films when you watch them?

KK: You know, maybe I don't watch my films. What I mean is that I watch them hundreds of times, but before I finish them; after I finish, I don't watch them at all. Unless I have to.

AO&JB: Can you talk in your films about your fears and hurts?

KK: This is what I usually talk about.

AO&JB: Don't you have any limits? Is it all effortless?

KK: [It requires] a huge effort. Herein lies the difficulty of this profession, among other things.

AO&JB: Could you please compare working in Poland with French working conditions?

KK: It doesn't differ much. I started to work in France when communism was just about to finish. I really saw [the difference] then. The fundamental difference has always been that if in France an actor signs a contract that he will act in a film, then he acts in that film and that's it. He doesn't do anything else.

AO&JB: Theater?

KK: Theater performance is out of the question. [In Poland] he has an audition in the morning, radio in the evening, and late at night a theater performance, and later still a cabaret. A French actor had the financial luxury of not having to do anything else in that time. When I came back to Poland with *White*, I already had the same conditions there [as in France]. Better tools, better organization, but much worse flexibility. If something is planned, it has to happen; however it is often the case it cannot happen for various reasons. Either the weather is not right, or someone gets sick, or something happens suddenly and suddenly something has to be changed. That is why we, who are badly organized and have a greater mess most of the time, can adapt much better and faster, and more intelligently. The French organize everything so well, everything is planned so precisely; for instance, they can ask me whether at the end of September they could move the lunch break from 1 PM to 1:30 PM. Good, let's schedule it. . . .

The tape ran out. The conversation continued.

Key Resources

We have limited this section to some additional resources available in English (or with English subtitles) in which Kieślowski speaks about his life and work.

Books
Kieślowski on Kieślowski. Ed. Danusia Stok. London: Faber and Faber, 1993.

Discs
The Decalogue. Facets Video, 2003. DVD.

Extras on these DVDs of all ten of the TV versions of the *Decalogue* include *On the Set of the Decalogue*, with Kieślowski answering the questions of a Polish reporter while production was underway, and *Kieślowski Meets the Press*, an episode of the Polish TV show *100 Pytán Do . . . (100 Questions for . . .*), in which Kieślowski responds to questions from the Polish press.

The Double Life of Veronique. Criterion, 2011. Blu-ray

Extras on this blu-ray (and on the Kino and Artificial Eye DVD releases) include Ruben Korenfeld and Elizabeth Ayre's *Conversation with Kieślowski* (1991). This film intercuts an interview with Kieślowski with documentary footage from the set of *The Double Life of Veronique*.

Three Colors. Criterion, 2011. Blu-ray.

In addition to the feature films *Blue*, *White*, and *Red*, these discs include three "Cinema Lessons" (originally) in which Kieślowski discusses his filmmaking choices, Krzysztof Wierzbicki's documentary about him *Krzysztof Kieślowski: I'm So-So* (1995), interviews with Kieślowski's collaborators, and a number of his student films and documentaries.

Films
1966–1988: Kieślowski, Polish Filmmaker. Dir. Luc Lagier. 2005.

Conversation with Kieślowski (Kieślowski—Dialogue). Dir. Ruben Korenfeld and Elizabeth Ayre. 1991. Included on blu-ray and DVD editions of *The Double Life of Veronique* (see above).

Krzysztof Kieslowski: A Masterclass for Young Directors. Dir. Erik Lint. 1995.

A transcript of the interview with Kieslowski included in this documentary is

available at http://zakka.dk/euroscreenwriters/interviews/krysztof_kies
lowski_03.htm.

Krzysztof Kieślowski: I'm So-So. Dir. Krzysztof Wierzbicki. 1995.
Available on discs of *Three Colors* (see above).

A Short Film about Decalogue: An Interview with Krzysztof Kieślowski. Dir. Eileen
Anipare and Jason Wood. 1996.

Interviews, Statements, and Profiles in Print

Abrahamson, Patrick. "Kieślowski's Many Colors." *Oxford University Student
Newspaper*, June 2, 1995.

Billen, Andrew. "Thou Shalt Not Show Any Optimism." *Observer*, May 6, 1990,
71.

Brunette, Peter. "A Film Maker Whose Range Is Wagnerian." *New York Times*,
November 20, 1994.

Cavendish, Phil. "Kieślowski's *Decalogue*." *Sight and Sound* 59, no. 3 (Summer
1990): 162–65.

Ciment, Michel, and Hubert Niogret. "On the *Decalogue*." *Positif* 346 (December
1989): 36–43. Rpt. in *Film World: Interviews with Cinema's Leading Directors*. By
Michel Ciment. Trans. Julie Rose. Oxford, New York: Berg, 2009. 221–36.

Dafoe, Chris. "Exit (and Onward), Kieślowski." *Globe and Mail*, October 11, 1994,
C2.

Greenberg, James. "A New World for East European Filmmakers' Movies." *LA
Times*, April 26, 1990, F1.

Greenberg, James. "Giving a Critical Look at the Ambiguities in Life." *LA Times*,
April 26, 1990, F7.

Gristwood, Sarah. "The Reluctant Auteur." *Guardian*, May 17, 1991, 37.

Harvey, Miles. "Poland's Blue, White, and Red." *Progressive* 59, no. 4 (April 1995):
38–39.

Insdorf, Annette. "The *Decalogue* Re-Examines God's Commands." *New York
Times*, October 28, 1990.

Kieślowski, Krzysztof. "About Documentary Film." *Krzysztof Kieślowski 1941–
1996*. Ed. Stanislaw Zawiśliński. Warsaw: Skorpion, 2006.

McKenna, Kristine. "A Look at the 'Double Life' of a Polish Director." *LA Times*,
December 10, 1991, F6.

Mensonge, Serge. "Three Colors Blue, White, and Red." Interview. *Cinema Papers*
99 (June 1994): 26–32.

Moszcz, Gustaw. "No Heroics, Please." *Sight and Sound* 50, no. 2 (Spring 1981):
90–91.

Index

Printed in the United States
by Baker & Taylor Publisher Services